Radicals in the Heartland

Local History
Endowment 2018

Lake Villa District Library

Radicals in the Heartland

The 1960s Student Protest Movement
at the University of Illinois

MICHAEL V. METZ

UNIVERSITY OF ILLINOIS PRESS
Urbana, Chicago, and Springfield

LAKE VILLA DISTRICT LIBRARY
847.356.7711 www.lvdl.org

© 2019 by the Board of Trustees
of the University of Illinois
All rights reserved
1 2 3 4 5 C P 5 4 3 2 1
♾ This book is printed on acid-free paper.

Cataloging data available from the Library of Congress
ISBN 978-0-252-04241-6 (cloth : alk.)
ISBN 978-0-252-08420-1 (paper : alk)
ISBN 978-0-252-05125-8 (ebook)

For Katherine, who challenged me to make it interesting

Contents

1960s Timeline: The University of Illinois and the World   x

1968 Campus Map   xiii

Preface   xv

Abbreviations   xxi

Introduction: Fighting Illini   3

PART I. THE PRELUDE

1 The New Yorker: George D. Stoddard   11

2 The New Guy: David Dodds Henry   17

3 The Communist TA: Edward Yellin   19

4 The Sexual Rebel: Leo Koch   22

PART II. THE FREE SPEECH ERA, 1965–67

5 The Civil Rights Movement and the University   29

6 Civil Rights, Free Speech, and War   32

7 A Spark: W. E. B. DuBois Club   38

8   The University Reacts   40

9   The University Delays   43

10 Passing the Buck   50

11 The Board Surprises   53

12 The Legislature Speaks   56

13 A Movement Is Born   61

14 Henry Responds   64

15 The Board Reverses   68

16 Students for Free Speech   72

17 Henry Reverses   77

18 Spring/Summer '67: Women Rising   83

PART III. THE ANTIWAR MOVEMENT, 1967–69

19 Fall '67: A Hectic Beginning   105

20 A New Focus: The War   111

21 Draft Resisters Act   115

22 Then There Was Dow   121

23 The Aftermath   130

24 1968: The Wildest Year   136

25 Race Returns to Center Stage   143

26 Spring Sputters to an End   150

27 Summer '68: The Turning Begins   155

28 Fall '68: Project 500   165

PART IV. THE VIOLENT TIME, 1969–70

29 Spring '69: Heating Up, but Not Boiling Over   173

30 Black and White Together   181

31 A Sign of the End: Weathermen Come to Town   185

32 Spring '70: The Final Semester   191

33 March: Patience Spent, the Storms Begin   194
34 April: Quiet between the Storms   199
35 May: The Final Month   202
36 Strike: The Final Days   207
37 Extra at the End   218
    Conclusion: On Agency   225

    Contributors: In Their Own Words   231
    Acknowledgments   241
    Notes   243
    Bibliography   261
    Index   265

Photographs follow page 92

1960s Timeline:
The University of Illinois and the World

1960
- UI student Edward Yellin convicted of contempt of Congress, later acquitted
- Leo Koch, UI professor, fired for letter to DI editor advocating premarital sex

- John F. Kennedy elected president
- Students sit in at Woolworth lunch counter, Greensboro, NC
- Birth control pill becomes widely available

1961
- Bay of Pigs Cuban invasion
- JFK "Man on the moon" speech
- Peace corps launched

1962
- Illiac II supercomputer operational

- SDS Port Huron Statement
- Andy Warhol soup can
- Rachel Carson's *Silent Spring*

1963
- Assembly Hall opens
- Big Ten basketball co-championship
- Big Ten football championship

- Medgar Evers, John F. Kennedy assassinated
- Four black children die in Mississippi church bombing
- Martin Luther King "I Have a Dream" speech

1964
- Dick Butkus, Jim Grabowski lead Illini to Rose Bowl victory
- SDS chapter formed on UI campus

- Cassius Clay wins heavyweight title
- Civil Rights Act
- Gulf of Tonkin
- Berkeley Free Speech Movement

1965

- First UI anti-war teach-in
- Student Committee for Political Expression (SCOPE) formed
- National SDS convention at UI

- LBJ sends troops to Vietnam
- Selma to Montgomery march
- SDS anti-war Washington march
- Malcolm X assassinated
- Los Angeles Watts riot

1966

- Ralph Bennett forms W.E.B. DuBois Club, threatens Clabaugh Act test with communist speaker on campus

- Black Panther Party formed
- Mao Zedong's Cultural Revolution
- National Organization of Women founded

1967

- Feb: Students Against Clabaugh Act (SACA)
- March: SACA -> Students for Free Speech (SFS), Louis Diskin speaks on quad
- April: UI women's midnight rally
- Sept: Jack Peltason named chancellor; SFS disbanded; CEWV, DRU formed; Schmidt, Soderstrom burn draft cards
- Oct: Draft Board sit-in, UI Dow sit-in

- March on the Pentagon
- Che Guevera killed
- First Super Bowl
- Newark, Detroit summer riots
- San Francisco summer of love
- UW Dow sit-in

1968

- May: Citizens for Racial Justice (CRJ) formed, Project 500 announced
- July: Clabaugh Act ruled unconstitutional
- Sept: Project 500 students arrested in Illini Union
- Sept: Anti-war activists plan "outreach and education"

- Jan/Feb: Tet offensive
- April: Martin Luther King assassinated, 100+ cities, towns riot, Columbia bldg takeover, Chicago peace march/police riot
- May: Paris student rebellion
- June: Robert Kennedy assassinated
- August: Chicago Democratic convention
- Nov: Nixon elected

1969

- Sept: Dohrn, Rudd, Jones speak on campus
- Oct: 9,000 person anti-war march from quad to Champaign West Park
- Dec: UI student/faculty anti-war march in Springfield

- June: SDS splits apart
- July: First man on the moon
- Oct: Weathermen Days of Rage
- Nov: Moratorium March in DC
- Dec: Fred Hampton, Mark Clark murdered

1970

- Jan: Champaign police station bombed, Illiac IV announced
- Feb: Armory ROTC bombed
- March: GE protest/riot, Henry retires
- May: post–Kent State student strike, riots, State Police, National Guard, mass arrests

- August: Cambodian invasion
- May: Kent State, Jackson State killings
- Jimi Hendrix, Janis Joplin die
- Beatles disband

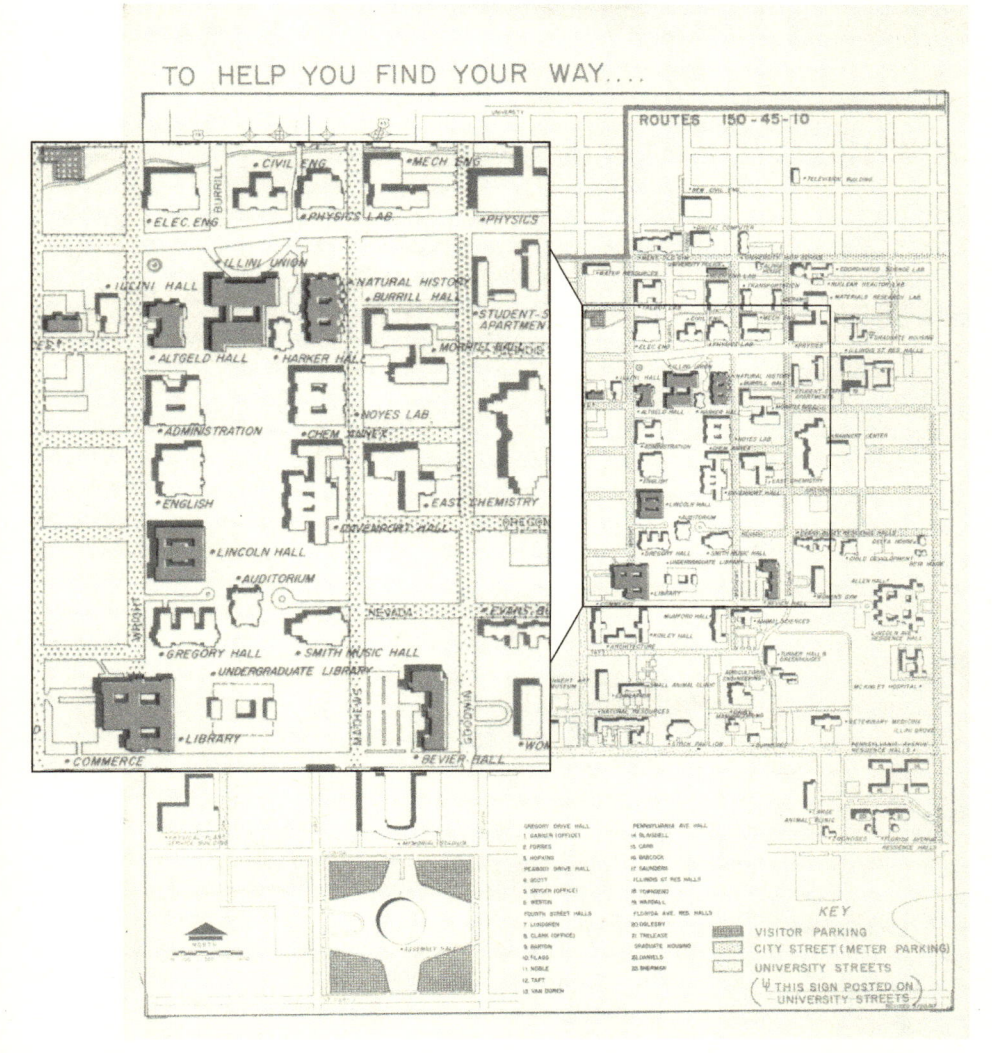

Campus Map, 1967–68. Photo courtesy of the University of Illinois at Urbana-Champaign Archives, image "Campus Map," 1967, record series 39/1/806.

Preface

Oskee-wow-wow Illinois,
Our eyes are all on you.

At the start of the sixties decade, I was twelve, the eldest of six children of an Italian Irish working-class Catholic family, an altar boy, a good student, and the neighborhood paperboy. Early one morning as I folded my stack of *Illinois State Journal* newspapers, one after the other, half-awake, a front-page photo of "Protesting Japanese students" caught my eye. The picture perplexed me, and eventually I paused and asked out loud, "Who are these students? . . . Are they students like me? . . . What are they doing?" The subject of the protest was unimportant; the idea of students publicly protesting authorities for any reason completely flummoxed me. The image simply did not fit into my worldview, formed by Dominican nuns at the Little Flower School in Springfield, Illinois. That worldview was largely shared by my fellow midwestern citizens, who believed the role of students was to study hard, listen to and respect teachers, and accept their parents' views. But that image of protesting students, so outside the midwestern norms of 1960, would soon become an iconic symbol for the decade.

Five years later I enrolled at the University of Illinois at the Urbana campus, ninety miles from home, and over time became one of those protesting students, much to the embarrassment, disappointment, and sometimes anger of Springfield friends and family. When I returned home on holiday breaks, my long hair would elicit anger from my father, an 82nd Airborne World War II veteran, my high school drinking buddies would look askance at me, and my little Italian grandmother would look crossly and mutter about "heepies." Within three blocks of my home lived two families whose sons would die in Vietnam. Sargent Michael Calandrino

xvi • *Preface*

New Student Guide, 1966. Photo courtesy of the University of Illinois at Urbana-Champaign Archives, image "Welcome to the University of Illinois," 1966, record series 39/1/806.

was my age, a star catcher on our little-league team. Private First Class William Hellyer was the minister's son at the Protestant church down the street. Hellyer, a few years older than I, had passed his paper route on to me.

Many of the norms I grew up with in Springfield, which my generation was taught so well, would be questioned and cast aside in our university experience, as large cultural upheavals—the civil rights movement, an antiwar rebellion, the drugs, sex, and rock and roll of the sixties—swept across the nation's campuses.

As a group, students of the movement were self-aware, excited, and even proud to be at the center of such tumult, and over time came to feel part of a worldwide, virtuous rebellion against a political and social order that was perceived as hypocritical, corrupt, and dying. These early baby boomers may have lacked historical perspective, but there was no lack of confidence nor righteousness, as Vern Fein and Vic Berkey, two leaders of the Illinois student movement, would make clear years later. Fein: "We knew we were right. And we were. About the war, they were wrong, and they knew they were wrong."[1] Speaking to the strong sense of moral clarity that drove the movement, Berkey added: "It wasn't even muddy . . . on civil rights . . . on bombing civilians with napalm . . . we were morally right."[2] The protesting students of the sixties were young, confident, and quite certain; the issues were clear, the conditions called for change, and their movement would be a catalyst for that change.

I was a part of the student movement on the Illinois campus for the most turbulent years, 1965 to 1970, participating in rallies, marches, sit-ins, and, I confess with mixed feelings, the riots at the end. Given my role as a participant in the drama, I've attempted to keep personal opinions confined to the front and back material, employing as much objectivity as possible in the body of the text, using newspaper records, university archives, interviews with participants, and academic dissertations as sources. The award-winning *Daily Illini* student newspaper, known as the "*DI*" on campus, with all back issues now available online, was an especially valuable primary source. During this period, the newspaper staff was blessed with some future journalistic stars such as Roger Ebert, Pulitzer Prize winner and forty-year film critic for the *Chicago Sun-Times*; Dan Balz, a *Washington Post* political correspondent; and Roger Simon, *New York Times* bestselling author and *Politico* columnist.

Why study the sixties? As divided as our country is today, it was just as divided, if not more so, a half-century ago. The most notable difference between then and now is that the hope, optimism, and self-confidence of the student movement of the 1960s is nowhere to be found today. In that earlier time, protesting students firmly believed they were about building a better world. Raised in an era of relative affluence and optimism, they had little reason to doubt themselves or the idea of American exceptionalism with which they were raised. They were children of a prosperous age, born amid a booming post–World War II economy of unprecedented middle-class growth, and as the privileged children of that class, they enjoyed the domestic calm of the Eisenhower years. That same Eisenhower, in his farewell address to the nation, would foretell the troubles of the sixties, warning of the rise of what he called the "military-industrial complex," the mutually beneficial relationship that had developed between the corporations and individuals who design and manufacture the nation's armaments, and the government officials and armed forces personnel who purchase those same products. A World War II hero, Eisenhower would warn his fellow citizens that they "must guard against the acquisition of unwarranted influence, whether sought or unsought" by these powerful interests. Years later, antiwar protesters would lay partial blame for the Vietnam War at the feet of that very group—corporations, the military, the government—accusing them of seeking economic gain from the conflict.

In contrast with the domestically sedate 1950s, the decade of the sixties brought major disruption—a civil-rights movement, assassinations, domestic riots, a foreign war, an unprecedented student-led uprising against that war—and the prosperity of the postwar economic times would end soon after, for some Americans never to return. Many of the issues born in the sixties remain unresolved in today's America: a collapse of trust in institutions such as government, media, big business, and the church; culturally disruptive forces that would come to be known as identity politics, feminism, minority rights, environmentalism; and the recidivist backlash against those forces, so evident in today's political zeitgeist. That certitude felt by the sixties students that a better world was within their reach is conspicuous today by its absence; indeed, today the notion seems almost quaint. By studying the period, we can better understand that spirit, where it came from and why it disappeared, as well as why and how it erupted into such a broad political and social movement when it did.

Jack Peltason, chancellor at the Urbana campus during the most intense years of student protest, claimed it was a mystery to him why the period of student unrest happened when it did. Perhaps he lacked perspective, as historical examination reveals obvious answers, as well as differences with today's situation. One activist of the time offered this analysis of the differences: "We were naïve, growing up in a time when the world was America's oyster. . . . We thought we could make it the country it was supposed to be. We thought if we changed America, we would change the world. Now what the kids see is years of bullshit, where America has been wrong time after time . . . dominated by corporate America in a way we could never have imagined. . . . They have no naiveté about America."[3] Naiveté was certainly one component of the sixties movement, but it came with a confidence born of affluence, youthful courage, and the clarity of the moral issues with which the students were confronted. This history explains how a small minority of self-confident, if naïve, and courageous, if sometimes arrogant, Illinois youth, facing intransigent government and university authorities and the existential threat of an appalling war, chose, in significant numbers, resistance over conformity to societal expectations.

Looking back, I'm extraordinarily grateful for my time at Illinois. As with many, those college years were some of the most intense and formative of my life. Of course, much of the education took place outside the classroom, at free-speech and antiwar rallies, on picket lines, at a 1967 sit-in against the Dow Chemical Corporation, and at the nearby 1968 Democratic convention, both described later in this book. But some of the most important learning took place in late-night dorm discussions, in marijuana-inspired conversations on the quad, and in candle-lit student apartments, with arguments about society, politics, economics, and what made the world the way it was, and an infinite number of memorable interactions with friends that I would remain close with throughout life. That education developed the critical-thinking, problem-solving, and analytical skills that helped make me successful in Silicon Valley, where I was fortunate to be employed for more than twenty years at two great companies, Apple and Cisco. Upon retirement, I returned to school at San Jose State University and earned a master's degree in history. It was there that, after reading history for three years, I was drawn to write about a largely ignored chapter of an otherwise well-documented era, the student rebellion at the University of Illinois at Urbana-Champaign. I thank the educators at Illinois and San Jose State and acknowledge a debt. And I especially thank the friends I made at Illinois, many of whom were interviewed for this book, for all I learned from them.

Abbreviations

AAUP	American Association of University Professors
BSA	Black Students Association
CEWV	Committee to End the War in Vietnam
CORE	Congress for Racial Equality
CRJ	Citizens for Racial Justice
CSA	Committee on Student Affairs
DI	*Daily Illini*
DRU	Draft Resisters Union
FUR	Faculty for University Reform
HUAC	House Un-American Activities Committee
PLP	Progressive Labor Party
ROTC	Reserve Officers Training Corps
RU	Radical Union
RYM	Revolutionary Youth Movement
SACA	Students Against the Clabaugh Act
SACB	Subversive Activities Control Board
SAR	Students Against Racism
SCOPE	Student Committee on Political Enlightenment
SDS	Students for a Democratic Society
SFS	Students for Free Speech
SNCC	Student Non-violent Coordinating Committee
YAF	Young Americans for Freedom

For most of my politically conscious life, the idea of social transformation has been the great taboo of American politics. From the smug 1950s to the post-Reagan era . . . this anti-utopian trend has been interrupted only by the brief but intense flare-up of visionary politics known as "the sixties." Yet that short-lived, anomalous upheaval has had a more profound effect on my thinking about the possibilities of politics than the following three decades of reaction. The reason is not that I am stuck in a time warp, nursing a romantic attachment to my youth, and so determined to idealize a period that admittedly had its politically dicey moments. Rather, as I see it, the enduring interest of this piece of history lies precisely in its spectacular departure from the norm. It couldn't happen, according to the reigning intellectual currents of the fifties, but it did.

—Ellen Willis, *Ghosts, Fantasies, and Hope*

To this day it remains a mystery why we went into the period of so-called student unrest or why we came out of it.

—Jack W. Peltason, *Reactionary Thoughts of a Revolutionary*

I am grateful to have been there and grateful for the people who were there too—good friends with a sense of purpose and belief. Do you think young people feel it is possible to change the world now? Do you think they care? We were very lucky. And no matter what history says, we did change the world. It is not the same. What is not better now is because we never fully understood the power of the military industrial complex that went into full attack mode post-sixties and so now . . . here we are. I wonder if this is what they all meant to happen?

—Patricia Engelhard, student activist, class of 1970

INTRODUCTION

Fighting Illini

In the final months of the final school year of the sixties decade, the University of Illinois at Urbana descended into chaos. Parents, administrators, and state officials looked on aghast as students defied authorities, took over the streets of their campus, and filled the air with cries of rebellion in language jarring to our ears today. Out-of-town radicals preached violent revolution from the stage of Gregory Hall, urging an overflow audience to "take up the gun" and "prepare for armed struggle"; firebombs were planted in Lincoln, Harker, and Altgeld Halls; the Armory headquarters of the Reserve Officers Training Corps (ROTC) were bombed, as was the Champaign Federal Building, and in Urbana an explosion completely destroyed a military recruiting office. Riotous mobs roamed the streets, throwing rocks, smashing windows, and fighting police, state troopers, and National Guardsmen for control of the campus. The *DI* reported, "Nobody is in charge of the University . . . groups roam around grabbing [power]. . . . The Board of Trustees grabs a chunk, the governor grabs a chunk, the mayors of Champaign and Urbana and the county sheriff take a chunk, and the kids in the street make a bid, too. President Henry and Chancellor Peltason are . . . ignored by all."[1]

The campus exploded in open revolt in the most turbulent period in the school's hundred-year history, as the university and the nation as a whole lived through an unprecedented weeks-long outburst of student violence from coast to coast. Then, on a rainy Saturday night in Urbana-Champaign, as the end of the last school year of the extraordinary decade neared, the riotous fever broke, the energy dissipated, and this tumultuous chapter of the University of Illinois story came to a quiet end.

Nationally, too, the violent campus disturbances soon ended, and the historic 1960s student protest movement stumbled to a close.

How could such a rebellion have happened at Illinois, of all places? The conservative U of I was one of the nation's largest public universities, hosting more fraternities than any campus in America, a leader in such noncontroversial fields as agricultural research, business education, engineering, and the new science of information technology, where only a few years before, faculty had built one of the world's earliest mainframe computers, the Illiac. Predating twenty-first-century diversity standards, the student population was white (90 percent), predominantly male (2:1), and represented the cream of the state's high school graduates.[2] The largest portion (39 percent) was drawn from the nation's "second city," solidly Democratic Chicago, and its suburbs; others came from "downstate" (to Chicago-area students, anything beyond the suburbs), midsize working-class towns like Peoria, Decatur, and Moline, still others from the hundreds of mostly Republican, small farming communities, such as the tiny hamlet of Lebanon, Illinois (1960 population: 2,863), across the Mississippi from St. Louis.[3] These students were the pride of their state; rebellion was the last thing expected of them. The midwestern heartland, more conservative than the liberal coasts, more liberal than the reactionary South, represented a sort of balance point for the country. Student rebellions in foreign lands or in more liberal parts of the United States might not seem surprising. But such disruption in the central core of the country, caused by such privileged students on campuses large and small, shocked and unbalanced the nation, threatening chaos. If the Midwest was the nation's stable center, then the University of Illinois was a major pillar of that stability. But now the center seemed not to be holding, and that which had seemed stable was shaken. How could this happen, at Illinois of all places? That is the story of this book.

That last nationwide eruption of student outrage had followed National Guardsmen's murder of four students at Kent State University in Ohio. Not everything about the movement would end immediately; related events would still occur, some significant—large demonstrations, Washington marches, bombings, arrests, capture and/or killings of self-described revolutionaries—but these were historical postscripts to a decade whose productive energy had been spent. Ironically, for a movement built on rational argument and nonviolent tactics—leafleting, rallies, teach-ins, gripe-ins, pray-ins, picket lines, peaceful marches, small and local to big and national—the end came with an unparalleled eruption of pointless, irrational violence. The targets were a government disinclined to change, a conservative majority adamantly opposed to change, and university administrators who could not change fast enough even when they tried. After years of students' peaceful efforts with little to show, student violence exploded against all levels of an establishment that had rejected the demands of a youthful minority, albeit a minority that had become too loud and too large to ignore.

And to be sure, the student movement always was a minority. As Illinois Chancellor Jack W. Peltason repeatedly assured his trustees, on his campus the core of the movement never represented more than 1 percent of the population, and that estimate likely held true nationally. But it was a minority with heft. Their protests helped end one presidency, mortally wounded another, and led the forces fighting to end a war. This is the story of a subset of a generation of students at Illinois and, by reflection, at campuses across the country, accurately self-described in the founding statement of the most influential of the sixties' student protest groups, the Students for a Democratic Society (SDS) in their Port Huron Statement: "We are people of this generation, bred in at least modest comfort, housed now in universities, looking uncomfortably to the world we inherit."[4] Young Illini, like college students elsewhere, were confronted with grave moral issues; in response, they questioned authorities, spoke out, and, in the end, made history.

Rebelling college students became commonplace in the sixties, not only in the United States but worldwide. French students rioted in the streets of Paris, Mexican students were shot down at their nation's Olympics, Chinese students led a raging cultural revolution at Chairman Mao's directive. In this country, students fought for free speech at Berkeley, were attacked by police in the streets of Chicago, and took over campus buildings at Columbia. The resulting backlash led to conservative and/or centrist American presidencies for the remainder of the century and growth of a global neoliberal political and economic order taken to a new apogee today under the guise of a rebellious populist movement.

The student movement took place during the Cold War, when the United States and Russia were sworn enemies. In the early years of that era, a "Red Scare," an intense and at times irrational fear of communist infiltration, swept the land. The period would come to be known as the "McCarthy era," after the most extreme of the anticommunist provocateurs, U.S. Senator Joseph McCarthy of Wisconsin, known for his wild and unsubstantiated accusations of treason and subversion. Yet even before the height of such red-baiting, anxiety-provoking stories of insidious "reds," of communist threats, of Russian domination in Eastern Europe filled the pages of Illinois's largest and most influential newspaper, the conservative *Chicago Tribune*. Russian spies were suspected of pilfering state secrets, communists were waging a civil war in Greece, and pundits talked of "losing" China to the enemy. Though many years later we would discover that threats of Soviet spies were in fact real, not imagined, at the time officials' and citizens' fears were often overblown as alleged threats seemingly became omnipresent. Overreaction to the communist danger was to become the norm in Illinois and across the country. State legislatures contributed to the hysteria under the auspices of protecting their citizens from the Red Scare; in this exercise, Illinois was no laggard.

Two examples of the Illinois legislature's aggressive approach to the exaggerated threat of communism took place in 1947, the year of my birth. In August, at the instigation of officials from the American Legion and under the sponsorship of Senator Paul Broyles of the small central Illinois town of Mount Vernon, the legislators created the Seditious Activities Investigation Commission, chartered "to investigate any activities of any person or persons, co-partnership, association, organization, group or society . . . suspected of being directed toward the overthrow of the Government of the United States or the State of Illinois."[5] The Broyles Commission, as it became known, would spend two years and nearly $100,000 seeking out communist influence in the state, particularly in the state's institutions of higher education. Said Broyles, "The greatest danger is in the over-liberal educators who have a tendency to glamorize the various -isms, especially communism, to our young people who are sent to our various colleges and universities."[6] The commission, whose hearings would be regularly publicized in the pages of the *Tribune*, would recommend half a dozen pieces of legislation intended to protect the state (none were enacted) and identify sixty-five hundred registered communists in the state—yet they would find no evidence of activities directed toward the overthrow of the government of Illinois. Robert M. Hutchens, chancellor of the University of Chicago, made clear his thoughts on the wrongheaded nature of the commission and the overreaction of the Red Scare, in his testimony to the commission:

> We hear on every side that the American Way of Life is in danger. I think it is. I also think that many of those who talk the loudest about the dangers . . . have no idea what it is and consequently no idea what the dangers are. . . .
>
> You would suppose, to listen to those people that the American Way of Life consisted in unanimous tribal self-adoration. Down with criticism; down with protests; down with unpopular opinions; down with independent thought. Yet the history and tradition of our country make it perfectly plain that the essence of the American Way of Life is its hospitality to criticism, protest, unpopular opinions, and independent thought . . .
>
> The heart of Americanism is independent thought. The cloak-and-stiletto work that is now going on will not merely mean that many persons will suffer for acts they did not commit, or for acts that were legal when committed, or for no acts at all. Far worse is the end result, which will be that critics, even of the mildest sort, will be frightened into silence. Stupidity and injustice will go unchallenged because no one will dare to speak against them.[7]

The Chicago chancellor would be pleased and relieved to know that, fifteen years later, his fears would prove unfounded, as students at Illinois and across the country would not be frightened into silence or allow stupidity and injustice to go unchallenged.

A second legislative act of 1947 would have a more direct bearing on our story and would plant the seed for the student movement at the University of Illinois.

The General Assembly passed a bill introduced by the Republican representative from Champaign, Charles Clabaugh, that demonstrated the era's deep concern about communism. Known by its namesake, the Clabaugh Act specifically targeted one school, the University of Illinois, a suspected hotbed of communist influence, and was intended to eliminate subversive activity on the state's flagship campus by prohibiting certain organizations from accessing university resources. The vaguely worded bill left it to university administrators and the courts to determine which organizations might qualify as "seditious," "subversive," and "un-American," and therein lay its fundamental flaw. The ill-defined language of the law foreshadowed the controversy it would engender for the twenty years it would remain in effect.

In the beginning, campus opposition to the Clabaugh Act would manifest in small and peaceful protests—letters to the editor, disagreements over administrative rulings, and faculty complaints about academic freedom. By the mid-1960s, Lyndon Johnson's escalation of the war in Vietnam would inject a second major theme, and a larger, more visible antiwar movement would displace the free-speech issue. Antiwar protests became common on campus, peaking in the fall semester of the pivotal school year 1967–68 with a large, nonviolent sit-in against campus recruiters from the Dow Chemical Corporation, manufacturers of napalm, a gelled petrochemical incendiary weapon used in the Vietnam War. The following summer, at the 1968 Democratic Convention in nearby Chicago, police introduced a level of violence into the decade that would prove to be a decisive turning point for the movement and thus initiate a transition to the final, violent phase of the era.

In this third phase, protest on the Urbana campus took a distinctly darker turn. Increasing student frustration with what had become the nation's longest war, exacerbated by perceived university administration support for the war, plus an ongoing draft that directly affected college-age males, led to students' political radicalization and rising emotions on all sides. These passions climaxed in campus riots, brought under control only with the introduction of Illinois State Police and Illinois National Guard troops, an overwhelming if not surprising reaction by the state to such disorder, effectively bringing an end to the sixties movement at Illinois. Students of the decade began to graduate, move on, find jobs, and shift into the next phase of their lives.

Of course, there was more to the student movement than the demand for free speech and an end to the Vietnam War. Youth of the era were in rebellion against an established order and conservative norms of thought, behavior, and dress that are hard to imagine today. Protesting students dressed differently, in jeans and army fatigues, grew their hair long, were more sexually active, smoked marijuana, and listened to a new kind of music, often played loudly. One student recalled, "It was such a remarkable time. You felt a kinship with people you didn't know, you knew how people thought, based on how they looked and how they dressed. We were creating a different culture . . . making the world a better, more peaceful place . . . rejecting the suburban normalcy we grew up with."[8] Drugs mattered: "They were a bonding thing, contributed to 'us versus them,' and increased the sense of estrangement from the authorities. We were outlaws, with all the thrill that brought, but also the recognition that we were different, that there was an us and a them."[9] Then there was the music, the soundtrack for the time—Jefferson Airplane, the Grateful Dead, Bob Dylan, the Beatles and Rolling Stones, and all the others: it could not and would not have been remotely the same without late nights in candlelit rooms with joints passing and youthful rebels hearing and feeling their music. And then there was "the Pill." For the first time in the history of humankind, young people could experience sex without the consequences of reproduction. And did they. But this story is not about the drugs, sex, and rock and roll; we should think of these factors as context—albeit critical contributors to the zeitgeist. Though such elements are not the focus here, we can only understand the period by remembering the part they played; the rise of radical politics cannot be divorced from such enablers.

Those who lived through the era knew their experience was unique, that they were about creating a new society, maybe even a new kind of person. "We called ourselves radicals for a reason. We weren't just angry liberals. We were change agents, catalysts for new, radical ways to look at reality. We were the ones who would change America and the world."[10] How and why did these youngsters ever come to think this? These University of Illinois students, privileged, white, middle-class sons and daughters of the midwestern heartland, would seem the most unlikely of rebels, the most improbable of radicals. That such a political and cultural uprising occurred in those conditions, at that time, in that place, defies logic. But it did. This is the story of how and why, when and where, this movement happened.

PART I

The Prelude

CHAPTER 1

The New Yorker: George D. Stoddard

The years preceding the sixties were not entirely without controversy at Illinois and are instructive in understanding how the university, the state, and the public would react to future controversy on the campus. The tenure of George D. Stoddard, named president of the university in late 1946, was quite contentious compared with those that came before. Born and raised in Pennsylvania, Stoddard was hired from New York, where he had been both commissioner of education and president of the University of the State of New York. Immediately following World War II, Stoddard served in Japan as head of the U.S. education mission under Douglas MacArthur and was appointed a founding U.S. delegate to UNESCO, the United Nations Education, Scientific, and Cultural Organization. He was an East Coast man, an internationalist, a political liberal, and a progressive educator, a seemingly odd choice for the University of Illinois. His style was direct and opinionated, and even a newspaper that was generally supportive of the man described him as having "a caustic temper . . . a tendency to go it alone . . . to discount the existence of other, different viewpoints."[1]

During the seven years Stoddard oversaw the university, from 1946 to 1953, numerous public disagreements arose with faculty, the board of trustees, and legislators in the General Assembly over a wide variety of issues. Early on, Stoddard named East Coast New Dealer and Keynesian economist Harold Bowen to the post of dean of the School of Commerce, challenging him to elevate the standing of the college to national recognition. In his first year Bowen added additional liberal, eastern faculty, and a mutiny developed among the majority conservative, classical economists. After two years the row ended with the faculty publicly rejecting newcomer Bowen with a vote of no-confidence, forcing his resignation. It so happened that one of the conservative faculty members who led the no-confidence effort was brother to an equally conservative state legislator, one who would later take the lead in opposing Stoddard in the legislature.[2]

Another area where Stoddard would raise concern, directly relevant to our story, was in his unabashed support for free speech. At the time, free speech was a particularly risky topic for liberal educators, one construed by conservative critics as tacit support for communism. Stoddard, like many liberals of the time, walked a fine line, publicly condemning communism while still supporting communists' right to free speech. He would carefully qualify such support; one of his favorite sayings was, "We are free in all respects save one; we are not free to tolerate the destruction of our freedom."[3] While proclaiming his anticommunism, Stoddard simultaneously voiced opposition to extreme anticommunist ideas, arguing against loyalty oath proposals in the legislature and opposing restrictions on what might be taught in university classrooms. He proposed to the board of trustees that they support repeal of a nineteenth-century state law prohibiting candidates for public office from delivering speeches on Illinois college campuses. The intent of the law was to keep university students sheltered from the tawdry corruption of politics. Stoddard argued that modern-day students no longer required such protection. His recommendation was declined by the board but received public support from Chicago newspapers, who brought the issue to light and criticized the trustees. Such public airing of disagreement between the president and his superiors did not please either the board or the legislature, and the ensuing discussion in Springfield led to proposals for further campus speech restrictions and anticommunist legislation specifically targeting Stoddard's campus. When Stoddard spoke out publicly, declaring such legislation unnecessary, the lawmakers were angered. Then, when he refused to ban a left-wing student organization from campus, they took action.

On July 1, 1947, the final day of that year's Illinois legislative session, House Bill 711, sponsored by Republican state representative Charles Clabaugh, sole proprietor of the Champaign Weather Strip Company, was passed through the General Assembly and onto the governor's desk as the country entered the post–World War II Red Scare. Clabaugh's bill fit the times: the anticommunist demagogue Joseph McCarthy of Wisconsin had just been elected to the U.S. Senate, Stalin was cementing his grip on Eastern Europe, communists were threatening takeovers in China, Italy, and Greece, and Hollywood stars were refusing congressional demands to name communists in their industry. Front-page newspaper stories reported on communist aggression, alleged infiltration and sabotage; the communist menace was beginning to seem ubiquitous. Clabaugh's bill was only one of many that typified the nation's overreaction to the perceived communist threat.

The wording of the bill was dark and unsettling: "The universities of America have been the breeding ground of a series of insidious Communist inspired organizations which have sought to instill in the hearts of American youth contempt and hatred for ideals to which the people of this great nation have been dedicated." Of all state facilities in Illinois, the new law prohibited only the use of University of Illinois resources "to any subversive, seditious, and un-American organization, or to its representatives." Its companion, the Broyles Bill, was passed the same day, sanctioning a communist-hunting commission. The governor's approval would come quickly for both. Broyles's bill included a loyalty oath for state employees and made public support of communism a felony throughout the state. Clabaugh's bill, less ambitious, was a straightforward attack on the university administration of George Stoddard and a direct response to the president's refusal to ban a student organization, Youth for Democracy, which Clabaugh characterized as a front for the Communist Party that "strives for destruction of the principles which democracy holds sacred."[4] The Clabaugh Act would remain on the books for more than twenty years, and would be the starter seed for the Illinois student protest movement of the early to mid-sixties.

The last of Stoddard's challenges was an odd one: his involvement in an international controversy over a sham cancer cure named Krebiozen. The substance had ostensibly been extracted from horses in Argentina by a Yugoslav refugee researcher who, in search of a patron, traveled to the United States on a Vatican passport, all aspects which made good material for newspapers.[5] The sketchy researcher found a champion for his alleged cure at the university in Dr. Andrew Ivy, a physiologist, respected at the time, who headed the university's medical college. The American Medical Association tested the substance and determined the so-called cure to be worthless, but Ivy refused to drop his support for the drug and the researcher, and he had the support of anti-Stoddard legislators as well as desperate cancer patients. Trustees of the university received letters from cancer survivors, one of which read in part: "Knowing that you are very much interested in the value of Krebiozen, I want to tell you that I honestly believe that I owe my life to this drug. Before I was given the injections I was so weak I could not walk a block without assistance. . . . The change has been remarkable. . . . This has been my only hope."[6] Despite such letters, Stoddard accepted the AMA findings, eventually placing Ivy on a leave of absence and ending Krebiozen experiments at the university. The legislature reacted by establishing a commission to investigate both the drug and Stoddard's actions. Not much came of the commission; according to the *Chicago Daily News*, the only thing established "was that horses are cheaper in Argentina than in America," and soon thereafter the issue faded.

Such public controversies as the business school affair, Stoddard's public politicking—first in favor of loosening campus speech laws and then against anticommunist legislation—and, finally, the Krebiozen affair did not fit with the traditionalist nature of those who oversaw the state university. His brash, opinionated style only further antagonized his opponents. The New Yorker had been appointed under a Democratic governor and board of trustees, but a statewide Republican sweep in the Eisenhower election of 1952 led to a more conservative governor and board, both less tolerant of liberals and controversy in the midst of the McCarthy era. The new board members had been nominated at a Republican state convention marked by a keynote speech from "gray-haired widowed homemaker" State Representative Lottie Holman O'Neill demanding the removal of the United States Secretaries of State and Defense for weakness toward Russia and the impeachment of President Truman for tolerating them, followed by a claim from the convention floor by Champaign representative Ora Dillavoux, brother of the commerce professor Stoddard had crossed earlier, that "Stoddard had countenanced the presence of 50 Reds, pinks and Socialists on the U. of I. faculty," an accusation in tune with the times but completely devoid of evidence.[7]

Stoddard vehemently disputed Dillavoux's accusation in the press. However, on a busy news weekend in summer 1953, with the Korean War ending and Cuban revolution beginning, the president, at the first meeting of the new board in the Illini Union, met his end. Following an evening budget discussion that rambled into the late hours, newly elected board member and former Illini football great Harold "Red" Grange—the "Galloping Ghost" gridiron star of the 1920s, lauded as "a real American" in Dillavoux's nominating speech—submitted a motion of no-confidence in the president. After nominating Grange, Dillavoux had told reporters he was "tired of hearing trustees say 'yes sir' to Dr. Stoddard," sending a clear message to Grange and an equally clear threat to Stoddard.[8] The Galloping Ghost, broadcasting a *Chicago Tribune* all-star football game at the time of his trustee nomination, claimed he had not sought the position but, understanding Dillavoux's intent, agreed to accept the position "out of duty to the university." This would be the only board motion Grange would ever submit; in fact, it would be the only board meeting he would ever attend. Stoddard, acknowledging that he served at the pleasure of the board, immediately wrote out his resignation on Illini Union stationery conveniently provided on the conference table.

The dismissal itself was not without controversy, nor was it a straightforward liberal versus conservative disagreement. Board member Wayne Johnston, outspoken president of the Illinois Central Railroad and an avowed conservative Republican, led the minority voting to keep Stoddard and called the dismissal "terrible and ridiculous." "I would," he said, "never dismiss a section foreman on the railroad the way Stoddard was dismissed, without a chance to hear the charges and present his case."[9] A former board president added, "Critics have made much of a few controversies. . . . His untimely departure will be a great loss to the University and the state."[10] Department heads of the College of Liberal Arts published a letter of protest, calling the board's action "technically, legally, morally unjust."[11] But Board President Park Livingston, spoken of as a possible backfill candidate for university president himself, responded, "These pets [sic] had best stick to their educational field or go elsewhere."[12]

Stoddard himself listed reasons for his dismissal in newspaper interviews, noting the Commerce College matter, his public opposition to anticommunist legislation in the assembly, and the Krebiozen affair, but he attributed his dismissal primarily to his unwillingness to "knuckle down" to legislators regarding alleged faculty "pinks and commies."[13] He also suggested "isolationists" in the legislature judged his United Nations role as "only one step from communism."[14] Responding, one Republican legislator claimed, "Stoddard surrounded himself with left-wingers at the University.... His dismissal serves as a warning to others in the state who have been flirting with leftists."[15] Livingston, the board president, tried to have the final word, calling Stoddard "a pain in the neck" and "an intellectual snob."[16] But Stoddard's words were the last recorded on the subject, quoted in his 1981 *New York Times* obituary:

> "I think what got some of them madder than anything," he said at the time, "was my connection with UNESCO." They regarded UNESCO as "pinko" and "socialistic." A year after his dismissal, the American Civil Liberties Union cited him for "resisting political interference in matters of educational policy and administrative discretion—even to the point of discharge from his post."[17]

The Republican governor, William G. Stratton, who admitted foreknowledge and support for the board's action, provided a simpler explanation. "There was a feeling on the part of the board that it would be better to have someone less controversial toward the legislature.... What it boils down to, however, is that the trustees had lost confidence in the way the university was being administered."

The *DI* reported that at least one trustee agreed with the governor, suggesting the dismissal was less about any one issue and more about the president's personality: "Stoddard was a stubborn man who could not keep out of controversial issues. It seemed as if he liked nothing better than to get into a big fight.... We've had one controversy after another since he came here."[18] But on the editorial page, the newspaper's editors revealed their true feelings:

> It's sickening to watch people play politics with our University. It's disillusioning to see a man cut down because he isn't afraid to fight for what he believes in.... The Board did not like Mr. Stoddard's principles or the way he stood up for them. In a part of the country notorious for its isolationism, his belief in the United Nations was odious. In a community not noted for a democratic spirit, his fight to keep

the University free from racial discrimination was dangerous.... In short, he was completely out of place in the choking atmosphere of conservatism and bigotry in the community, the legislature, and the state as a whole.[19]

To the board of trustees, the Illinois governor, and the General Assembly, and likely most central Illinois citizens, such controversy was simply an undesirable attribute for the state's flagship academic institution. Representative Dillavoux—he with the commerce faculty brother and the source of the "50 Reds" accusation—suggested that publicity in itself was a bad thing for such an institution. "The university ... would be better off if newspapers would quit writing stories about it," adding for good measure, "There's still a lot of those screwballs and crackpots there, and there's a chance to get rid of them now that Stoddard's gone."[20]

Grange, a successful Chicago-area nightclub owner and insurance salesman who, once his sports eligibility expired, had left college without graduating, articulated his idea of a good university administrator: "Other universities undoubtedly have troubles, but the public doesn't hear about them. An able administrator handles his problems quietly."[21] Such a quietly managed institution, displaying a worldview consistent with the legislature and citizens of central Illinois, was the midwestern ideal for the state's flagship university. Stoddard saw it differently: "Many persons will shrug off these events as so much spilled milk. They will crave a period of peace for the university. The aim is laudable, but there could be a peace of the graveyard."[22] The *Chicago Sun-Times*, in an editorial headlined "Politicians Finally Liquidated Stoddard," supported the ousted educator and pulled no punches in its condemnation of the legislators and trustees:

> The Statehouse politicians have been after George D. Stoddard's scalp almost from the very day he took over.... After seven years of stalking, almost to the day, the men who want to use the state's university of higher learning for political advantage, got him.... From this, we take it, the board wants as president a Mr. Milquetoast, who will let the politicians push him around.[23]

After two years of interim leadership, a new president, David Dodds Henry, judged by some a good match for the *Sun-Times*'s suggestion, would be in place. It would be Henry's role to lead the university through the decade of the sixties, a period when problems could not be handled quietly, controversy could not be avoided, and the conventional midwestern worldview would not prevail.

CHAPTER 2

The New Guy: David Dodds Henry

Following Stoddard's firing, the university functioned without incident under the acting-presidency of former financial controller Lloyd Morey, a churchgoing, classical music aficionado, and former Rotary Club president. It was a period of relative calm. In 1956 a new, more liberal board of trustees finally settled on Henry as a sufficiently qualified replacement for Stoddard. Henry was another eastern import, the chief educational officer at the nation's largest private university, the prestigious New York University. However, this easterner did not share his predecessor's inclination toward controversy. Recognizing Stoddard's ongoing conflicts with the board and the state legislature, Henry from the start established excellent relationships with those parties and worked hard to maintain them throughout his tenure.

Ironically, Henry and Stoddard both faced nearly identical challenges in their presidencies. At Illinois, under Stoddard, the Youth for Democracy group had received recognition on the Illinois campus despite angry denunciations from conservative legislators, who in retaliation had passed the Clabaugh Act. At Wayne State University in Detroit, where Henry had previously served as president, he, too, had allowed recognition of a branch of the same student organization, despite threats from Michigan legislators that the school's budget could be withheld as a result. Henry "refused to back down," and said "he would not disband the group until charges against it were proved."[1] With this courageous stand, Henry garnered the strong support of the two Detroit newspapers, the state board of education, the Wayne State faculty, and students. When the federal government eventually determined that the student group was in fact directly connected with the Communist

Party USA, both presidents succumbed, withdrawing recognition from their respective student groups, and the groups disbanded. While Henry seemed to gain in stature from the incident, Stoddard's actions had drawn the wrath of the legislature, simply adding to his list of troubles.

This incident would arise again for Henry during his hiring process at Illinois. With Henry's name at the top of the list of candidates, Illinois Superintendent of Public Instruction Vernon Nickell, an ex officio member of the university's board of trustees, announced that he and the committed communist hunter Paul Broyles would visit Wayne State to look into Henry's behavior in the handling of the alleged communist student organization. Not surprisingly affronted at the news, Henry immediately withdrew his name from consideration for the Illinois position. However, with two other candidates having already turned the Illinois job down, common sense prevailed and the board overruled their superintendent, unanimously offering Henry the position. The diminutive administrator hesitated a bit: "I appreciate the honor [but] my first reaction is to say no," then elected to talk it over with the board in person. After an apparently quite positive meeting with the members (it is unclear if Nickell was present), Henry decided to give the Illinois "hotseat" a try.[2]

For students at the university during Henry's tenure, it would be difficult to characterize the president, since he was rarely seen by students in person and would be best known on campus throughout his career by statements, proclamations, and announcements in the student newspaper. Fifty years later he remains almost as difficult to characterize. Robert Goldstein, today a university professor who was a *DI* reporter at the time, says, "Henry was a non-presence. Nobody ever saw him. . . . He was just a cipher, this invisible person . . . dealing with the students just wasn't part of it [for him]."[3] The president was clearly well thought of by his peers—"It was a measure of the confidence he instilled in his fellow administrators that he was chosen to head six of the nation's leading organizations of higher education, including a stint as president of the Association of American Universities."[4] In modern terms he was a man who managed up, not down, and maintained his focus on the sources of the university's funding, the trustees and legislators. Not surprisingly, his career would be lauded by those bodies, but to students at the university during his tenure, the small balding man with the slight mustache seemed to pretty well fit the *Sun-Times*'s suggestion of a "Mr. Milquetoast."

CHAPTER 3

The Communist TA: Edward Yellin

As the decade of the sixties began, David Dodds Henry was presented almost simultaneously with two opportunities to demonstrate how he would deal with controversy during his tenure. In 1960 Edward Yellin, an engineering graduate student at Illinois, presented Henry with the first such occasion. Years before, as an undergraduate in Colorado, Yellin had been subpoenaed to testify before the House Un-American Activities Committee (HUAC) regarding his past membership in the Communist Party, and he had declined to answer the committee's questions, creatively claiming First Amendment privileges. By now a recipient of a PhD fellowship at Illinois, he was described by the head of the fellowship committee as a student of "genuine achievement and great promise."[1] The fellowship award included teaching-assistant employment in the engineering department, and as a university employee, Yellin was required to take a newly enacted loyalty oath prior to assuming his teaching duties, stating, "I am not a member of nor will I join any political party or organization that advocates the overthrow of the government of the United States by force or violence."[2] Since Yellin had long before left the party, he felt perfectly able to comply with the oath. However, because of his undergraduate decision to refuse to answer HUAC questions and his unwillingness to "name names," Yellin was now charged with contempt of Congress and called to trial in Hammond, Indiana, in March 1960.

Yellin was not a typical student. In 1960 he was thirty years old and a father of three children. As a youthful Communist Party member, he had been selected to participate in a program that placed young party members in industrial jobs, with the goal of enlisting new recruits for the party. In that role, he had worked in various Gary, Indiana, steel mills for several years doing party organizing. In 1956 he made the decision to leave the party and enrolled as an engineering student at the University of Colorado, where he received an undergraduate degree prior to being accepted for graduate work at the University of Illinois. The intent of the HUAC committee was to have Yellin identify members of the party from his younger days, to "name names," as it was described in the press, but Yellin had no intention of doing so. However, instead of appealing to his Fifth Amendment rights, ensuring he would not face contempt charges, Yellin chose to stand on the principle of free speech, embedded in the First Amendment, as his rationale of refusing to testify. This placed him on untested constitutional grounds, and the decision was to punish him with a lengthy legal battle, eventually won at the Supreme Court of the United States many years later, dramatically affecting Yellin's career at Illinois in the meantime.

March 11, 1960, found the young TA in U.S. District Court in Hammond, Indiana, facing four counts of contempt of Congress. Yellin stated to the court:

> The House Committee on Un-American Activities has proved by its past actions that it functions not as a bona-fide congressional committee for the purpose of developing legislation, but rather as an inquisitorial body dedicated to expose to public scorn anyone who has the courage and conviction to dissent. To me, cooperation with such a group would be tantamount to being a party to the transgression of our personal freedoms.[3]

The U.S. District Attorney said Yellin "fit the category [of communists] described as colonizers, who left homes to get jobs in basic industries," and described Yellin as "a hard core colonizer of the Communist Party who was sent to the Gary steel mills to organize for the party."[4] In short order the judge rejected Yellin's First Amendment defense and found him guilty on all four counts, sentencing the graduate student to one year in federal prison on each count.

When the university received word of the conviction, Yellin was immediately suspended, his fellowship placed in question, and his case submitted to the Faculty Committee on Graduate Student Discipline. The committee informed Yellin they intended to ask him direct questions regarding his activism in the Communist Party and his current beliefs but made it clear they would not ask about any past associations; that is, they would not ask him to provide names. Thus, Yellin took a different approach with the faculty committee, acknowledging his party membership and activities of the past and fully answering the committee's questions to their complete satisfaction. As promised, the committee did not ask about past or present associations, and, said Yellin, this was the determining factor in his decision to cooperate.[5] The decision of the committee was that since his conviction was now under appeal, Yellin was at the moment fully compliant with all university requirements. Thus, within two weeks of his suspension, in the afternoon following the committee's morning recommendation, the dean of the Graduate College announced Yellin's reinstatement as a student in good standing, with full privileges, including access to his critical financial fellowship.[6]

Before the decision, the student paper equivocated editorially, citing Yellin's "brilliant five-point average in engineering," while acknowledging, "There are people who do not cater to having sons and daughters in the same institution where men refuse to identify past associates and associations." The paper ultimately came down on the student's side: "[Yellin] was standing on a principle, and if a man cannot do this and remain in the University, there is something drastically wrong with the University's attempt to keep open the avenues of free exchange in the academic marketplace of ideas."[7] The paper characterized the final decision as "a refreshing spring breeze in the sometimes stale atmosphere . . . on campus."[8] President Henry kept a low profile throughout the case and accepted the decision of his faculty committee. If he had an opinion on Yellin's case, there is no mention in the record.

It would be three years and many court appearances before the U.S. Supreme Court would overturn Yellin's district-court conviction. In the meantime, when HUAC members retaliated by having Yellin's National Science Foundation grants rescinded, friendly sources at the university ensured he received loans, which were written off over time as he continued his teaching internship. Yellin credited the dean of his department, among others, with the necessary support that allowed him to finish his doctoral work.[9] This formal and informal support for a former communist might be seen as a turning point at the university, away from the anticommunism mania of the Cold War years and toward a new phase. Joseph McCarthy had been dead for several years when the decade began, and though his shadow was still present over ongoing HUAC hearings, the university and its president chose to support the former communist student. Henry did this by default, accepting the decision of his faculty committee, although a second incident occurring in the same month would showcase a different attitude and would prove to be much more controversial for the president.

CHAPTER 4

The Sexual Rebel: Leo Koch

In the week before Yellin's reinstatement, on March 18, 1960, the *DI* published a letter to the editor from Leo Koch, assistant professor of biology, advocating premarital sex for "mature" students. The letter criticized "decrepit," "inhumane," and "Victorian" standards of the era, with Koch suggesting that for consenting university students, "mutually satisfactory sexual experience would eliminate the need for many hours of frustrating petting and lead to happier and longer lasting marriages.... With modern contraceptives and medical advice readily available at the nearest drugstore ... there is no reason sexual intercourse should not be condoned for those sufficiently mature."[1] Koch's comments, coming years after the publication of the controversial Kinsey Reports—nationally renowned research papers on human sexuality published by an Indiana University zoologist—might seem tame today. But such public discussion of premarital sex on the part of university students was scandalous to central Illinoisans of the time, and the missive was described by the newspaper as "the most controversial letter to the editor in *Daily Illini* history."[2] Koch's use of the words "sexual intercourse" may have been the first time such words had ever appeared in the newspaper.

Responding to hundreds of letters from angry parents and other citizens, the Executive Committee of the Liberal Arts College soon recommended Koch's immediate dismissal, and the still relatively new President Henry, perhaps with Stoddard-era controversies in mind, immediately approved the recommendation and announced the firing, stating, "Koch's letter expressed views offensive and repugnant, contrary to commonly accepted standards of morality, and their public espousal may be interpreted as encouragement of immoral behavior."[3] Koch replied, "I thought the University of Illinois was too intelligent to do something like this. . . . I hope the people of the country have enough intelligence to know that democracy depends upon freedom of speech."[4] He would be disappointed in that regard. The dismissed assistant professor followed with, "This action is in the same class with those of the late Sen. McCarthy. . . . I gladly take my stand with Bertrand Russell, George D. Stoddard and other forward-looking thinkers."[5]

Some fellow forward-looking thinkers came to his defense. A faculty senate committee pushed back on Henry's decision, voting for reprimand but not censure. A student group, the Committee on Liberal Action, met, drawing an audience of two hundred, and voted to demand a public apology to Koch from the university. Other students hung an effigy of Henry from a tree in front of the McKinley YMCA, "a well-dressed mannequin, complete with spectacles and moustache," and adorned it with signs, "Not for Free Sex, but for Academic Freedom."[6] Forty-nine faculty of other universities—including Harvard, Yale, Princeton, Oxford, and Cambridge—formed a Committee for Leo Koch, to no avail. *Playboy* magazine publisher and Illinois alum Hugh Hefner wrote an essay defending Koch, to even less effect.[7] Rev. Ira Latimer, speaking for the University of Illinois Dad's Association, sent a letter to the parents of Illinois *women* students, calling Koch's ideas "an audacious attempt to subvert the religious and moral foundations of America . . . standard operating procedure of the Communist conspiracy."[8] The Dad's Association passed a vote of confidence in Henry's handling of the case, adding, "The State of Illinois is indeed fortunate in having a man of the caliber of Dr. David D. Henry."[9] At the same time, the group went on record favoring the upcoming $195 million dollar bond issue scheduled to appear on the ballot the following November and pledged to support it enthusiastically.

University students organized a three-hour campus protest against what they called "intellectual contraception," drawing a crowd that started at a few hundred and then swelled to several thousand at a Saturday afternoon campus carnival. Demonstrators sang protest songs, defended Koch and freedom of speech, shrugged off counterprotester calls of "Go home, beatniks," and charged that Henry had "pandered to the popular pressure exerted to remove Dr. Koch so that the passage of the bond issue might more easily be secured." Henry went on record later the same day, vehemently denying the suggestion, and declared that drawing a connection between the dismissal and the bond initiative was "perfectly absurd."[10]

Koch, a graduate of the University of California at Berkeley and a World War II navy veteran, stuck to his guns and explained his position further in newspaper interviews. "Koch sees no reason why students planning marriage should not rent apartments and live together. 'If we begin to practice what we preach as a society, I see no problem in having young unmarried couples living together like anyone else. . . . If this were allowed, I believe that the appeal of the forbidden fruit would be lessened.'" However, he emphasized, "For heaven's sake don't say I'm for free love," which he defined as "sex after any casual, accidental encounter." "What I advocate is that couples try out living together for a few months. This is the scientific attitude." When asked about his wife's reaction to the controversy, Koch admitted, "Naturally she was dismayed that the university fired me . . . she had been doubtful about [the wisdom of] mailing the letter." He added that Mrs. Koch was unavailable, having "spent the weekend . . . at an obedience dog show, and was still out of town."[11]

A campus Presbyterian pastor, Rev. James Hine, laid it on Koch: "This is the grossest oversimplification of facts and the most inadequate treatment of a complex and important aspect of human existence that I've ever had the agony to read." Hine went further, declaring, "If he [Koch] would care to elaborate on his theories, he might do so under the title 'Life in the Zoo.' On second thought, the animals might object, as they seem to observe a sex life governed by considerable order and restraint."[12] Not surprisingly, the university's board of trustees lined up behind their president:

> We do not condemn Assistant Professor Koch's actions in issue here merely because he expressed in his letter views contrary to commonly accepted beliefs and standards. We condemn it because of the manner in which he expressed those views. We do not consider that letter as a "responsible" and proper expression of the views stated in it.[13]

Twenty-five student leaders, including the editor of the student newspaper, petitioned the board to reconsider the university's decision. Twenty-year-old Elizabeth Krohne, a junior student senator and English major, requested five minutes of a meeting of the board to discuss Koch's sentence, in light of a well-publicized American Association of University Professors (AAUP) censure of the university. The trustees voted unanimously to deny Krohne her five minutes. The AAUP declared the university's action "outrageously severe and completely unwarranted," but there is no indication in the record that either Henry or the trustees were disturbed by the censure.[14]

Even the *Sun-Times*, one of the more liberal Chicago newspapers, supported the president's decision in this era of tight sexual mores:

> [Henry] did right in discharging Koch. It would have been better if he hadn't hired him in the first place. . . . The professor may be a specialist in biology . . . [but that] does not give a biologist the right to advise students in controversial areas involving religion and morality. . . . Freedom of speech? He has it. He exercised it. [But] he can no longer exercise it as a member of the faculty of the University of Illinois. . . .

Koch has a right to his views. He has a right to express his views. He has done so. And in doing so he has demonstrated his lack of fitness for the post he occupied. Dr. Henry did right in booting him out."[15]

Coincidentally, the week following publication of Koch's letter, a husband and wife author/lecture team, co-sponsored by the University YMCA and YWCA, delivered a weeklong series of well-attended presentations on "Sex, Love, and Marriage" at various university venues. The student newspaper reported packed houses as the speakers provided such wisdom as, "There is no easy answer to whether sexual intercourse before marriage is permissible," and "The modern woman is clearly confused about her identity . . . [while] the American man . . . feels threatened by the emancipation of American women . . . unsure of his masculinity. He reacts either with passivity or aggressiveness. . . . The woman's problem . . . [is] whether to achieve or to be loved. . . . For the student who wants to know how far to go . . . [there is] no pat answer." The lecturers helpfully suggested students pause at decisive moments of intimacy to ask themselves, "What am I doing here?" with "careful consideration of social and moral obligations."[16] Such a cautious, considered treatment of the subject was certainly more in accord with the mores of central Illinois citizens. According to the student newspaper, the lectures were delivered to packed houses and, as judged by letters to the editor, were considered a rousing success, providing a sharp contrast to the unacceptable behavior of the fired biologist.

Leo Koch was relieved from teaching responsibilities immediately upon Henry's approval of the committee's decision. He would appeal to the Illinois Supreme Court and the U.S. Supreme Court, but both denied him a hearing. Following his departure from Illinois, and from academia, Koch would make a career as a leader in the sexual revolution, founding "The League for Sexual Freedom" in New York City, with Allen Ginsberg, among others.[17]

Though Leo Koch's call for sexual revolution was seen by some as a communist attack on American morals, Yellin's treatment by the university was gentler, demonstrating a new era, one that would be focused on freedom of speech. The sign hung on Henry's effigy suggested that Henry might well support such freedom of speech, even for a former communist, but that public advocacy of sexual freedom for students was beyond all limits. Henry squashed the public discussion of sexual mores with unhesitating support for his committee, while in the same month managed to avoid controversy in the Yellin affair by accepting a gentler decision by another faculty committee, without comment. Henry would frequently utilize this technique, adroitly standing behind faculty committees, and would have many opportunities to demonstrate such nimbleness, as freedom of speech would become a larger and more central issue on the Illinois campus.

PART II
The Free Speech Era, 1965–67

CHAPTER 5

The Civil Rights Movement and the University

Central Illinois newspapers of the early 1950s, during the university presidency of George Stoddard, often featured front-page stories of threatening communist aggression worldwide and/or domestic communist infiltration. McCarthy hearings, Soviet oppression in Eastern Europe, communists in North Korea, Red China, and Greece, and blacklisted movie stars all made up the news background of the times. By the sixties, that background was fading, and another ongoing story, the civil rights movement, was becoming pervasive in Illinois newspapers, beginning with bus boycotts in the late fifties, lunch-counter sit-ins and freedom rides in the early sixties, and voter-registration drives and peaceful marches, some turning violent, by the mid-sixties. Tactics of this grassroots movement spread throughout the southern states from the late fifties on. The violent response by southern police, who used fire hoses, dogs, and batons to control protesters, only served to spread news of the movement faster and provided garish fodder for the nation's newspapers and the nightly news programs then growing in popularity on the three television networks.

As this new force for change was sweeping across the South in the early sixties, the Illinois campus was not immune. In fact, on one occasion in 1963, Illinois even contributed leadership to the movement in a small way. Racial tensions were high across the country throughout the summer of that year. A "March on Washington for Jobs and Freedom" occurred in August, climaxing with Martin Luther King's "I Have a Dream" speech. The following month, on a Sunday in Birmingham, Alabama, a church bombing killed four young girls, shocking the nation's moral conscience. The day after, a memorial vigil was organized on the University of Illinois quadrangle, attended by 350 students and faculty. Local priests, ministers, rabbis, and student leaders addressed the crowd. Pleasantly surprised at the turnout, leaders announced they would extend the vigil to every day of that week. Other campuses across the country picked up the idea of a weeklong campus vigil; more than twenty-five schools as diverse as the University of Washington in Seattle and Wellesley in Massachusetts joined in. Students and faculty marched in picket lines on the Illinois quad from 8:00 A.M. to noon every day of the week. Numerous deans, along with future chancellor Jack W. Peltason, expressed their support for the vigils, and President Henry himself announced that he was hard at work on a "very concise and thorough statement on the University's relationship to the area of civil rights."[1]

Within a week of the vigil, twenty-five university students participated in an all-night sit-in, led by the local chapter of the National Association for the Advancement of Colored People (NAACP) at the Champaign City Council building, protesting the defeat of an antidiscrimination open-housing ordinance the council had rejected. Kenneth O. Stratton, the council's only African American member, had introduced the measure, and his was the only vote in favor when the ordinance went down to a 6–1 defeat. The sit-in tactic was an old and trusted tool of protesters, used in the United States by civil rights and labor organizers even before World War II. As far back as 1939, the *New York Times* reported peace activists and cafeteria workers using the tactic at a Forty-First Street sandwich shop, where protesters purchased five-cent cups of coffee, occupied all available seats, and settled in, preventing any other customers from finding places—and, according to the Times, "conducted what might best be described as a customers' nickel sit-down strike."[2] In more recent years black and white college students had used the sit-in tactic at segregated lunch counters with great effect in more than a dozen southern cities, including Greensboro, North Carolina; Nashville, Tennessee; and Rock Hill, South Carolina. Their actions were, of course, broadcast regularly on the evening news across the nation's television networks. The children who would grow into the activists of the student movement would learn of this protest tool as they watched the evening news with their parents in their middle-class living rooms. A sit-down strike that could paralyze a New York sandwich shop or a Greensboro Walgreens lunch counter would certainly have an impact in quiet Champaign, Illinois; it is no surprise, then, that the city-council sit-in was the highlight of Champaign-Urbana media for several days, bringing publicity to the protesters' cause, just as they had hoped.

There were no arrests at the Champaign sit-in, as amiable police allowed the students and accompanying NAACP members to remain in the lobby of the building all night. "The police were very understanding and cooperative," said Rudy

Frank, a member of the NAACP executive committee. "We appreciate their attitude very much." The *Daily Illini* reported that about a third of the student protesters, female "co-eds," chose to leave the sit-in early to comply with the university's curfew for women dorm residents.[3] Commentary about the sit-in ran in the newspaper alongside the now-completed statement from President Henry on the university's new civil rights position:

> It is clear that everyone is called upon, by the horrors of Birmingham, by the obvious cumulative injustices in our social system, and by the imperatives for enforcement of basic policy, to make a personal decision on how he will cast his influence for racial equality. Merely hoping for improvement in the normal course of events is not enough. Each student, like each member of the faculty, must decide for himself what he can do, by himself and with others.[4]

The following week, on November 8, Senator Strom Thurmond, leader of the conservative southern Dixiecrats in the U.S. Senate and a vociferous opponent of civil rights legislation recently proposed by President John F. Kennedy, was on campus to deliver a speech regarding alleged communist influence within the civil rights movement. Students, perhaps heeding Henry's advice, heckled Thurmond's speech and formed rowdy picket lines that impeded his departure from the campus building where he had spoken and, after the senator was finally in his car, from the campus itself. Within days the student senate convened and passed "emergency legislation," issuing an apology to the senator for his treatment.[5]

The week following the senate's apology to Thurmond, a sometime-student-turned-fundamentalist-Christian-bookstore-owner, Richard McMullin, was arrested outside the university library for distributing religious literature on campus without approval of the administration. A broad coalition of student groups rose to his defense, including the campus Young Democrats, the YMCA, the Student Peace Union (an antinuclear group), the NAACP, and Friends of SNCC (supporters of the Student Non-violent Coordinating Committee, a civil rights organization that led voter-registration drives, lunch counter sit-ins, and other protest actions in the southern states).[6] In a letter addressed to President Henry, the coalition demanded "a centrally located area where literature may be handed out . . . [provision for] any speaker to address students from the Auditorium steps . . . [and that] leaflets and handbills be allowed distribution anywhere on University grounds."[7] In short, the letter suggested that the university's proper role was to stimulate rather than discourage the spread of ideas. Such demands for greater sanctioning and protection of free speech on campus would become a consistent theme in the coming era of student unrest. The protest over McMullin's arrest occurred November 22, 1963, the day President John Kennedy was assassinated in Dallas, Texas, and the tumultuous sixties now began in earnest.

CHAPTER 6

Civil Rights, Free Speech, and War

The tumult of the civil rights movement continued to dominate the national news for much of 1964 and 1965 while the war in Vietnam escalated in the background. Related stories on both topics were well represented in the pages of the *Daily Illini*. In January 1964 the paper reported on several former university students headed to Albany, Georgia, to join a peace march in support of jailed civil rights protesters. A February follow-up recounted that one of those students had been jailed for twenty-five days and was released after losing thirty pounds in a jailhouse fast. March brought front-page reports of interracial violence in Jacksonville, Florida, along with stories of Illinois students, SNCC members, training to join voter-registration drives in Greensboro, North Carolina, and Atlanta, Georgia. In April the paper reported on the opening of the New York World's Fair, where a thousand advocates from the Congress for Racial Equality (CORE), a twenty-year-old, nonviolent civil rights organization, interrupted a speech by President Lyndon Johnson, shouting, "Freedom, freedom!" The *DI* continued to report on civil rights protests across the country, including an incident in May when demonstrators disrupted a rally for the staunch Alabama segregationist and presidential candidate George Wallace in Cambridge, Maryland, with thirteen arrested by the Maryland National Guard. Later that same month the paper reported on the arrests of fourteen Illinois students sitting in at the Champaign County Board of Realtors, demanding support for a local equal-housing ordinance.

However, in the fall of 1964 the focus began to change when the paper began coverage of students at the University of California at Berkeley protesting a ban against on-campus political activity and elimination of a free-speech area, resulting in the formation of what would become a years-long student effort known as the Free Speech Movement. Like the earlier McMullin incident at Illinois, the Berkeley movement in its early days was broad based, with even the conservative Young Americans for Freedom joining more liberal groups in protest against the university restrictions. On the day following the mass arrest of 801 students and sympathizers on the Berkeley campus, seventy-five Illinois students gathered on the quad under the leadership of campus Young Democrats, Friends of SNCC, and Students for a Democratic Society (SDS) to show support for the Cal students. Former *DI* editor Roger Ebert spoke, berating the student body for the small turnout and bemoaning the student apathy rampant on the campus: "[At Illinois] we don't even have 801 students who would understand why 801 students would want to be arrested for denial of a free speech area."[1] To the contrary, and perhaps to Ebert's later surprise, the issue of free speech would indeed arise at the university.

In January of the new year, with a national focus on civil rights and the Berkeley free-speech movement, not many noticed the account of Gene Keyes, pacifist son of a U of I professor, who was found guilty of burning his draft card outside the Selective Service office in Champaign to protest the war in Vietnam. The judge in the case delivered a light sentence, entering an application for probation.[2] Eight months later, in August, as Keyes's act became more common among draft protesters across the country, the U.S. Congress would enact a broad law to punish anyone "knowingly" destroying or mutilating his draft card, with lengthy prison sentences attached. The act of burning a draft card would soon attain great symbolic meaning among draft protesters and defenders of the war alike. However, at this time the national civil rights movement still maintained front-page position in the student newspaper.

In February 1965, Martin Luther King Jr. asked President Johnson to place Selma, Alabama, under martial law; in Champaign, local SNCC supporters marched on the local Federal Bureau of Investigation (FBI) office in support of the request.[3] In March, President Henry spoke to students in a large ballroom at the Illini Union on the topic of "International Dimensions of Higher Education," but the student paper lamented that only twenty-eight showed up to hear him speak.[4] Later in the month, three hundred students gathered on the steps of the Auditorium to show support for protesters in Selma, where the university was represented by several students.[5] The themes of civil rights, student rights, and the war now began to overlap, as reflected in the March 27 issue of the *DI*, with reports of graduate students demanding more liberal dormitory policies, students returning from Selma celebrating at the Latzer Hall YMCA, and a bomb exploding at the U.S. embassy in Saigon.[6] A small article appeared on page 2 of the April 6 issue, noting that a

"Student Committee on Viet Nam" was forming on campus to "protest against the United States policies in Viet Nam."[7]

Another indicator of growing concern about the war came in early May, when a second new committee, the Ad Hoc Faculty Committee on Vietnam, announced its participation in a nationally televised "teach-in" to be broadcast on the CBS network on May 15. The teach-in concept had originated at the University of Michigan two months earlier, when more than three thousand gathered for an all-night affair of lectures, debates, and movies about the war. The May 15 teach-in would include a distinguished list of speakers for and against the government's policies, including McGeorge Bundy, Arthur Schlesinger, and Hans Morgenthau. The Illinois faculty committee arranged for the broadcast to be piped into the Gregory Hall auditorium for an audience of more than a thousand students and faculty; loudspeakers carried the audio of the broadcast to an overflow crowd listening on the lawn outside. Following the televised program, local speakers, including political science professor Eqbal Ahmad, delivered remarks and commentary on "The Nature of Guerrilla Warfare"; economics professor Russell Moran on "Containment: For What?"; economics professor Fred Gottheil on "What Are Our Stakes in Vietnam?" Nine additional seminars, facilitated by journalism, English, history, and mathematics faculty, ran on into the early evening. The *DI* reported, "students either listened attentively, slumped in their seats or wandered downstairs to the Coke machine" throughout the day's events, with the audience seemingly "equally divided between the supporters and the critics." In these early days of Vietnam war debates, calm prevailed, and "little violent difference of opinion" was noted, between the "polite professors and calm spokesmen for the administration's policy in Viet Nam."[8] Such relatively tranquil discussion would be less common in the years to come.

For five days in the summer of 1965 the worst rioting since the American Civil War erupted in the Los Angeles neighborhood of Watts, resulting in thirty-four deaths, millions of dollars in damages, and mounting racial tension across the country. At the start of the fall term at Illinois, reports of civil rights protests and the war continued to dominate the *DI* headlines. In October seventy-five Friends of SNCC members gathered on the Auditorium steps to protest an acquittal in the trial of a part-time deputy sheriff who shot and killed civil rights worker Johnathan Daniels in Hayneville, Alabama. A jury of twelve white men deliberated less than two hours before returning their verdict. Rick Soderstrom, president of the campus SNCC organization, told the group, "This type of thing cannot go on without some form of protest. There is no place to turn for justice except the federal government, but they say 'we can't act.' The federal government won't act if we don't. We must act!" Mack Jones of the Champaign chapter of the NAACP also spoke, bringing in the local angle: "This acquittal is nothing new. Western civilization has been predicated with white supremacy. This supremacy is manifested in many different ways, whether it be murder in Alabama, housing in Champaign-Urbana or indifference in the University president's office."[9] Stalled court proceedings in another case of a slain civil rights worker in Alabama were reported on the same page.

On October 15, at a gathering sponsored by SDS, nearly four hundred students and faculty gathered on the quad to debate the Vietnam War, followed by a smaller all-night vigil at the Armory. A week later, members of Sigma Alpha Epsilon announced a blood drive, labeling it a "blood crusade," for U.S. soldiers in Vietnam. Initially, the effort was described as "strictly a humanitarian gesture ... neither in support or opposition to U.S. policy in Viet Nam, but rather to show support for the soldiers."[10] The idea, which spread to other campuses with support of the national Red Cross, the Defense Department, and the White House, quickly lost its apolitical nature. The Illinois SDS chapter issued a response to the fraternity blood drive, in a letter released by co-chair Vincent Wu:

> To all those who believe that measures such as the blood drive indicate support for our soldiers in Viet Nam: You mean to furnish blood for our soldiers in Viet Nam. We share your concern for their welfare but would like to go farther than that. We would like to bring the boys home. You would like to ignore the real issues underlying our being in Viet Nam. We would like to bring these issues to light, in the hope of getting out of the mess. You would like to furnish blood for bleeding people. We would like to stop and prevent their bleeding, in the first place. The Red Cross and the Pentagon have stated that there is no shortage of blood either here in the United States or for our soldiers in Viet Nam. (The Vietnamese probably are short though—so why don't we give it to them on both sides? Or, better, why not stop the bleeding in the first place, by stopping the war?)....
>
> Therefore, we refuse to take part as a group in prolonging the war by joining you in missing the point. As a group we shall continue to work for an end to the bloodshed. The situation is as though men were falling off a cliff. You are at the bottom administering first aid. We are trying to stop the men from falling off.[11]

Wu, a graduate student in mathematics, was born in China, brought to the United States as a child by his parents, and raised in San Francisco. A member of the Quaker congregation, he was the son of a Christian minister, "a preacher's kid," as he put it, with strong religious, moral, and ethical convictions. He would later obtain the first conscientious-objector status granted by his draft board in San Francisco. A veteran of the civil rights movement, Wu had participated in early voter-registration drives in Mississippi as well as a fifty-mile antisegregation march from Selma, Alabama, to the state capital in Montgomery in 1965. With a deep faith "in the American ideal, I truly believed in it," he felt that both the civil rights and the antiwar movement "were founded on hope, that if we reviewed factually for people what was going on, they would change their minds. It turned out not to be."[12] A regular speaker at protest rallies on the campus, he played a leadership role in the local movement both within SDS and on the steering committees of various ad hoc groups. Wu would sign letters to the editor of the *DI* with his full name, Vincent Hau-Leong Wu; he stood out not only for his beliefs and speaking skills but also because Asian students made up such a small minority of the Illinois student population in the sixties and were even rarer in the movement. He would joke with his fellow activists that, given most Americans' limited familiarity with Asians, he could easily pass himself off as a Vietnamese orphan if it would be helpful. The few other Chinese students thought him "foolhardy." "They didn't know what to make of me," he said. "They thought I was stupid to expose myself in an American community." A second Asian American, law student Bob Hasagawa, would also speak at rallies on the quad, often reminding his audience of the West Coast internments of the Japanese during World War II. This would be the first that many in his audience had heard of such camps. Within weeks of publication of the SDS letter, as if to validate Wu, the national Red Cross would publicly admit they had no way to ascertain if blood collected as part of the campus donations would actually find its way to Vietnam.

In the spring the issue of free speech raised its head at the University of Illinois campus in Chicago, known as the Chicago Circle campus, when Louis Diskin, an admitted member of the American Communist Party, was denied permission to speak on campus. Diskin had been invited by the Student Humanities Club, which had refused to sign a statement saying the speaker would not advocate the Communist Party platform. President Henry approved a committee decision that Diskin's speech would violate the "subversive, seditious and un-American" clause of the Clabaugh Act. The next month, faculty of the law school submitted a resolution to the trustees, asking their support in repealing the Clabaugh Act, arguing the law "interferes with the educational functions of the University by denying students, faculty . . . freedom to hear divergent views . . . [and] embodies the idea of censorship and prior restraint."[13] The board sent the request to a committee for consideration, but no further action followed.

The spring term would end with a portentous front-page story, given the conservative nature of the campus. Phillip Durrett, an Air Force veteran, student member of the Young Socialists, and a future leader in the Illinois antiwar movement, announced plans to open a Green Street coffeehouse where "disciples of Karl Marx and Robert Welch may find themselves meeting face to face. . . . [It would be] a place for radicals of both the left and right to come and air their ideas. . . . We want it to be a place of inquiry where everyone can come and talk." Echoing Ebert, Durrett complained, "Right now we have such widespread apathy that anything would be better."[14] On the same day the paper reported that President Henry was requesting support from the faculty senate for a new position, that of chancellor at the Urbana-Champaign campus, citing the president's increased workload of recent years. In his request, Henry cited the lengthy hours required "for keeping good relations and close coordination between the University, the governor and the General Assembly."

During that summer there were signs that Illini apathy was beginning to wane. In early July, when Johnson escalated the war by bombing North Vietnam's major cities and harbors, three hundred protestors gathered on the quad to hear several hours of antiwar speeches. In an ominous sign of the violence that would come much later, an "aerial bomb" was detonated near the group, though no one was injured.[15] Occasionally, small groups of protestors would gather on the back steps of the Illini Union. Vern Fein remembers, "In those first demonstrations there would be maybe twelve of us, and people would come by and spit but we just kept marching around. I remember once it started raining, and we'd made signs but the rain got on the signs and the marker ink ran, so you couldn't read them. We looked like bedraggled cats. But within two years we had thousands marching for the moratorium."[16] Even at Illinois the times were beginning to change.

CHAPTER 7

A Spark: W. E. B. DuBois Club

The 1966 fall term began against a multilayered, tension-filled, political background, both nationally and on campus. On the most basic level at the university, the fight was about whether students were to be treated as children or adults. At this time American public universities largely set rules for student behavior using the concept of in loco parentis, the university acting in the place of parents to determine appropriate dress codes, living conditions, and personal conduct. At Illinois, this effectively meant a code consistent with the standards of the strictest of parents. Dormitories were unisex, and visits of men to women's dorm rooms or vice versa was strictly prohibited. Men and women students were allowed to visit each other only in the lounges of the women's dorms, where a notorious three-foot rule was enforced—that is, a couple was required at all times to keep three of their four feet on the floor. To enforce the rule, supervisors patrolled the lounges, which, as closing time neared, would transform into frenzied, passion pits teeming with entwined students. Women were required to be inside their dorms by 10:00 P.M. on weeknights and by midnight on weekends, after which doors were locked and not reopened till 7:00 A.M.; overnight stays were forbidden, and violators were subject to disciplinary punishment. Throughout the decade, student-government leaders pressured the administration, with painfully slow progress, to loosen some of the Big Ten's strictest housing rules. The legal basis of in loco parentis *in* colleges and universities had been defeated in a federal court in 1961, but at Illinois, housing administrators doggedly held tight to the concept.

Demonstrating similarly slow progress the civil rights movement continued atop the national news, while on campus the student NAACP chapter dissolved and re-formed as a local unit of the less conservative Congress for Racial Equality, indicating "a shift toward increased militancy."[1] The student SNCC group, a racially mixed organization still led by Rick Soderstrom, applauded and supported the shift. The antiwar movement continued to build across the nation's campuses, and at Illinois the first SDS meeting of the semester spilled out of its scheduled room and moved outdoors to accommodate the overflow.[2] But neither the tensions around student housing, nor civil rights, nor the war would be the major story of the new school year. That honor would belong to a student rebellion against the nearly twenty-year-old Clabaugh Act.

In September, Ralph Bennett, an assistant flight instructor at the university's Institute of Aviation, formed a local branch of the W. E. B. DuBois Club. The club's namesake, William Edward Burghardt DuBois, was a well-known, Harvard-educated, African American historian, sociologist, civil rights activist, and anti-Stalinist communist who had died in 1963. In spite of DuBois's quite public negative feelings about communism as implemented in the USSR, the Communist Party USA, leveraging his popularity on the left, adopted the name for a new, national youth organization in 1964, not long after his death. Bennett knew that selecting such a name (associated as it was with the Communist Party) for his group would provoke a significant reaction in the conservative environment of Illinois. Going even further though, he announced his intention to apply for university recognition of the new group. The response of the university, the legislature, and the public was just as he expected. Representative Charles Clabaugh, interviewed on the subject, did not mince words: "The club is a first-rate communist organization, they're no damn good." He called for Bennett's immediate firing. A conservative student group, which occasionally published the *Rubicon Review* bulletin, called for a letter-writing campaign to trustees and government officials, declaring, "With God's help we will succeed in setting His enemy back." Bennett responded, "Any group, right or left, has the right to establish itself. We disagree with groups on the right but recognize their right to establish themselves," adding that in his estimation, the *Review* was somewhere to the right of the John Birch Society.[3] To add fuel to the fire, Bennett suggested that his club was considering extending an invitation to Bettina Aptheker, communist student leader from Berkeley, to speak on campus, testing the Clabaugh Act. A university administrator announced that no application had yet been received from the club, but that the Clabaugh Act would have to be taken into consideration, and that without speaking to the merits of the club, the university certainly could not be expected to violate a state law prohibiting any "subversive, seditious or un-American" organization.[4] The Clabaugh Act and Bennett's DuBois Club would combine to create a spark that would set off the Illinois student protest movement.

CHAPTER 8

The University Reacts

The university administration reacted tentatively to the DuBois Club application. The group's request for recognition marked the beginning of a months-long struggle by President Henry and his fellow administrators to find a path through an obstacle course of conservative legislators and public opinion, a more liberal faculty, a student body at first indifferent but eventually quite engaged on the issue, and a small group of student activists intent on creating a confrontation. Compounding the administration's situation were public statements by Attorney General Nicholas Katzenbach and FBI director J. Edgar Hoover labeling the DuBois group communist and subversive, even before any such official determination had been made. A fundamental issue was that the name "Du Bois Club" was used by both a national organization that was under federal investigation and a loosely related collection of similarly named smaller groups on the nation's college campuses. The relationship between the national and the local clubs was intentionally kept vague, adding complexity to the already unclear situation that confronted Henry and his fellows.

The federal body chartered to make determinations regarding communist-front organizations was the Subversive Activities Control Board (SACB). The board was established in 1950 at the height of the Red Scare, as part of the Internal Security Act—also known as the McCarren Act, after its author, an ardent anticommunist and anti–New Deal conservative Nevada senator Pat McCarren. The SACB was made up of five appointees named by the president; they reported directly to him but worked in conjunction with and at the request of the Justice Department.

When the Attorney General decided an organization merited investigation, his department submitted a petition to the SACB, which conducted the investigation and made a final determination. If and when the SACB determined a group was subversive, it then reported its decision to the Attorney General, who was responsible for enforcing the decision. In March 1966 Katzenbach formally petitioned the SACB to declare the DuBois group a communist front. His request was made public along with accusations about the seditious and subversive nature of the club. However, as of September, the SACB had not yet completed its investigation, creating an ambiguous situation for Illinois administrators. Bennett's repeated claim that there was no formal affiliation between his club and the national organization would become a central point of dispute in the university's (and later, the trustees') decision-making process. Available evidence seemed ambiguous, and based on that evidence, there seemed at best only an informal relationship between the two. More important, even if such a relationship did exist, the national organization had not yet been determined subversive by the SACB, despite the public, accusatory statements by Hoover and Katzenbach.

On the night of September 26, with the university still undecided on how to proceed, Bennett seized the initiative by bringing together representatives from a number of sympathetic campus groups, including Students for a Democratic Society, Young Socialists, and another liberal campus group, Americans for Democratic Action, asking their support in his drive for recognition. All the groups responded positively and began to work together to put plans in place that would soon develop into a test of the Clabaugh Act.

The following day, Durrett, now president of the Young Socialists, along with a member of Bennett's club, met with William K. Williams, an administrator on Henry's staff who would later receive a title of "Ombudsman" and would become very familiar to the students as an intermediary between the activists and the administration. At this initial meeting, the *DI* reported that Williams told the students that Henry was completely opposed to the DuBois group's presence on campus, but Williams later denied both that he had said that and that such a statement accurately reflected Henry's position.[1] Williams did indicate the university would likely table any decision regarding the local chapter until after the SACB had made its formal decision regarding the national organization. He also warned the two activists that Henry would not hesitate to invoke the Clabaugh Act if faced with a confrontation, but for the time being the university's position was that more review of the situation was necessary.

At this time Bennett's group included only five members—five short of university requirements for recognition—so Bennett began actively recruiting more members, even some who might be opposed to the club's principles but were still willing to support him in the drive for recognition. In newspaper interviews the

Aviation Institute employee admitted his political activities were beginning to complicate his life, even creating tension at his workplace. He noted that he had encountered "silent stares" from his fellow employees but no open hostility yet. His wife was more forthcoming, admitting that if her husband were to lose his position, she "would love to move," adding for emphasis, "I hate this town."[2]

CHAPTER 9

The University Delays

Only one more day of administrative review was needed after the Durrett-Williams meeting, as the following day Dean of Students Stanton Millet, who would assume a central role in the handling of the club, released a statement through the Public Information Office:

> I have informed representatives of the W. E. B. DuBois Club who are seeking to organize a chapter of the national parent organization on this campus that I will defer any consideration of their request for use of university facilities until the status of the national organization has been clarified. I am advised that the nature of the parent organization is being reviewed by the Subversive Activities Control Board on the initiative of the Attorney General of the United States, and the action of that committee will be relevant to the matters presented by this request for university facilities. In my judgment, it is not appropriate for the Dean of Students to take action on the request without further clarification. The representatives of the W. E. B. DuBois Club have not been willing to assert that there would be no connection between a local chapter and the national parent organization, and in any case, I believe that such separation of a local chapter from its national organization would not be tenable.[1]

With this statement the university attempted to delay the decision indefinitely, passing the buck to the SACB. In response, the DuBois Club members, with the support of other campus groups, announced creation of an "ad hoc committee in defense of free speech," in order to "defend the rights of all individuals and organizations to express themselves in accordance with the First Amendment and the

Bill of Rights of the United States of America." Representative Clabaugh did not hesitate to provide his opinion: "We don't need any people who want to destroy this country meeting in public places and I'll do everything I can to prevent that. That's all that law of mine does—I'm just being a patriotic citizen."[2] The following week Bennett announced that he had managed to sign up the required ten club members and planned to apply for recognition soon. It took another two weeks before he found a friendly faculty advisor, as required for the application, but on October 13 he announced he was ready for formal application. Finally, two years after the Free Speech Movement at the University of California at Berkeley had roiled the nation's academic community, a similar group was birthed at Illinois. The university had entered into the free-speech era.

The next month Henry formally announced a new governance structure for the three university campuses, with chancellors to be appointed for each of the separate campuses. This meant that beginning the following year, campus responsibilities such as management of the DuBois matter on the Urbana campus would not come to Henry's desk but to that of Jack W. Peltason, a former professor of political science at the university, now named chancellor of the Urbana campus. This action was intended to remove Henry from the day-to-day management of the three UI campuses and allow him to focus on the trustees, the legislature and other, more strategic responsibilities. The coincidence of the growing DuBois controversy and Henry's decision to add a layer of management did not escape attention. "Henry wanted Peltason as chancellor to sort of figure out how to fix this, to take care of it so it didn't blow up into something . . . like Berkeley. Henry had bigger fish to fry," recalls then-undergrad Steve Schmidt.[3]

In addition, in December 1966 a scandal garnering nationwide interest in the sports world erupted within the university's Athletic Department when it was discovered that for some time athletes of the three major Illinois sports programs had been receiving illegal cash payments from a "slush fund" of donor contributions, managed out of the back office of a local sporting-goods store. Dealing with the media, the public, and the Big Ten over this scandal would consume much of Henry's attention for the following year. Beginning with the next school year, the president's delegation of management of the main campus to Peltason would be a relief. This would put the new chancellor in charge of the campus as the free-speech era played out and for the even more tempestuous days of the late sixties. But until September of the following year, Henry would remain in charge of the Urbana campus, with its developing controversies, both athletic and political.

Stimulated by the publicity surrounding the DuBois situation, numerous student groups began lining up to support repeal of the Clabaugh Act. In late October the Student Senate Committee on Student Rights voted to support repeal of the law and began lobbying other student groups to join them. In late October the Men's

Independent Association, made up of representatives from the men's dormitories, was one of the first to announce support, followed soon by the Women's Independent Association, a parallel organization for women's dorms, and eventually by many other groups. In November, even the conservative Young Americans for Freedom (YAF) considered the issue, though eventually voting to table a decision. The more libertarian YAF members, critics of the law, argued it violated both the state and national constitutions: "It takes away the liberties of individuals . . . to impose the will of the majority on a minority." However, the majority of the YAF, Clabaugh supporters, rebuffed them, saying the law "provides a necessary check on the leftist infiltration of the campus" and noting that "there has been a marked influx of leftists on campus this year . . . a lot more beards, a lot more sandals, you know the type." The Clabaugh supporters went further, claiming, "These infiltrators are trying to make the University another Berkeley, and the Clabaugh Act will help to check their attempts. . . . Students should be protected from subversive speakers . . . this is a basic principal of survival."[4]

On the same day the reports of the YAF debate surfaced, the *DI* editorialized against the law, presciently noting that while supporters suggested the act would prevent a Berkeley-like movement—characterized as "riots"—the law was in fact more likely to have the opposite effect:

> Riots don't occur when there are no causes for discontent. Satisfied people don't take up causes and revolt against the law. But people who feel their rights are being abridged, people who feel that someone else is doing the thinking for them do get angry. This anger often extends beyond rational limits and explodes in everyone's face. . . . Clabaugh might have thought he was doing a good thing for the University in 1947 when he introduced his famous law, but if any single person has contributed to the growing discontent of students, faculty and administrators at the UI, it has been Charles Clabaugh himself. If the law is not abolished because it violates basic rights, it should be to avoid a major confrontation on campus.[5]

These arguments around the Clabaugh Act were not conducted in a vacuum, and as the Vietnam conflict continued to heat up, campus antiwar activities were growing commensurately. In November, Keenan Sheedy, president of the campus SDS, announced a Vietnam War "speak-out," to be held at a space identified the previous year by the administration as a "Free Speech Area," off the quad, specifically set aside for the exercise of such rights. The irony of one specific location on the campus so designated was not lost on either faculty or students, and as the spot was somewhat hidden, it would never become a favorite gathering place of protesters.

The speak-out was planned to coincide with nationwide antiwar rallies and marches collectively labeled the "Mobilization against the War," organized by a group of old and new leftist groups acting together in an umbrella organization called the National Coordinating Committee to End the War in Vietnam, based in Madison, Wisconsin. The committee included older, antinuclear pacifist groups such as Women Strike for Peace and the National Committee for a Sane Nuclear Policy, and joined with more recently formed student groups such as SDS, which, not surprisingly, had been one of the first groups to respond to the student senate request for support in its call for the Clabaugh repeal.[6]

Faculty speakers slated for the Illinois Mobilization event included law professor Herb Semmel, psychiatrist John Werry, economist Fred Gottheil, and student speakers Phil Durrett, Vic Berkey, and Vincent Wu. Durrett, the older veteran, spoke with a sincere, unpretentious style. His political education began while he was stationed in Georgia, where he came face to face with the blatant racism of the southern United States. His wife, employed by Emory University, "was trained by her black co-worker," Durrett said, who, he claimed, "earned half of what my wife earned." He recalled "people cheering in Atlanta when JFK was assassinated" and was made aware there would be a "[Christmas] party for 'white' [Emory] employees, and a separate one for 'Negro' employees. . . . We were invited by her black co-workers to their party. [My wife] was . . . threatened with firing for attending the 'wrong' party."[7] Robert Goldstein, then a *DI* reporter assigned to cover the student movement, remembers Durrett as someone who came across as "authentic and genuine . . . a fully realized person in his public persona . . . a solid, decent person of integrity."[8]

Berkey, a more histrionic speaker, was a graduate student and teaching assistant in biology from California, where his political action had begun with participation in a sit-in at the U.S. Attorney's office in San Francisco, demanding federal protection for civil rights workers in the South. Born in Mexico City, Berkey was raised in Los Angeles by Democratic parents who nonetheless voted for Eisenhower. Goldstein remembers the bearded grad student from one of the first Illinois antiwar rallies: "This unknown guy got up to speak and became a leader of the student movement in five seconds by saying, 'I'm Vic Berkey and I went to the University of California at Berkeley.'"[9] He was an eloquent and rousing orator; Rick Soderstrom would call him "a spellbinder"; he would continue as one of the primary leaders of the Illinois student movement throughout its duration, though later he admitted he had actually missed the Free Speech Movement at Berkeley by a semester. After receiving his undergraduate degree from Berkeley he had moved on to San Diego for graduate school when the Berkeley movement erupted, then left California for Illinois.

Though the audience at the speak-out event was thin, there was no shortage of speaking out. The *DI* reported that Wu, representing SDS, declared that "U.S. policy was illegal in light of the 1954 Geneva accords on Indochina and immoral because of American use of 'modern technology and fearsome weapons against a small country.' The war is also stupid," Wu added, saying the "best way to fight an ideology is to replace it with a better ideology.... The U.S. should seek to negotiate an 'honorable withdrawal as soon as possible' and then follow a policy of supporting all social revolutionary movements in the world." Gottheil decried the "military-industrial complex," while Werry judged U.S. intervention had benefited no one in Vietnam. A supporter of the war, Henry Karlson spoke for the government: "The only alternative to a limited war now is a total war later ... we have to draw the line somewhere." Another war supporter, representing a Republican student group called the Conservative Coordinating Council, complained to Sheedy that he'd not received sufficient notice of the event and had no time to prepare any remarks. Sheedy said that he "wasn't able to notify" all the conservatives.[10]

Groups across the campus continued debating the student senate request for support in their call for the Clabaugh repeal, spreading interest in the topic. Those stepping up in support were not only the more politically active groups but also included mainstream groups. In addition to the Men's and Women's Independent Associations were such organizations as the Inter-Fraternity Council and Pan Hellenic (sorority council), the groups together likely representing a majority of students by this time. Not all joined in, though; on the day of the SDS event even the student Ag Council argued the issue, eventually turning down the senate request, choosing not to take a stand and saying simply, "We should not be bothered." Only one lone agriculture student, Bill Condon, representing the Dairy Production Club, voiced opposition to Clabaugh's law, arguing that the issue was one of academic freedom, which affected them all. Despite Condon's brave stand, the vote was not close.

That week, national elections indicated a major electoral shift in the nation with the beginning of the end of the historic "solid South," that block of southern states that had voted Democratic since the days of Reconstruction. The beginning of a coming white backlash and a Republican southern strategy could now be seen. In Florida Claude Kirk became the first southern Republican governor in eighty years. Kirk had accused his opponent of "ultra-liberalism" and "favoritism toward Negroes"—damning accusations in the southern states. In Alabama, Lurleen Wallace, standing in for her segregationist husband George (constitutionally prevented from a third term), won handily, officially becoming the country's first woman governor in forty-two years, though her husband would in effect continue to run the state government. Other outspoken segregationists won contests across the South in a regional reaction to the strife of the civil rights movement.

Back in Urbana, on November 18, 1966, the Dean of Students Committee on Student Affairs (CSA), composed primarily of faculty but with some student representation, surprised many by announcing their unanimous decision that Bennett's

DuBois Club request for university recognition should be granted. The key factor in their recommendation was that when asked, Bennett vehemently denied any affiliation between his local club and the national organization. This was the deciding point for the committee, who qualified their recommendation by stating that if that relationship should change at any time in the future, they could reconsider their decision. Their input was passed on to Dean of Students Millet, who announced he would take their recommendation under consideration and, likely feeling some pressure to make some decision, predicted a final verdict on the matter within a week, contradicting his earlier statement that he would wait for the SACB to act.

The CSA report to Millet declared first that they had "found the nature and application of the DuBois Club to be in accordance with existing University regulations" but then went even further, stating, "There is no substantial basis or clear showing that either the national or local DuBois organizations come under terms of the 1947 Clabaugh Act." Representative Clabaugh, who had previously denounced the club as a "first-rate Communist organization," was asked if the CSA recommendation changed his mind. "Hell no," he replied, adding, "The University is not going to recognize them. They're not going to listen to any faculty committee or anybody else which sits around in pompous conclaves making great decisions." Bennett responded, "We don't think we're subversive—the actions of the CSA seem to indicate we are not."[11]

Millet, the man on the spot, continued to delay by asking for various clarifications—from the CSA, from university legal staff, even from the federal government, regarding the timeline for an SACB decision. Though the SACB investigation was still underway, Hoover and his boss Katzenbach continued to make their opinions known about the club, the latter stating flatly, "The DuBois group was created, and is dominated and controlled by the Communist Party USA, and is primarily operated for the purpose of giving aid and support to the Communist Party."[12] In spite of these public comments, the CSA stuck to their decision and suggested that until the SACB—the legal body chartered to make such determinations—did so, Millet should ignore such statements, move forward, and approve the local chapter. CSA members noted, again, that if a later SACB decision went against the organization, the university could always change its position and revoke the approval.

Millet was caught in the middle, with serious pressure coming from all sides, and came down firmly in favor of continued delay. "It should be clear that the charges made by the Attorney General, presumably based on careful investigation, provide strong notice or warning that careful study of the club's present status, of their petition to the university, and of the possible relevance of the Clabaugh Act, are required of us." At this point a second university committee, the Faculty Senate Committee on Academic Freedom, weighed in and placed even more pressure on Millet by declaring wholehearted support for recognition of the club and even raised doubts about the university's right to "question the purposes and nature of such an organization."[13] Bennett continued to argue that his local club related to the national organization only in "general aims, but not in any formal manner," and he affirmed to anyone who would listen that he had no intention of applying for a charter from the national office. This critical disavowal of a formal connection with the national DuBois organization placed the university and Millet in a difficult position. The dean explained the dilemma in this way:

> On the one hand, it would appear that if the club has not applied for a national charter the club is not, in fact, a W. E. B. DuBois Club as described by the Attorney General. On the other hand, the choice of the W. E. B. DuBois name by the local club could be assumed to be a declaration of intention to establish an identity with the national group regardless of the technical requirements of affiliation.[14]

On the same day Millet made this statement about his dilemma, a small item appeared in the back pages of the *DI*, announcing a lecture sponsored by SDS, in an on-campus university building, that would feature a professor from Communist China (and thus a communist, one would assume), speaking on the Chinese Cultural Revolution. No question was raised regarding the applicability of the Clabaugh Act to the professor's event. On the same day, James Meredith, the first black student to enroll at the University of Mississippi, and now a civil rights activist, also came to the campus to speak. In his talk he challenged Illinois students to stand up for their beliefs. "The only way you're going to count is to get into the arena, make a decision and take a stand."[15] The growing publicity surrounding the DuBois Club controversy and the Clabaugh law combined to provide an excellent opportunity for UI students to heed Meredith's advice.

CHAPTER 10

Passing the Buck

Peltason's appointment as chancellor would not take effect until the beginning of the next school year, so Henry remained the man in charge on the Urbana campus. On December 13, the president rewarded Millet's delaying tactics and announced that a decision had been made (by whom was unclear) to move the decision on the DuBois matter to the board of trustees. Specifically, the issue had been referred to the board's General Policy Committee. An obviously relieved Millet said, "[Henry] did not take the DuBois question to the committee, but the committee has asked for it," though it seems more likely that Henry initiated the move. Millet added, somewhat hopefully—but incorrectly, as it would turn out—"I now have no more to do with it."[1] On the same day, the Faculty Senate Committee on Academic Freedom made public a letter to Millet denouncing the Clabaugh Act and called for its repeal.[2] The situation Millet and Henry found themselves in remained an awkward one. They were chartered with enforcement of a law of questionable legality, with pressure from the legislature and public on one side, students and (now) faculty on the other.

Like many university administrators of the Red Scare era, Henry was not inexperienced in managing issues of communism on campus. In 1947, both he and George Stoddard had coped with the issue of Youth for Democracy, later declared an arm of the Communist Party, on their respective campuses. Both had to deal with their respective state legislatures threatening to become involved. Henry had come through his test better than Stoddard, thanks to Henry's greater diplomatic talent and the positive relationships he had built with his board and legislature.

Henry's political skills would be tested throughout his career, and he would repeatedly demonstrate his aptitude for diplomacy.

Later, at Wayne State in 1950, Henry was faced with a second challenge involving alleged communists on campus. Herbert Phillips, a philosophy professor at the University of Washington, had been fired as a result of a statewide witch hunt for communists in the ranks of state employees. Though Phillips's political affiliations were unclear, he refused on principle to answer questions put to him on the subject by a legislative committee. His resulting dismissal by the university administration, along with two other faculty, for refusing to answer the committee's questions was a precedent-setting event for other legislatures' campus investigations across the country, a not-uncommon occurrence during the Red Scare. Following his dismissal, Phillips began a nationwide tour, speaking on the topic of academic freedom or, in the caustic words of a Detroit newspaper, displaying the prevalent animosity of the era, "in the role of political martyr and champion of academic freedom." Henry decided that Phillips, once tarred with the allegation of communist sympathizer, should not be allowed to speak at Wayne State. He voiced what were probably the feelings of many of his fellow Americans of the fifties:

> In other years I have held that even a Communist should be heard in an educational setting. . . . [But] it now is clear, I think, through actions of the U.S. Congress, the attorney general of the United States and court decisions, that the Communist is not to be regarded merely as an ordinary citizen of a minority political party but as an enemy of our national welfare dedicated to violence, disruption and discord.[3]

Questioned in 1966 amid the DuBois controversy as to whether his opinions regarding communist speakers on campus had changed, Henry declined to answer, citing that both the University of Illinois Board of Trustees and the courts were at that time considering the merits and the constitutionality of the Clabaugh Act. In his defense, the president said his "1950 decision must be considered within the context of the 'laws and situation' of Michigan at that time."[4]

The increasingly tense attitudes of both university administrators and activists in the era are evident in the report of a December 1966 SDS meeting on the Illinois campus, at which Dean Millet accepted an invitation to speak. He had been asked in advance to address such provocative questions as "Why does the University have the authority to tell you where to live until you are 23? Why is the University an accomplice in deciding which students qualify to be sent to Vietnam? Why is it university policy to release names of students to the HUAC?" And most bluntly, "When will the Clabaugh Act be flushed?" The questions had been distributed on a flyer advertising the meeting, under the heading "Time to Confront." However, while accepting the invitation to speak to the group, Millet neatly avoided such confrontation by claiming that a "prior commitment" left him with no time to take questions from the floor. He did answer all the flyer's questions, one by one, if not to the students' satisfaction. Why must students live in dorms? Because the university has construction bonds that must be paid off. Why cooperate with the Selective Service? Some students were fine with the university doing so. Why cooperate with HUAC? Well, as a matter of fact, a request from the ACLU to refuse such cooperation was on Henry's desk at that moment and under consideration. Millet did make one extremely controversial statement, presumably based on the in loco parentis principle, which by that time had been legally discredited: "There are no student rights—just student privileges," he stated, even if "any institution with its wits about it acts as though there were student rights, especially the right of due process."[5] In an unambiguous editorial titled "What's the Deal?" the *DI* responded to that comment with a mix of shock and warning. "If he wants a Berkeley riot here, claiming that students deserve only privileges is the way to get one."[6]

CHAPTER 11

The Board Surprises

In January, in their first board meeting of the new year, the trustees took up the DuBois issue. The board's General Policy Committee questioned faculty representatives from the two university committees regarding the nature of the local club. The faculty members argued intensely for approval of the club, noting that the group had complied with all university regulations and that there was no evidence that the organization could in any serious way be considered "subversive." They contended that the university's academic environment depended on open and free discussion of ideas, that an academic institution needed "wide powers of student activity" in order for the university to fulfill its role. One suggested that for the board to accept and acknowledge the academic freedom requirement of the campus was the only way to avoid "an embittering confrontation between the administration and the faculty and student body."[1] However, the trustees' questions revealed they were less interested in the issue of academic freedom and much more concerned with the presence of communists on campus, and they took the faculty counsel "under advisement."

However, one month later, surprising nearly everybody, the board announced that it had accepted the recommendation of the two committees, and by a vote of six to three, they returned the decision on the DuBois Club back to "normal administrative channels," effectively supporting university recognition of the club. In response, Millet announced he would soon approve the club's application. The board statement said that "no proof that the DuBois Club is subversive, seditious or dedicated to the violent overthrow of the government of Illinois or the United

States exists."[2] However, the decision was not a unanimous one, and dissenting board members spoke their minds freely to the press. One argued for a path of further delay: "The board should defer any action until the Attorney General of the United States has resolved charges that the club is a communist front organization." A second opponent of the decision added, "There is no urgency about the issue." But a third went further with his opposition, calling the decision "weak and dangerous" and warning that the board should not be taking such chances with "a potentially dangerous organization." However, legal principle prevailed for the moment, as board president Howard Clement pointed out that "basic philosophies were involved" and that the trustees "had the responsibility of insuring that the DuBois Club was not treated as though it were guilty before any charges could be proven." Six of the nine members supported Clement, emphasizing that the most important issue involved was one of "due process, the very basis of our system," with one explaining that "until it can be shown the club is subversive, it must be allowed to exist at the University." The board cautioned that should the subversive, seditious accusations ever be proved against the club, recognition could and would be immediately withdrawn.[3]

The *Chicago Tribune* attacked the decision immediately, speaking for many Illinoisans with an editorial titled "Berkeley Comes to Illinois": "The thin opening wedge to possible campus anarchy in the state universities of Illinois was attained when the board of trustees of the University of Illinois granted recognition to the W. E. B. DuBois club at the Urbana campus." The conservative paper warned that worse was yet to come: "When a university administration begins yielding to the demands of student leftists it simply invites new and more excessive demands, until academic freedom becomes a cover for license. That is precisely what happened at the Berkeley campus of the University of California." The editors suggested a clear remedy: "The people of Illinois, who have poured hundreds of millions of dollars into the universities of the state, have a stake in this. Are they going to control the universities through their agents, or are they going to allow the inmates to take over these institutions? We have no doubt the people will demand a firm rein over the campuses."

Not unexpectedly, Ralph Bennett was ecstatic:

> We have brought before the University and before the students the issue that the club should be judged on its merits and its views and not on some anti-communist act. . . . We have made people aware of the nature of the Clabaugh Act and its repressive features, and our fight has helped unite students to fight the act. We now have the right to exist despite our beliefs.

He announced the focus of the newly recognized club would be threefold, neatly tying together the major issues of the day: opposition to the Vietnam War, promoting civil rights issues in the local community, and (likely most alarming to legislators, university administrators, and the public) inviting a communist to speak on campus to present a direct challenge to the Clabaugh Act.[4]

President Henry declined to elaborate on the board's decision, stating simply, "I concur." When asked about reports he had influenced the board in their decision, he replied, "I discussed the matter with board members, arranged for the presentation of all points of view and encouraged the general position finally taken by the board." In hindsight, the entire episode might be seen as an act of adept diplomacy on Henry's part. The decision to move the question to the board, likely the president's, rather than making the call at his level, provided him with a degree of political cover. Henry's "encouragement" to the board to make the decision that they did, subtly indicating his support for their position, avoided an outright decision on his part that might have antagonized the board and certainly the legislature. It is no surprise that Representative Clabaugh was unmoved: "I think the Board of Trustees acted just as juvenile and irresponsible as the kids.... I think the whole thing is ridiculous," adding ominously, "I do not regard the matter as over."[5]

On a side note, some hard feelings between Bennett's group and the campus SDS organization appeared in the aftermath of the decision. Bennett castigated SDS for what he considered their lack of adequate support in his club's effort for recognition. Sheedy, speaking for SDS, explained to the *DI* that Bennett had attempted to force reluctant SDS members into joining his club in order to enlist the required number of members. The DuBois vice president fired back, calling SDS members "Uncle Tom radicals ... a bunch of middle-class students who like to think of themselves as radicals.... When it comes to gut issues, they're worthless." A frustrated Sheedy responded, "The DuBois Club is actually a conservative, coalition-ist-oriented group.... [T]hey supported Pat Brown against Ronald Reagan in California on the thesis of lesser evil. As a result they're always bought out even if they have left-oriented goals."[6] At this point the two defenders of free speech seemed to be using their free-speech rights largely to disparage each other.

CHAPTER 12

The Legislature Speaks

Clabaugh's prediction that the matter was not ended soon came back to harass the principals. Less than a week after the board's announcement, the state senate shocked the university administration and the board by passing a nearly unanimous resolution "asking" the trustees to rescind their decision, citing the attorney general's statements about the DuBois Club. Board president Clement responded hopefully, saying, "The legislature obviously has the right to express itself" but "perhaps they don't have all the facts before them." Bennett, in an understatement, said, "I think the resolution reflects the hysteria of anti-communism." Victor Stone, chairman of the Faculty Senate Committee on Academic Freedom, suggested that the legislature was threatening political interference with the university. "If that time comes . . . the University of Illinois will certainly be on the skids," adding optimistically, if unrealistically, "When Illinois citizens are fully informed on the DuBois Club issue and consider it unemotionally they will appreciate the wisdom and propriety of the action by the University Board."[1]

If the board needed further convincing, other senators threatened direct budgetary retaliation if the decision was not reconsidered, warning, "If they don't [reconsider], the appropriation bill is coming up and I assure them it would get a good working over." Another legislator jumped on. "If the club were allowed to form, we would have another Berkeley," adding, in a less than comforting manner, "I will always protect the right of free speech, but when it goes against the principles of the government you have to step in."[2]

Lines were drawn and the battle commenced. Governor Otto Kerner, a Democrat, came down fully in support of the board's decision. "I am as anticommunist as they come but I think prohibiting such a group, which is a small one, sends them underground and tends to increase their membership."[3] The local American Legion, aroused, urged all its members to write to the board opposing the club. The letters poured in to Henry and to the board, largely critical of the decision. "It is inconceivable that we can sanction, much less associate with, an avowed enemy who is right now killing our young men and planning for the destruction of our freedom." A second was even more direct, indicating some serious paranoia about Bennett's group. "Are you prepared to hand over your authority as President of the University of Illinois to the Dubois boys? They will be satisfied with nothing less than complete control. . . . Our center of higher learning will become a center for Marxist, Leninist, Russian revolution!" And a parent warned, "They [DuBois] spew forth treason against the United States. If it wasn't my daughter's final year I would have her transferred."[4]

Finally, taxpayers made clear just whose institution it was. "You guys must be crazy giving recognition to the W. E. B. DuBois clubs on our campus. As Illinois taxpayers, we vigorously protest," and, "The voters of Illinois . . . will hold you responsible for these decisions and their dire results. You are elected to serve a State university—not an international institution for . . . minorities preaching anarchy. Your responsibility is solely to the people of Illinois."[5] In days before the internet and cable television, this level of criticism was as intense as could be for public officials.

In March, after another electoral swing, three new Republican members of the board were to be sworn in, replacing three exiting Democrats, likely changing the opinion of the board. Recognizing this, CSA members urged Millet to act immediately and approve the club's application, warning, "Even the slightest delay in recognizing the club might lead to a major divisive confrontation between the University Board of Trustees, the faculty, and the state legislature." Some observers might suggest that such a division had already occurred. Meanwhile, Anthony Scariano, a liberal state representative from Park Forest, Illinois, did the previously unthinkable and introduced a bill in the state senate to repeal the Clabaugh Act, stating on the floor of the General Assembly:

> The obligation of the University to its students is to expose, not protect them—to expose them to man's mistakes as well as his triumphs, to teach them to grapple with ideas, to train them in reasoning, in evaluation, and in intelligent exercise of choice. An educational policy which shelters students from the seamier side of life, which filters the dregs from the wine of wisdom, is both blind and an insult to the learner. It indicates no faith whatever in the student's judgment nor in his family background nor in the society which bred him.

Clabaugh laughed off the repeal bill. "It's not gonna pass, nobody with any brains would vote for it," while admitting there might be a few votes in favor. "You've got a lot more kooks in the legislature today than we had in 1947, just like you've got a lot more kooks in the University."[6]

As feelings around the Clabaugh Act roiled, the antiwar situation also began heating up, and in mid-February a small group of protesters came together to demonstrate against an Air Force event in the Illini Union. The gathering, co-sponsored by SDS and the newly formed Committee to End the War, grew as it moved from inside the Union to the south terrace, where Sheedy and others spoke atop the balustrade. Though numbering fewer than fifty at most, the demonstrators' signs showed creativity, with messages such as "Kill for Peace," "Escalate Brotherhood," and "Is God Really on Our Side?"[7] The committee, only a week old at the time of the demonstration, was formed "to promote education and action designed to end the war," said Kitty Cone, the group's first president. Unique among the protest groups, the committee issued membership cards that stated: "We condemn the Vietnam War as illegal, immoral and unjust. We feel an obligation to promote discussion and actively oppose this cruel war." According to Cone, also a founding member of Bennett's DuBois Club, the new group already had about thirty members and, like the DuBois Club, had submitted application for formal university recognition.[8] Sheedy, speaking for SDS, expressed support for the committee's aims but made clear that there was no formal relationship between SDS and the new group.

Ignoring the CSA suggestion for immediate action on the DuBois application, Henry, always cognizant of relations with the legislature, responded to the senate's demand to the board by announcing he would ask Millet to hold off on any action regarding recognition until the board had time to reconsider their decision. The next board meeting, with the new membership present, would be held in March. Bennett predicted, "He's knuckled under to quite a bit of political pressure. The decision is not being left up to the University community—it's now being left up to which group can exert more powerful political pressure."[9] Members of the CSA were equally harsh on the president. James Carey, professor of journalism, said, "The action is outrageous—a violation of all administrative procedures in a case which has seen violation piled upon violation." Bernard Karsh, sociology professor, agreed. "I view the statement as raising some of the most serious questions which could confront the University . . . interference of the legislature in the heart and substance of what a university is."[10] Scariano called a press conference in Springfield to ridicule Clabaugh and his allies in the legislature. "People who think like Clabaugh . . . are well on their way to making the University of Illinois a cow college. They have ignored the fact that academic freedom and the freedom to speak, listen and read are integral to the wholeness of a University community."[11]

The *DI* agreed with Scariano's comments but blamed the administration and specifically Millet for the current predicament by not acting quickly to recognize the club. "The administration of this University has messed around and dallied and double-talked its way into a corner from which all the possible exits seem to point toward a crisis." The paper claimed the legislature's reaction was only to be expected, given the "legislature is basically conservative in nature," implying Millet should have known better and acted quickly. "Knowing of possible reaction in the legislature which would again blow the issue into crisis status, Millet should have had the foresight to grant recognition immediately.... [I]nstead [he] wormed his way around that final act by claiming there were certain details he thought he ought to iron out." The paper somberly judged, "We can think of no details so important that they warranted letting the University be placed in the compromising position in which it now finds itself."[12]

Later that week, Millet met with Bennett for what became an in-depth interview. At Millet's request, a stenographic record of the meeting was made, as Bennett declined to be recorded on tape. In the meeting, Millet quizzed Bennett repeatedly on the local club's relationship with the national organization, an issue around which Millet expressed skepticism. He thought Bennett was hiding something. Bennett thought Millet was fishing for any information that might allow the board to rescind its decision. "Rather than seeking to defend the Board of Trustees' action (which found there was no evidence the UI club is a 'subversive' organization), he was trying to give them ammunition to reverse their action." Millet, for his part, opined, "I am becoming the great midwestern expert on the DuBois Club," while denying that there was any "nefarious police work" in his preparation for the board meeting.[13] Millet's interpretation of the Bennett interview would be critical to the board's reconsideration of the matter, and his testimony about the meeting, made to the board's General Policy Committee, indicated he had serious doubts about Bennett's stated lack of a relationship with the national organization.

As an indicator of rising tensions on the campus, that same week the local SDS group voted to begin withholding lists of its members from the university unless the administration agreed to not provide such lists to the House Un-American Activities Committee in response to subpoenas. Such lists had been subpoenaed from the University of California at Berkeley and the University of Michigan, SDS claimed. There was no immediate response from the administration.[14] Similar rising tension was noted at Madison, Wisconsin, in that same week when seventeen student protesters were charged with "abusive, violent and otherwise disorderly conduct against the Dow Chemical Corp" during a campus recruiting visit by the company. Dow's incendiary product, napalm, widely used by American forces in Vietnam, often caused horrific injuries and excruciating deaths for innocent civilians. As the military's sole supplier of napalm, the company would become an ongoing target of student protest, and its recruitment efforts would be a catalyst for antiwar activity on campuses across the nation. The director of Wisconsin's Placement Office, who signed the complaints, ignored his own university administration's recommendation that the charges against the students be dropped. He expressed his frustration by saying, "I have complete and overwhelming support of the faculty. I'm tired of this. We're not backing down on this one."[15] The Madison protest lasted three hours, ending only after the interviews were completed. The protesters did nothing to prevent interviews from being conducted. At the Illinois campus on the following day, a smaller group conducted a similar protest at Dow's recruitment efforts in the Illini Union, again without interfering with the interviews. One of the protesters, Jocelyn Werry, wife of psychiatry professor John Werry, expressed the feelings of many of her fellow protesters. "I feel sickened when I realize that most people don't care a whit about what napalm is doing to children in Vietnam."[16] These spring 1967 visits by Dow to the two midwestern campuses would be repeated in the fall, with more significant consequences.

The university involvement in the Vietnam War was not limited to support for on-campus recruiting by military contractors. In 1966 Illinois was among the top recipients of defense-related grants awarded to public and private institutions across the country, receiving more than twenty million dollars from defense-related federal agencies, representing more than a third of all federal awards to the university. Illinois ranked third in such receipts among public universities, behind only Michigan and UCLA.[17] Eisenhower's military-industrial complex might now more accurately be described as a military-industrial-academic complex, and the university's involvement with the nation's military efforts extended much further than simply allowing distribution of armed-services literature, on-campus recruitment by military contractors, and accreditation of ROTC classes. Such university collaboration with the military-industrial complex was becoming more common across research universities nationwide and would become a central theme of campus antiwar activists.

Only a few faculty members were aware that the university's historical contribution to the Vietnam War effort ran even deeper, and if they had known, such history would have further appalled both Werrys. During World War II, a University of Illinois graduate student in botany, John Galston, had discovered in his doctoral research that the acidic compound TIBA, used in small amounts as a growth stimulant for soybean plants, could be an extremely effective plant defoliant when used in higher volumes. Army scientists embraced Galston's research and developed it into a powerful defoliant called Agent Orange (for the orange stripe painted around the metal drums that contained it), widely used by the United States in Vietnam to destroy dense jungle overgrowth. Later it was discovered that the millions of civilian and military personnel exposed to the compound, Vietnamese and American alike, would have major long-term health problems as a result. Galston, deeply affected by the military's use of his research, would later turn his career to bioethics, and as a professor at Yale he would help influence the United States government, after many years, to stop all military use of the defoliant.[18]

CHAPTER 13

A Movement Is Born

Nineteen sixty-seven would be a watershed year for the student movement at the University of Illinois Urbana campus. Sparked by the administration's Dubois Club dithering, stoked by the questionably legal Clabaugh Act, and with the civil rights movement and an increasingly unpopular war simmering in the background, that spring witnessed the largest protest rallies in the school's history to that point, and an Illinois student protest movement was born. While previously the campus had witnessed small demonstrations with, at most, a few dozen activists, the months of March and April would see hundreds of students, with supportive faculty, staff, and administrators, gathering regularly on the south side of the Illini Union in a movement that began around opposition to the Clabaugh Act but grew from there. They named themselves Students Against the Clabaugh Act (SACA) and were soon handing out thousands of copies of an eight-page newspaper produced on a hand-cranked mimeo machine.

The new effort would grow to include not just the usual core activists—SDS, SNCC, and Young Socialists—but previously apolitical, uninvolved students—independents, representatives of student government, fraternity brothers and sorority sisters, even university athletes. The effort would become a popular, broad-based movement, though certainly the numbers never exceeded more than a small percentage of the total student population. But with the Vietnam conflict escalating and draft calls of young men increasing, student political awareness was growing, and the issues raised by the Clabaugh Act and the DuBois Club, such as academic freedom and free speech, were easy to comprehend and broadly supported. As spring progressed, the concerns SACA raised received increased publicity and popularity as student and faculty support grew, leaving no simple way for the university administration to defuse the situation.

The events of spring in Urbana-Champaign were triggered by an action at the university's Chicago Circle campus, where on Monday, February 27, fifty students began a spontaneous sit-in at the office of the chancellor. The sit-in followed a campus speech, unapproved by the administration, by a leading American communist writer and intellectual, Herbert Aptheker, an honorably discharged World War II artillery major later blacklisted in academia for his membership in the Communist Party. Aptheker was a regular speaker on college campuses during this period and could be counted on to provoke public controversy. The Marxist veteran had been invited to the southwest Chicago campus as a test of the Clabaugh Act by a coalition of campus groups, including, as would be expected, SDS, SNCC, and the Committee to End the War, but also by more mainstream groups: student government, Young Democrats, and even the campus YMCA. Following the speech, at the suggestion of SDS leaders, about fifty audience members walked to the chancellor's office to demand a statement supporting free speech and the repeal of the Clabaugh Act. The chancellor declined the opportunity to meet the students and left the building via a "secret elevator," at which point the students announced a twenty-four-hour vigil outside his office and demanded a statement. However, not all the demonstrators supported the sit-in, among those the student government president, who, though fully supporting the Aptheker speech, condemned the sit-in. "This will jeopardize everything we've tried to do. . . . I have received quite a bit of encouragement from the University [regarding Clabaugh repeal] . . . but now all that is shot to hell."[1] This split, between moderate and extreme protesters, would soon be evident at the downstate campus too.

SDS leaders on the Urbana campus decided a sympathy demonstration was in order and called it for the next day, on the south porch of the Union. An audience of approximately two hundred showed up, carrying signs reading "We Can Do Our Own Thinking," and "Free Speech, Yes—Clabaugh, No!" After listening to speeches, they followed Keenan Sheedy, still SDS president, on the short walk to the Administration Building, where they demanded that the Urbana administration also issue a statement opposing the Clabaugh Act. When informed that President Henry was not in the building but in Chicago, the students declared they would return the following day. When informed via telephone of the students' planned return, Henry replied that he would have no comment on the Clabaugh Act and would be out of town again the next day. Regarding the students' demonstration, he said blandly, "I have no reaction. . . . The students are free to demonstrate at any time on any issue so long as they comply with University regulations."[2]

The next day, the crowd size doubled. Four hundred students, faculty, and bystanders listened to a variety of speakers, all demanding that the university back opposition to the Clabaugh Act. Associate Provost John Briscoe and Dean Millet appeared unexpectedly at the gathering. Briscoe, attempting to placate the group, complimented them, saying, "This demonstration is entirely within the spirit of our academic community."[3] The crowd was unappeased and quickly rejected the pair's offering of a meeting between representatives of the group and administrators. Instead, they demanded that the president himself come to a public gathering to speak to all of them. Vern Fein, an early SACA leader, dramatically placed an empty chair on the terrace balustrade to represent Henry's absence.[4] The press dubbed the affair "the empty chair demonstration."

Fein, a graduate student in the English Department, would be an articulate and passionate leader in the campus movement for many years, in his words, "protesting everything that moved until the movement ran its course." Born and raised in the Chicago suburbs, he was the son of a "non-participating Jewish Father and a closet Catholic Mother," both Eisenhower supporters in his youth. He had started his college career at Cornell in Iowa, where he remembered jeering at nuclear weapons protesters because, as he said, "I thought they were communists." Transferring to Illinois, Fein began his political transition: "I began to learn about the Vietnam War and how wrong I'd been."[5]

Since President Henry was still out of town, the SACA students voted to gather once again the following day. In response, the president's office quickly announced that Henry would be out of town that day, too. The day's demonstration, like the previous ones, progressed in a haphazard but peaceful manner. Anyone who wished to speak simply jumped up onto the terrace pillar and spoke his or her mind. The audience listened and cheered enthusiastically. It was an excited crowd, beginning to feel its strength. The momentum was building.

CHAPTER 14

Henry Responds

On Friday morning, President Henry offered to meet with two SACA leaders, Sheedy and Student Senate president Bob Outis, as representatives of the larger group. Both refused the offer. At noon, a crowd of more than six hundred students and faculty gathered in an "orderly and businesslike" manner and voted to demand that either Henry or his representative meet with the group to discuss the Clabaugh Act. After the crowd dispersed, Henry issued a statement to the *DI*, which reported, "It would be 'highly improper' for him to voice his views on the Clabaugh Act 'at this time.' . . . a statement now would be 'an act of discourtesy' and 'a professional impropriety' since the University Board of Trustees is presently considering [the issue]."[1] Henry was attempting to shift the responsibility of taking a position on the Clabaugh law, as he had with the DuBois recognition, to the board. "In general, I am opposed to legislative restrictions on the University's management of its educational affairs. However, whether it is timely, wise or desirable for the University to advocate the repeal of the Clabaugh Act . . . is clearly a matter for the trustees to decide." SACA and SDS leader Vic Berkey, commenting on Henry's continuing unavailability, suggested to the crowd, "I'm beginning to wonder if he exists." Another speaker, Howard Rothman, pointed out the obvious, that "Henry is afraid to speak on the Clabaugh Act because he is afraid of an unfavorable reaction from state legislators."

On Monday, the administration attempted to take the initiative and quell the unrest. Millet announced that he would be inviting twenty student leaders to a meeting with him and the university's chief legal counsel to discuss the legal implications of the Clabaugh Act and the university's responsibilities. Results of the meeting would be publicized so that all students would hear. Separately, he offered that President Henry was also willing to meet with the twenty representatives to discuss the DuBois and Clabaugh situations, which Millet and Henry saw as very distinct issues. SDS leaders announced a gathering on the south terrace for Tuesday and a planned vote either to accept the administration proposals or to reject them and then initiate a sit-in at the Administration Building, and/or, a third choice, to consider a demonstration at the upcoming trustees meeting scheduled for the Illini Union later in the week. The SACA gatherings were largely organized and led by SDS but featured a significant presence of and support from student-government representatives, who provided a small stipend that paid for SACA flyers and newsletters.

The Tuesday meeting was chaotic. The crowd was the largest yet, still reported as "orderly and peaceful," but was unable to reach a "consensus," which was the preferred way of making decisions at the rallies. The group did vote to accept Henry's proposal for a meeting with the twenty student representatives, but they noisily attached conditions; first, that the meeting with Henry should be broadcast live, so that all students might feel a part of it; and second, that any students who wished to could meet with Henry in an open meeting following the meeting with the twenty. The administration was unlikely to accept the crowd's conditions, and following the rally, opinions differed sharply over how to proceed. One more moderate group of fifteen students, representatives of the student senate, Inter-fraternity Council, and Pan Hellenic, wrote a letter rejecting the meeting's conditions; they felt that Henry's offer to meet with the student representatives should have been accepted without conditions. Another group, moving in the opposite direction, felt that Henry's offer should have been rejected entirely; they wanted to stick with the original demand for Henry to meet with all the students in an open assembly. The movement was dividing into separate camps, representing sharply differing positions of moderate and more extreme views, with student government leaders most prominent in the former, SDS members in the latter.

Meanwhile, in Springfield, Clabaugh described the demonstrators as trying to "put a horsehair shirt on the administration" and suggested they ought to find a better use of their time than to "trollop around in the rain and snow." He laughed off talk of repeal of his law. "Student efforts to repeal the statute will meet with about as much success in the General Assembly as moving the State House to Moscow." The legislator made clear whose university it was: "The University of Illinois belongs to the people of this state, and the University must act within the guidelines of their beliefs. The University can't run cross-wise to the will of the people in this state." If they tried, Clabaugh pointed to Berkeley as an example of what would happen. "Take a look at California, the red-pinkos haven't made a peep since Ronald Reagan was elected governor."[2]

Even the more liberal of the town newspapers, the *Courier*, expressed frustration with the students, saying in an editorial, "Unshorn, bearded students paraded in front of the Illini Union . . . ill-mannered . . . boorish . . . [with an] absence of emotional maturity self-evident. . . . Someway or another, the idea has gained a foothold among these people that permission to register in the University is tantamount to being given control over its destiny."[3] More influence over their destiny and that of their university was certainly a goal of the students, but from their point of view such aspiration was not unreasonable. With university conduct rules based on outdated ideas, with campus speech inhibited by laws that seemed to be and would soon be proved unconstitutional, and with a seemingly endless war in which they and their peers might be drafted and killed, the idea of more control over their lives, their government, and their university did not seem unreasonable.

Of course, there was another side, and many citizens of central Illinois held a different perspective, especially the older ones, those who had lived through a world war and now found themselves in the midst of a cold war globally and a hot war in Asia. They felt terribly threatened by the world around them. One expressed such a feeling in a letter to the editor in the *Courier*: "The American public must come to realize that we are dealing with a world-wide conspiracy the like of which we have never seen before . . . bent and determined on the total destruction of our way of life. . . . How gullible must we be to allow this sort of thing to go on in the name of 'academic freedom.'"[4] Another was even more direct: "Being a taxpayer in Illinois, I feel that I have the right—no the obligation—to . . . speak my mind. . . . God willing, the citizens will now take a stand. Back the Clabaugh Act with vigor. Force the scum, those who would despoil the very principles of our democracy, out of our schools. By their actions they forfeit the right to be there!"[5] And in another, more accusatory missive, a citizen wrote: "To those of us watching and listening from the outside it looks very much like your biggest want [is] freedom from discipline. . . . It is a little hard to understand how a few hundred immature students can be so right and the majority of voters of this state can be so wrong."[6]

Undaunted by such letters, editorials, or warnings from Clabaugh, on Friday morning the SACA leaders went ahead with their meeting with Millet and the university legal counsel, hearing once again that only the board of trustees could make an institutional statement on the Clabaugh Act, and that no university administrator would be doing so until the board had acted. Millet told the group, "President Henry may not agree with the position the board takes, but he can't make a public expression of his personal views until after the board takes action."

Millet did assure the students that Henry would be accurately presenting the SACA group's views to the board. "The president is an agent of the board and it is the president's responsibility to see that all views on issues are presented to the board."[7]

Friday at noon, at a SACA rally chaired by Outis, the more moderate camp dominated, and the audience, reversing its vote of the previous meeting, agreed to accept Henry's offer to meet with twenty SACA representatives without preconditions. They then agreed to come together again the following Tuesday, when the board would be meeting at the Illini Union, to consider further action.

CHAPTER 15

The Board Reverses

The following Tuesday the board met, and things did not go in SACA's favor. The trustees opened their meeting on the second floor of the Illini Union with testimony from students, faculty, and representatives from the Association of University Professors (AAUP), all speaking in support of the board's decision for DuBois Club recognition. William MacPherson, professor of economics and representative of the AAUP, told the board that they would do less harm by recognizing the DuBois Club, even if they were truly communist, than by barring it and damaging the principle of free speech on the campus. His comments had exactly the opposite effect that he desired, however, as board member Howard Pogue responded, "If I had any reservations about how I would vote on this matter, they were resolved when I heard that man say we should recognize this group even if they're communist."[1]

Looming over the trustees was not only the ongoing "war with communism" in southeast Asia but also the threats from the legislature, letters from taxpayers, and the feelings of much of the Illinois citizenry, strongly opposed to their previous approval of the DuBois Club. To one of the faculty presenters, a trustee replied bluntly, "I am impressed with your presentation, but we are in a shooting war with communism."[2] After listening to all the testimony, the board went into session and came out with an announcement of a complete reversal of its previous DuBois position, directing Henry, Millet, and the administration to deny the club's application. The board attributed the reversal entirely to Millet's "new evidence," allegedly discovered in his meeting with Bennett, regarding the relationship between the local and the national organizations. Millet had submitted his new evidence in testimony to the General Policy Committee prior to the board meeting and claimed that after his conversation with Bennett he arrived at the opinion that there was a definite connection of some sort between the local and the national organizations, even if only an informal one. Millet agreed that though Bennett's local was "autonomous and independent" from the national organization, he believed that regular communications did occur between the two, that the national office had regularly provided pamphlets and other materials to the local, and that several common members across the two groups contributed to evidence of a relationship. On this basis he concluded that an informal relationship existed, even without formal affiliation. Wayne Johnston, chairman of the General Policy Committee, announced the final judgment, that "Millet's evidence showed the local club is 'subversive and communist.'"[3]

Sheldon Plager, professor of law, dramatically expressed the feelings of many faculty and students:

> The trustees have in this one vote undermined the historical tradition of academic freedom that is the touchstone of every great university. They have seriously damaged the morale of the faculty and students; they have tarnished the reputation of the university in the eyes of those who measure a university by its commitments to the search for truth. . . . For those who urged this decision upon the trustees, I can only say that theirs is a hollow victory—their success is the university's shame."[4]

Not surprisingly, Henry took the opposite position and supported the board's decision by explaining, "I would have preferred to have had the DuBois Club recognized, but I agree with the trustees it would be unwise for the University to recognize the DuBois Club at this time." His reasoning was straightforward and transparent, concerned less with the affiliation issue and more with the harsh realities presented by the legislature's threats, the newspaper editorials, and the taxpayer letters. "Such action would be widely misunderstood and misinterpreted by the general public, and the University program would significantly suffer as a consequence. . . . the University would suffer loss of both support and dollars." He attempted to explain the dilemma as he saw it. "The public has two major misunderstandings on the question: the Attorney General's request [for an SACB investigation] is regarded as tantamount to proof, and the University is seen not as dealing with political ideas in the DuBois issue, but with enemies of the state."[5] On the quad, a disappointed and angry SACA rally jeered the decision and then escalated the matter with a vote to bring a communist speaker on campus to test the Clabaugh Act.

At this point within SACA the wedge began to deepen between the SDS activists and the more moderate student-government representatives. The two groups had been, at best, tentative partners in the SACA movement to this point, with the SDS members leaning toward more radical action while the student government representatives generally supported a more cautious path. The decision to invite a communist speaker to campus had been advocated by the more aggressive SDS members, who carried the vote, perhaps on the wave of emotion following the trustees' reversal. The day after the rally, however, the moderates from student government began having second thoughts. The student senate, after lengthy debate on whether to support the SACA decision, chose to table the issue and wait to see if other student groups would support the call. SDS leaders in SACA criticized the senate vote as timid and divisive. In compensation, the senators did vote to offer the DuBois Club the use of its facilities in the Union, in open violation of university regulations.

In other reactions, various faculty members voiced condemnation of the board's action, as did the president of the local AAUP. The law faculty met in emergency session and declared that the action "represents a serious lack of perception of and commitment to fundamental principles of academic freedom," while also questioning the constitutionality of the action. State Senator Robert Mitchler, sponsor of the senate resolution demanding the board rescind their decision, hailed the board's action, declaring, "We may have averted what could have developed into another Berkeley." Pointing out that all of the three new Republican trustees had voted to bar recognition, Mitchler said the second board vote "reflects directly on the individual thinking of the new members and the party that placed them in power."

In Springfield, Representative Clabaugh crowed, "The people are tired of all these crazy goings on at college campuses." When asked about the issue of academic freedom, Clabaugh said, "Bull. There's no more connection between academic freedom and the right of a bunch of bums to come in and preach sedition than there is between academic freedom and the price of rice in China."[6] A local conservative coalition, speaking for the Daughters of the American Revolution, the Urbana American Legion, and the conservative campus Liberty Council, announced it would be sending letters to the parents of all Illinois students, rallying support for the Clabaugh Act. The group made the lofty claim that "this will change the entire direction of the present protest movement." The following Sunday, Clabaugh appeared at the American Legion dinner meeting in Champaign, speaking on "the whys and wherefores" of the Clabaugh Act. He explained that his law had nothing to do with freedom of speech or academic freedom. "These are smokescreens being used by the left-wingers, the ultra-liberals and the campus monkeys to cloud the true issues. . . . If Academic freedom has been degraded to the point of defending treason, then I want no part of it."[7]

Meanwhile, Millet, preparing for the potential of a subversive speaker appearing on campus, began publicly parsing exactly what might and might not be a violation of the Clabaugh Act. Making use of the vagueness of the law's language in an apparent attempt to avoid confrontation, he made clear that in the university's interpretation, the law was not directly targeting either students or speakers but rather university officials and employees. "Unless one of the people who extends the use of University space to a communist speaker is an employee of the University, there will be no violation of the Clabaugh Act." He went further in watering down the law's impact, saying, "The leadership of the organization sponsoring the speaker might be assessed and action might be taken if the Clabaugh Act were violated . . . but I'm not sure that even then a violation would have occurred." Millet and the administration appeared to be bending over backward to avoid a confrontation with SACA over the law. Their words presented SACA with some difficulty in determining exactly what actions would have to be taken to actually violate the law in order to test it.[8]

In what turned out to be a reasonably amicable meeting, Friday morning, after the board's decision, Henry met with SACA members, as promised, and did his best to explain the difficult position he was in. "We are living in a public climate," he explained. "We are not free agents." With the Vietnam war raging, a war the general public perceived as an all-out fight against communism, students wanting to offer university space to subversive speakers was seen from outside the campus, the president suggested, as "Not free speech, but treason." He admitted that the students' impatience was understandable: "You can't be patient because you're here for only four years." But he counseled caution. "The University is a law-abiding place and it will enforce the law." Although he claimed he had advised the board to allow the DuBois Club to be recognized, he did assert, "The board's position rules. I just work for it." In one of the more prescient comments in the meeting, SACA leader Vern Fein suggested to Henry that he was badly misunderstanding the significance of the protests, that what had started as a straightforward reaction to the Clabaugh Act was now becoming something larger, not a one-issue movement but a "free speech movement," that, harking back to Berkeley, would encompass larger social and political issues. Henry's reference to the students' impatience struck a chord with the activists. There was a real impatience on their part, a feeling that in this unique time, they must strike while the opportunity was clear; the time might well pass, and the chance for change might not last.[9]

CHAPTER 16

Students for Free Speech

Fulfilling Fein's prediction, at the next SACA rally on the quad the group took a major step to enlarge their focus, voting to change their name from SACA to "Students for Free Speech" (SFS), mimicking the Berkeley movement. The vote was not close, yet votes such as these at the SACA rallies were very informal, rarely counted, and whoever happened to show up on a given day was included in the voting. Voice votes were the norm, and only a few votes were close enough to need counting; whichever side seemed to be in the majority carried the day. About three hundred showed up for this day's rally, and the name change carried easily. Joe Allen, student senator, spoke in favor, arguing that the board decision on the DuBois decision "demonstrates that the issues go beyond the Clabaugh Act," adding that the movement was now larger than just students and involved supportive faculty. SDS leader Berkey had a more skeptical reaction to the faculty support, cautioning, "We won't ask the faculty or the Student Senate or any other group for anything. If they want to help, fine. But it's more important to retain our independence."[1]

The name change indicated a transition for the movement toward concern with much broader issues. Signaling that larger scope, the new organization soon published a "manifesto," setting forth its philosophical positions:

> SFS is formed to exercise our freedoms—human, Constitutional, and educational—and to resist, from whatever source, attempts to negotiate or abridge these rights. We seek nothing, we request nothing, we demand nothing from the Board of Trustees and the Administration. We simply declare our intention as human beings, as citizens, and as students to act on our rights.[2]

In addition, the new group created a steering committee of thirty, who voted to establish formal relations with other campus groups, of students and faculty alike, to review student movements at other universities for ideas, and to work for the Clabaugh repeal bill in the legislature. Most critically, SFS affirmed the vote to bring Louis Diskin, avowed communist, to the campus. Since an invitation from a recognized student group was needed to formally test the law, and SFS had no formal standing with the university, SDS, at their next meeting, voted to extend the formal invitation.

Such SDS meetings were at times exciting but could also be lengthy and tedious affairs, as indicated by one member, David Ransel, an assistant professor of history and, for a time, faculty advisor for SDS. As the group was committed to agreement by consensus, the meetings "went on half the night, so that everybody had a chance to say something," and even among committed members, "the view at the time was that SDS was very good at mounting tomorrow's demonstration and very good on the ultimate ideals with its Port Huron Statement, but in between there was nothing, no scaffolding, to get us from here to there. That's the way [SDS] was."[3] Despite SDS's inefficiency, the leadership of such radicals in SACA, the transformation of SACA to SFS, and the expansion of the movement's focus disturbed many of the more moderate SACA members; the *DI*, perhaps overdramatically, spoke to those concerns:

> The time has come to step back and take a long look at the Students for Free Speech (SFS) movement.... [T]he movement has suddenly taken a new turn, one which threatens its existence.... It would be one thing ... if free speech was the goal of the SFS. But they are now talking in terms of other campus issues—hours, the grading system, etc.—and seem to be trying to become the governing body of the campus.... [T]hey are not a body willing to listen to reason.... SFS is preparing to act without thinking.... The original goals of SACA have been lost in the cries of "Remember Berkeley," "free speech," ... terms used to stir up emotion. SFS has decided it is time they took over the campus, and not worry about what anyone says.[4]

Despite the growing division in the movement, the student senate soon agreed to follow the SFS initiative, voicing support for the Diskin invitation and, regarding the university's required documents, announcing that if SDS chose not to sign them, the senate would. In self-protection, one senator quoted Henry staff member William K. Williams as saying that "no students or organizations would be punished or reprimanded for having Diskin speak on campus, even if he does violate the Clabaugh Act" and added that Henry himself had authorized Williams to sign a statement to that effect.[5] Clearly, Williams and Henry were of mixed feelings about the Clabaugh restrictions and found themselves in an uncomfortable position. Williams's statement indicated that Henry was not interested in stirring up more student emotions over the law.

In addition, the senate went further than simply supporting the SFS action and voted to extend their own, even if only symbolic, recognition to the DuBois Club, and for a second time offered meeting space in their own campus offices to the club. "We are not saying we believe in the principles of democratic socialism as espoused by the DuBois Club," just their right to speak, said the senators. The senate decision to sign the necessary paperwork was to become a source of friction, as the SFS steering committee, after two hours of debate over the wording in the university documents, voted to direct Keenan Sheedy, SFS steering committee member and also SDS president, to not sign the documents required by the university, intending to provoke a reaction from the administration. However, once it became known that SDS would decline to sign, senate representatives stepped forward and signed off, avoiding a confrontation on this issue.[6]

This series of actions set the stage for the most dramatic event of the semester and perhaps one of the more remarkable moments in the university's history, when, at noon on Friday, March 23, on the south terrace of the Illini Union, student president Robert Outis introduced an avowed member of the Communist Party of the United States of America, Louis Diskin, to a crowd of more than two thousand students, faculty, and bystanders. Diskin's speech, likely more remembered by the crowd for its occurrence than for its content, was titled, "The Smith Act, McCarren Act, and the Clabaugh Act," drawing a pattern across decades of restrictive and questionable government actions. One portion stood out relative to the Clabaugh Act. "For 25 years I have advocated the central idea of Marxism . . . that the most rational way to solve the deep problems facing the American people is through a great political, social and economic revolution in our land, a socialist reorganization of American society."[7] Whether such a statement should have been considered subversive or seditious was less sensational to the crowd than that a real, live communist was speaking the words while standing on the quad of the University of Illinois campus. It was a momentous event, and, by advocating for such a "great revolution," Diskin certainly seemed to test the subversive and seditious criteria of Charles Clabaugh's law.

Coincidentally, several justices of the Illinois Supreme Court were on campus for a College of Law event and happened to be crossing the quad during Diskin's speech, on their way to an Illini Union luncheon. The judges stopped and listened to the communist but declined to offer comments to reporters. Diskin, using a microphone powered by a generator brought in when electric power to the Union porch was shut off, surprised the crowd by expressing sympathy for the difficult position of the university's president, caught between a conservative legislature and a restive campus. "I feel sorry for Dr. Henry; the task of administration is not easy."[8] He recommended that Henry trust his students more, involve them in the university's administration, and have confidence in their wisdom. He remarked that the Communist Party had faith in the nation's students, and Henry should too. When asked by reporters if the Communist Party had anything to do with the local DuBois group, he admitted, "I regret to say I know of no Communist Party members who have anything to do, inside or outside, with the DuBois Club on campus." Regarding the Clabaugh Act, Diskin commented, "I have no doubt that in the course of time the Clabaugh Act will be struck down as unconstitutional." Diskin, a World War II veteran of the Battle of the Bulge, failed to live up to the dangerous, threatening image many held of a communist. "[He] described himself as a happily married man who likes sports, lives in an integrated neighborhood... has never seen a dope addict, has little personal wealth, who sleeps soundly and considers himself a 'decent human being.'"[9]

Following Diskin's appearance, the university went to great lengths to explain to the public that despite appearances, the speech had not violated the Clabaugh Act in any way. James Costello, chief legal counsel, stated that the university "interprets the act as applying only to the Communist Party, and that for a violation to occur a Communist Party representative would have to advocate the violent overthrow of the U.S. government." However, when Diskin was asked directly if he was carrying on the activities of the Communist Party, he replied "Of course." It seemed that finally, the general lack of clarity in the Clabaugh law had at last become obvious. Did Diskin's speech violate the act? As Charles Clabaugh intended the law, it was certainly violated. But was the university, whose president would soon come out publicly in support of repeal, likely to enforce the law, even when faced with a direct violation? The evidence shows that he was not so willing. In fact, there were no legal repercussions to anyone as a result of the Diskin speech. The final words of the communist's speech were telling: "Fear is vanishing from our land and nowhere is this seen more clearly than on our campuses."[10] Irrational fears of a communist speaker on the Illinois campus had finally been put to rest, and the SACA/SFS students were to be credited with the achievement.

However, fear, or at least fear-mongering, was still very apparent in a newsletter reportedly mailed to parents of students soon after the speech, authored by a group calling itself "The Champaign Urbana University Committee," and signed by Robert Wells, secretary of the group. The letter chronicled the activities of SACA and SFS and castigated President Henry for tolerating such activities and for suggesting to the board in any way that they should allow recognition of the DuBois Club. The letter warned of numerous suspicious student leaders—Senate President Outis, who "approves of civil disobedience to pressure the University"; SDS leader Berkey, a "bearded refugee from the Berkeley campus"; and SFS leader Durrett, guilty, as "president of the Socialist Club"—while praising Clabaugh and other conservative members of the legislature, and finally, alerting the public to general "communist encroachment" at the university. The group asked parents to write to administrators and legislators "to demand strong, effective action to be taken to curb Communist activity at the University."[11]

It is unclear how many such letters were actually sent, but a version was delivered to the parents of student president Robert Outis in the tiny farming community of Ramsey, Illinois (1960 population, 815), causing not insignificant apprehension in that household. Outis had begun his college career as a traditional Republican, a Goldwater supporter in the 1964 presidential election, and an applicant for the Marine ROTC program in his freshman year. However, by his senior year, elected president by the students, he saw it as his duty to argue for free speech rights not only for his fellow students but also for communists on the state campus. The transformation led to his role as a leader in the SACA/SFS movement and his introduction of Louis Diskin on the quad. His mother, a staunch Roosevelt New Deal Democrat, proud of her son's achievements at the university, was, however, sufficiently concerned by the letter to take it to her Methodist minister for guidance. The cleric reassured her, advising, "Bob knows what he's doing." Mrs. Outis, apparently comforted by this advice, chose not to mention the letter to her son until after the passing of her husband many years later.[12]

CHAPTER 17

Henry Reverses

On April 6, 1967, a month after Diskin's speech, Henry met in closed session with the faculty senate, a body that was in the process of developing a strong public statement against the board's DuBois Club reversal. The senate opposition was based on familiar grounds: that the board decision violated academic freedom and free inquiry, that it was arbitrary and of uncertain constitutionality, and that it violated faculty primacy in such matters. During Henry's meeting with the senate, intended as a confidential discussion of the controversy and his handling of it, Henry revealed a more liberal point of view than he had previously shown. Though not intended for the public, his comments were soon leaked by faculty members, who reported that Henry had disclosed that he had written to the trustees expressing his personal opposition to the Clabaugh Act.[1] His letter, marked confidential, can be found today among the president's personal papers in the university archives; it showed that his position was based on three principles. First, as necessary as it might have been in 1947, Henry believed that today's students and faculty were more attuned to, and better educated about, the dangers of communism, and therefore less susceptible to its attractions:

> In the late 1940s, the typical university was unprepared to deal with the Communist-front organization.... [However,] it is fair to say that today, the American people, in general, and the campus community in particular, are much more sophisticated about the aims, purposes and nature of the Communist Party, both internationally and in America. There is little possibility that students or very many others will be deceived or misled by expressions from Communists or Communist-front groups.[2]

Second, he considered the law practically unenforceable, as it carried no sanctions and thus, by his judgment, was meaningless. "I do not believe that there is any way for the University to adequately enforce the law against those who willfully undertake to violate it." His third objection was the familiar one—interference with academic freedom and free inquiry—with the law forcing "the University to apply procedures that are contrary to accepted academic practice."

Behind the closed doors of the faculty senate, Henry also revealed that he had recommended to the board that the DuBois club be recognized and still felt that way, despite Millet's alleged "new evidence" of an informal connection with the national organization. Henry shared that Millet's evidence regarding the local-national affiliation had weighed "very heavily" in the board's decision to reverse, despite the flimsiness of the evidence. The president told the senate that he had "worked hard to convince the trustees that the club should be recognized," going so far as to claim that he had successfully "convinced several trustees who originally opposed recognition of the club to change their minds."[3] These statements on the Clabaugh Act and the DuBois Club indicated a significant turnabout by Henry, putting him at odds with the board, the legislature, and his own dean of students, and essentially conceding to SACA's request of a month earlier that he support their request for public opposition to the Clabaugh Act.

To review: In early March, Henry had said that "it would be highly improper . . . to voice his views on the Clabaugh Act," suggesting it would be "an act of discourtesy [to the board] and a professional impropriety." Soon after, speaking to the group of student leaders, Millet had confirmed Henry's position, suggesting, "[He] can't make a public expression of his personal views." And then, one week later, speaking to the SACA representatives, the president had said, "The board's position rules. I just work for it." But in truth, as shown by his letter to the board, the president had chosen to "voice his views" to the board regarding the Clabaugh law, effectively siding with the protesting students, and had also worked to influence their DuBois Club decision. All in all, Henry's change of heart demonstrated a significant victory for the students. The day after his meeting with the faculty, as his comments were leaked out, Henry decided to share his letter to the board in its entirety with the *DI*, which published parts of it the following day. Despite Henry's change of position, Representative Clabaugh displayed no such flexibility. The colorful legislator pronounced that "the Clabaugh Act has about as much to do with violation of the nature of free inquiry and discourse as it does with horse stealing" and suggested that "as far as the students being so sophisticated enough not to need the protection of this act, the kind that attend those meetings and demonstrations need the protection that the Clabaugh Act provides them."[4]

The SACA victory, represented by the Diskin speech on campus, plus the dramatic shift in Henry's position, left the SFS rebels feeling triumphal, if a bit disconcerted. A successful rebellion was one thing; determining how to follow up on such victories was to prove more difficult. Some SFS leaders suggested a second communist speaker be brought to campus, this time without any prior documentation being filled out, either by SDS or the student senate. Student-government leaders attacked this as straightforward confrontation simply for the sake of confrontation. More radical members suggested that the issue was one of "student rights," that students should have the right to invite whom they wanted, when they wanted.

Casting about for a way forward, SFS voted to ask the senate to follow through on its offer of space to the DuBois Club, and if the administration interfered, a sit-in might follow. Discussions were held on the effectiveness and logistics of various sit-in locations, such as Henry's office, or the Union, or the Administration Building. At a climatic and chaotic steering committee meeting in the Channing Murray Foundation building on April 18, nearly half the committee members walked out in frustration over the group's inability to reach a decision. At one point, Durrett, now editor of the SFS newsletter, dramatically wrote out his resignation from the committee, handed it to Berkey, and walked out. Berkey, even more dramatically, pulled out a lighter and burned Durrett's resignation, indicating his refusal to accept it. More committee members then walked out, feeling the group was caught in an endless discussion loop, unable to make a decision. Finally, the remaining members took a vote, again agreeing to ask the student senate to open its office to the DuBois Club, and if the university locked the doors, SFS would then meet to decide on a course of action. Not the most decisive vote, to be sure. As it turned out, the DuBois Club did hold a brief meeting in the senate office, in open defiance of university regulations, but the administration, after a tense hearing for the senate officers who had facilitated the meeting, took no action against them, effectively ignoring the infraction, and successfully heading off yet one more SFS attempt at confrontation.

That same week, in a surprise move, the trustees, meeting on campus, invited student leaders into their meeting to hear their views. Among others, Vic Berkey spoke, calling the university "a free society, which cannot have any type of thought control" arguing that "the Clabaugh Act was a matter of thought control, and so vague as to be dangerous." He added that although he disagreed with the DuBois Club, "I'd like to get them recognized and into the open because I would like to debate them." After listening to Berkey and other students, some trustees suggested that it might be a good idea to continue such open communications. "I guess I don't fully understand academic freedom and free speech the same way the students and faculty do," said one trustee.[5]

Such open communication by the board only added to the SFS conundrum. At a subsequent meeting later that day, the uncertainty continued over how to move forward. Steering-committee member Bob Solomon expressed his feeling that retribution for the office space infraction could be imminent, although it would likely be against the student senate as a whole, not individuals. Durrett, by now returned to the organization, suggested that if there were retribution, other groups might repeat the senate action, reserving rooms and then turning them over to the DuBois Club. Vince Wu disagreed with the entire direction of the discussion, arguing that it was not a proper SFS responsibility to find space for the club. Some members complained that SFS had shifted into a reactive mode, waiting for the university to act. Others suggested an effort to focus on education, to bring more students into the movement. Berkey recommended a petition in support of the senate action. Fred Landis, in exasperation, demanded that the group "do something." "We're not moving forward," he said.[6] The student movement, a victim of its own success, seemed to be foundering.

The week following the board's effort to open communications with students, the state legislature made it clear that nothing had changed in Springfield, firmly voting down in committee the Scariano bill to repeal the Clabaugh Act. Eight individuals—students, faculty, and alumni—had spoken in favor of the repeal, but the committee vote was not close, twenty-three to seven. Clabaugh spoke to the press following the vote, suggesting that if such a vote were put to the citizens of Illinois, 90 percent would vote against repeal. He said the law was no curtailment of students' rights. "It is utter nonsense to say that, when you're keeping subversive, seditious and un-American organizations from using facilities. That's no curb on academic freedom." In a reminder targeted at the students and faculty speakers in support of repeal, he stated what was obvious to him and to the legislature, but certainly not to the activists, that the university didn't belong to the students or faculty: "The university belongs to the people of Illinois."[7]

As the semester drew to a close, the campus was far from unanimous in its thinking on the future of the student movement. Dean of Students Millet took a harmonious tone, thankful that the university had made it through the year. "SFS has unquestionably had a constructive effect on the campus and student government. The actions and rallies of SFS have been constructive and responsible."[8] He added, hopefully, "In many ways SFS has now done its work. What is needed now is careful consideration of rules, regulations and administrative structure." From the movement side, Fred Landis agreed with Millet that the organization had served its purpose by successfully bringing a communist speaker to campus and essentially defanging the Clabaugh Act. "The time for agitation and propaganda is over. . . . Right now the movement is dead." Landis, irritated, suggested that the movement, built with widespread student support and democratic procedures, had now degenerated into "Vic Berkey and a small group who follow him right or wrong." Not unexpectedly, Berkey disagreed. "What's been developed is a lot of awareness among a small but significant minority that students can be the impetus for changing the University." Berkey foresaw big happenings in the future. "I see direct exercise next year . . . civil disobedience on the highest level . . . acting directly against the law."[9]

In the final days of the semester, a noon-hour SFS "gripe-in" in the Illini Union raised the issue of activists' files supposedly held by the university's security department and would lead to the first student sit-in of the era. Millet had denied that any such files existed, but undeterred, one student suggested that a march on the office of Chief Security Officer Thomas Morgan would resolve the issue, and off the protesters went. Once crowded into Morgan's small office antechamber, the group of about fifty were refused appointments with Morgan, so they decided to stage a sit-in until given access to their files. The protest lasted about an hour, gained no access to any files, and resulted in no disciplinary action. But the precedent of the sit-in tactic, though neither thought through nor planned, was now established at Illinois and would become significant. The same week the Illini activists staged their sit-in at Morgan's office, the Defense Department announced that, in the worst month yet of the Vietnam War, 443 Americans were killed and more than eight thousand were wounded. The escalation of the war and the newfound protest tactic would come together in the next school year.

In the final trustee meeting of the semester, Henry introduced Millet to the board, praised his service during the tumultuous year, and asked him to deliver a report on the state of student unrest. The dean announced that the previous year had proved conclusively that in loco parentis was dead at the university, that today's students had an unprecedented degree of maturity and common sense, and that they were deeply offended by university and legislative limitations on their freedom of speech. Today's students "are smarter than in the past," Millet suggested, and were not to be considered "boys and girls, but men and women." In a poke at the Clabaugh Act, he said, "There is educational benefit in exposure to those with different commitments—even to eccentric or antisocial causes," adding, "I am confident students can judge better than we have previously supposed." Henry added optimistically, "I'm happy to say we have not had any physical destruction during protests, which has characterized other campuses. . . . Students have not broken rules; there have been only technical and incidental violations."[10] Clearly Henry and Millet had hopes that the most challenging moments of the Illinois student protest movement were behind them, but in reality, the movement was only just gathering steam, and the administrators' optimism and confidence in their students would face severe tests in the following school year.

Later that summer, the *Chicago Tribune* would interview President Henry regarding modern college students and campus unrest. His comments demonstrated a reasonable understanding of his students. "[The students] are disturbed about the war in Viet Nam . . . about not making more rapid progress in solving civil rights problems . . . about the materialistic goals of our civilization . . . that problems of poverty have not been solved." He accurately described the students' feelings toward the university: "Young people today have a very sensitive social conscience and believe more progress should have been made in solving the problems I have mentioned . . . they look upon [the university] as part of society's establishment. They want the university to take up arms on the social scene." Regarding the unrest: "Modern students have grown up with much more freedom in their homes," and they've "learned the techniques of the civil rights movement, labor unions, and other organizations. The young people have adopted [*sic*] this to campus life and they know how to make it work." The reporter asked, "Where do you draw the line?" Henry responded, "The university can't draw the line. In drawing a line, it would defeat the concept of the right of demonstration and picketing." In the coming year, Henry and his fellow administrators would be forced to draw lines in order to deal with Vic Berkey's visions of "direct exercise" and "civil disobedience on the highest level."[11]

CHAPTER 18

Spring/Summer '67: Women Rising

Despite the claims of 1960s student activists to be radical champions of cultural, social, and political change, the movement was slow in confronting traditional gender roles, which remained largely unquestioned by activists at Illinois and elsewhere for much of the decade. The women's liberation movement, which would become such a powerful force nationally in the seventies and eighties, was not yet visible at Illinois, but in the spring and summer of 1967, suggestions of the coming change could be seen within the movement at Illinois and nationally.

As hard as it might be to imagine today, at Illinois in the sixties virtually all student leaders of the Left—of SACA, SFS, SDS, CEWV (Committee to End the War in Vietnam), and even student government—were men, and nearly all white men. In 1967, a typical year, the student body was composed of almost twice as many men as women, 66 percent male to 34 percent female.[1] Indications are that the proportion of women in the student movement was somewhat higher, but they were still a minority, and an oppressed one.[2] Women in the movement were treated as a second class, at times ignored, at times relegated to clerical tasks, and at times sexually exploited. Some male activists were known to use their leadership positions for sexual advantage, and language disparaging to women was not uncommon among movement males. Sexual attacks were no less a problem on the college campus in the sixties than today, although discussed much less openly, and there is no evidence to suggest that their occurrence was any different within the movement than in the student body as a whole. It is noteworthy that in the research for this book two of the six women activists of the era who were interviewed reported they were raped, the perpetrators men within the movement. One victim commented, "I was caught up in and confused by the 'free love' movement that seemed to tag along with the political movement we were all involved with. At the time, I felt some pressure that if you supported the politics, the sex would follow." Neither of the victims reported the crimes to the police. "I knew they would call me a 'hippie girl' and not believe me." The second added, "I did expect better behavior of men in the movement. I don't know why."[3] In the treatment of women there was little evidence of the sense of justice so avidly displayed toward other causes by the privileged, white-male-dominated student protest movement.

Paula Shafransky, a woman activist of the time, laughs when asked about the role of women in the movement, "Well, we could type up the *Walrus* [the underground newspaper]" but it was men who wrote the articles. "It was still a male-dominated society.... Women were just starting to get their own voice."[4] Activist Joanne Chester recalled, "[At meetings] guys were always doing the talking; it was hard for women to talk. They thought an awful lot of themselves... thought they were really important [and]... attractive to women... some women hung on them just because they were in charge."[5]

Chester grew up in a Chicago suburb; her parents were immigrants from Hungary and Russia. "They were leftists... my mother would pull me out of school to go on demonstrations... to ban the bomb... to pass out anti-war flyers at the train station.... In the 1956 election, my mother hated Richard Nixon. So I hated him too, and I hated him again in 1960." In her high-school history class she would become known as "the class arguer," she said, "because I talked about the Vietnam War all the time."

After arriving on the Illinois campus, she went to a few SDS meetings but didn't think much of them. "I didn't want to belong to a group, I'm not a joiner.... I had a lifetime of antiwar activities before I came to college.... I was reading *The Nation* in junior high." But she had her limits. "I never wanted to get arrested... never wanted to get kicked out of school; my parents were spending money for tuition." She lived in dormitories for a year and a half, but the strict rules were not much of a problem for her. "It was easy to get in and out.... People would always open the doors for you." Later, she would be housemates with draft resister Steve Schmidt, a "really good friend," and a houseful of other activists.[6]

While Chester was among many who ignored dorm rules, in loco parentis oversight was the norm on the campus. Women were required to be in by ten o'clock on week nights, midnight on weekends, had to wear skirts for Sunday dinner, and, according to at least one resident, were not eligible for seconds in the dormitory cafeteria. "Men were allowed [seconds]... I guess they were trying to watch women's weight." Chester laughed when reminded of the rule, "Who would want seconds of that food?" Yet another remembered, "We had to wear *skirts* to the gym class freshman year—for bowling."

Awareness of their second-class status in the movement came gradually for some women, suddenly for others. Patricia Engelhard recalled her moment of recognition: "I had to be awakened to the realities of gender roles and discrimination. I was part of the 'movement,' but despite our radical politics our roles were in every way traditional." When antiwar activist Vivian Rothstein, a Mississippi voter-drive veteran and national SDS organizer, visited the campus to speak to students, Engelhard was asked to take her to dinner. At a meal in a campus pizza joint, Rothstein "opened my eyes," she said, "with one simple question," affecting Engelhard in a way that still resounds:

> She looked at me and asked, "So what's the role of women (a word we did not yet use—'chicks' was the term of the day) in the movement here?"
>
> Perhaps it makes no sense in the world we inhabit now, but that one question would be depicted in a movie by clouds parting, music playing, and the sun shining. It took my breath away. I knew instantly what the question meant. My answer was something like "The women have no role other than to support the men." It may not have been that profound an answer, but I was changed forever.
>
> We talked for hours. She suggested that I invite women to my apartment and not tell them why because men would hijack it. She had a tape for me to play that was a message from the women of North Vietnam to the women of the U.S. It was simple. This is not OUR war. We are sisters. We all want peace. Vivian said just play the tape and let the conversation happen. I did that. . . . Men were unnerved because they could not imagine why women were gathering without them and no one could explain it.
>
> That was my first step as a feminist.[7]

Engelhard's sister Nancy, a year younger and also a member of the Illinois student movement, recalls the sexual climate of the era:

> There was this beautiful thing that happened—the birth control pill—that freed women from getting pregnant and allowed us all to interact in a radically new way compared to our parents' generation or, in fact, any generation up to that point. Sex was an enormous part of the sixties; it was a freeing and truly liberating part of our lives. I remember my mother worrying about women's "reputations"—and I had to explain to her that we were living in a new time and that these concerns were not our concerns.
>
> Sadly, upon reflection, some of the beauty of that time is tainted by the fact that women were sexually harassed by men—broadly speaking, of course. Not all men by any means, but particularly the major movers and shakers in the movement [who] put pressure on women to have sex with them. Women were often willing partners, but there were definitely incidents—I remember one movement "leader" (we tried not to have leaders but we had them anyway) telling me that I shouldn't "lead a man on" unless I was willing to have sex with him, because it caused men

physical pain and was unacceptable. I was seventeen and completely clueless and in way over my head.

So there was that aspect to it. And then the day-to-day work of the movement was truly run by the men and carried out by the women. I remember working on the mimeo machine in the [Channing Murray] basement—making leaflets, whatever. That was the women's job.

As far as women's liberation as a term, that did not come to me until much later—the early seventies. Nor did the word feminism. I remember that when Patsy told me she was having a "women's meeting" I thought, why would you have a meeting with just women? I had no understanding of the big picture at that time.... The sixties were about us being chicks and girls and helpers. I also remember in the seventies when I realized for the first time the importance of calling women "women" and not "girls"... [but] this was not in the consciousness of anyone I knew in the sixties.[8]

Shafransky remembers the women meeting in Engelhard's campus apartment. "It was really powerful for me... talking with women and thinking about what was going on... feeling some empowerment.... It's not to say [the male domination] was [only] because of the males. It was also because the women hadn't yet got to the point where they could really roar, really speak their mind, really take charge, get into the middle of the action.... That took a while and is still taking a while." It was a hint of what was yet to come. "The very, very beginning of the women's movement, understanding what your place was, feeling your power, feeling that you could talk in front of people, that you had independence, a right to your own life, that you didn't have to get married and have kids... it was just the beginning."[9]

Years later the women's movement would grow in strength on the campus, but in the sixties there were only these hints of the movement that was yet to form. Another significant indication of what was to come occurred in April 1967, when Patsy Parker, a senator in student government, announced her surprise candidacy for president of the student body. No woman had ever been elected to such an office at Illinois. Parker would prove to be a dramatic exception to the rule in this male-dominated era when, in May, in a tightly contested two-person runoff, she was elected the university's first woman student body president.[10] However, she was by no means an overnight sensation, as she had built a long and remarkable record as a student government leader prior to the election.

As a freshman, Parker had joined the Young Democrats and from there would move to a position on the steering committee of the Student Committee on Political Enlightenment (SCOPE), a group of liberal students focused on university policy reform and student government, with student senator Joe Allen at the head. Particular issues of interest to SCOPE were living conditions in the dormitories, loosening of housing rules, and extension of the extremely limited women's hours. The group held small rallies, but their issues received limited enthusiasm from the majority of students, who largely ignored the reform effort as they did student government, traditionally controlled by members of the campus fraternities.

By her sophomore year Parker had become president of SCOPE and found the issues that would be hers—liberalization of housing rules and key privileges for women in dormitories. Speaking to a small crowd of thirty at one of the sparsely attended SCOPE rallies, she focused on the plight of women students: "You [women] don't become a pumpkin after 12, you don't automatically become bad at a certain hour.... It doesn't make any difference what side of the hour you're on." She argued, "In some states, women can vote and drink at 18, but at the University, you're not able to regulate your own hours." She ridiculed in loco parentis, arguing the university was less like a parent and more like an authoritarian government: "It has a legislature, it has 10,000 committees, it has a president ... that isn't a mother, that's a state," and "when a state tries to control the individual lives of students, it becomes a police state."[11]

By spring Parker had turned her focus to electoral politics, at one point seconding an SDS suggestion that the students would be best served if the student senate were simply abolished altogether. She criticized that body's convoluted rules of representation, which at times resulted in the oddity of fraternity men representing women's dormitories. "I question Senate's ability to do all the things it's supposed to be doing because it's not really representative.... I can't see how a man from ZBT [a men's fraternity] can represent Allen Hall [a women's dormitory]."[12] In spring of her sophomore year, she won election to the senate of which she had been and would continue to be quite critical.

In her junior year, Parker was elected vice president of the Women's Independent Student Association (WISA), an organization representing women's dormitories, giving her a platform with which to advance the issues she cared for most. Soon she was leading a committee developing a plan for a gradual, incremental program of women's key privileges. By spring, she had it approved; implementation began. Then, in March, in a great surprise to her peer senators, Parker announced her long-shot candidacy for president of the senate, effectively the student body president, for the following year. She won with the largest majority of votes in the school's history, succeeding a long line of fraternity men in the post.

When the official decision was announced, Parker and her team reacted with unrestrained joy. "The tension finally gone, the weeks of sacrificed sleep suddenly felt, the small group of friends ran down the stairs from the WISA office informing everyone along the way they were looking at the new student body president." Parker, exuberant, sprinted away from the group onto the grassy quad. The *DI* reported, "Breaking into a run as she pushed through the south doors of the Illini Union Miss Parker bounded across the quad into the mild spring night." Then she stopped. "Sticking a sprig of flowers in her coat lapel, relaxed for the first time in weeks," Parker calmed herself, struck the proper tone for a newly elected president, and admitted, "I'm terribly excited and a little scared thinking about the tremendous responsibility ahead."[13]

Given her previous hostility to the senate, Parker's victory was seen by the largely conservative male student senators more like a victory over the senate than as a victory for her presidency. She had campaigned on a somewhat nebulous but still dangerous-sounding platform of "Student Power." Vic Berkey called her win "a victory for student rights," and her opponent had charged that Parker would let "SFS run wild."[14] Not surprisingly, her reign as president would be rancorous, marked by conflict and discontent with the senators, and over the course of the year Parker would slowly transition from her reform issues toward more radical ones, offering support for Dow sit-in participants against the university's closed disciplinary process, for local draft resisters against the government, and for African American students against the administration. At one point the *DI* reported that she was "fed up" with the student senate strife, considering resignation and disavowal of campus politics, but in the end, she stayed to fight.

In her presidency Parker would face attacks from all sides, both from the fraternity-dominated senate as well as from some activists on the left. Because she was the first woman in her position to the head male-dominated senate, it is safe to assume some of the attacks were related to gender. Though she fought for due process for protesters, demanded the Security Office open student records, and marched with draft resisters, this was insufficient for some leftists. SDS leader Landis would characterize her as "a wishy washy bowl of jelly. She used to carry picket signs and talk about . . . the DuBois Club. Now that she has felt the so-called burden of office she is going out of her way to be responsible."[15]

Nonetheless, her successful advancement of student and especially women's housing issues, her precedent-setting victory, and her progressive stances as president all made for an extraordinary record at a time when the women's movement was still a vague and distant rumor on the campus. By any measure Parker was one of the most impressive of Illinois student leaders, male or female, before or after the sixties. Though in her campus career she would not identify as a feminist or a liberated woman, as it was too early for such language, she and other women students of the sixties were harbingers of a coming wave that would gain momentum in the seventies, when a substantial feminist movement would develop on campus. In the sixties, however, traditional male dominance remained the norm within and without the student movement.

Such stereotypical male domination would be on full display as the spring '67 semester came to a close in one last gathering on the quad, a fiasco of a late-night rally intended as yet one more protest against the university's restrictive women's hours. Flyers for the midnight rally announced:

MIDNIGHT MEETING

For all girls who like to take walks at 2:00 A.M.; Who like to leave parties when they're over; Who get hungry in the middle of the night; in other words, for everyone who is fed up with women's hours.

Why wait for the administration to <u>grant</u> us <u>privileges</u>?

We must exercise our <u>rights</u>.

Come to the quad Friday night at midnight and decide what course of action we will take.

Bring guitars, kazoos, banjos, bodies, friends, etc.[16]

A crowd of three hundred showed up, according to the *DI*, mostly "security officers, newsmen, and male students."[17] Keven Roth, an organizer of the event, saw the crowd differently. "You know who showed up? All the frat boys, and they were drunk, hooting and hollering. I looked out and saw some women, and some normal guys, but it looked like every frat house had emptied onto the quad to disrupt the meeting." Sophomore Carla Fortney kicked off the rally, asking, "Where does the Administration get the authority to control the social regulations of students?" She was immediately met with heckling and ridicule from the predominantly male audience. Gail Pohlman stood to beg the crowd, "Give us a chance." But soon a frustrated Roth, recognizing the reality of the situation, rose, thanked the women for coming out, and admitted, "This is not working, I'm afraid the guys have taken over our meeting, let's get back to the dorms," then turned and left the demonstration.[18] Soon the crowd dispersed. It was an event most noteworthy for the male harassment in the days before the feminist movement.

The evening was particularly galling for Roth, who years later would reflect on the event, as well as her participation in New York and Washington protest marches, claiming to be a participant in "nearly every anti-war event on campus." She remembered with special rancor the ongoing, frustrating campaign "to liberalize 'women's hours' that would have allowed us to stay out after 10:00 P.M." Roth came from an intellectual, suburban household south of Chicago; her father worked on the Manhattan Project and her mother was a former actress. "Graduate students and foreign professors were frequent visitors in our home," she recalled. As for the midnight rally, "Like many women, I found that locking women up at 10:00 P.M., while the men could do what they wanted around the clock, was unfair." Roth spoke of her background and her involvement in radical politics:

> We were serious Democrats. My [Republican] grandmother said she prayed for us every night, because we didn't go to church and we were Democrats. We had a mock election in my third-grade class, and I was only one of two who voted for Adlai Stevenson. I started college at the U of I in 1966. My roommate was my best friend from high school. Our first semester was rather boring until we discovered that the

more interesting liberal students hung out in the Union cafeteria. After that, I'm pretty sure we were part of nearly every anti-war event on campus.

I would like to say that a feminist awakening led me to protest our restrictive hours, but the actual case was less clear cut and more reflective of the times. . . . While women muttered about this among themselves, at a meeting of SFS in the back lounge of the union, the usual leaders of meetings, the guys, started talking about successful efforts at other colleges to abolish women's hours and maybe we should do something. . . . I asked what we could do [and] I became the leader of the effort.[13]

The following year, Parker's plan for extended women's hours, key privileges, and loosening of visitation rules in dorms would be implemented for seniors, with gradual extension of similar privileges to younger students over the next several years. Roth would graduate from the university before the liberalization would extend to freshman.

The national SDS convention took place that summer in Ann Arbor, Michigan, and was a harbinger of the next stage of the national movement, yet to arrive at Illinois. Several SDS members from Urbana made the trip north and brought back new thinking with them. The conference heralded a sharp turn away from issues such as free speech, and toward more radical ones. The *National Guardian*, a New York–based newsweekly, described the attendees: "The major political tendencies appear to be these: On the one side are the left-wing socialists and neo-Marxists, on the other the anarchists of various persuasion, including hippies, and to the middle a combination of both."[20] The attendees showed a new, complete disdain for conventional politics. "The left-liberal tendency had vanished as a serious factor," Vic Berkey recalled years later. "We couldn't align with the Democratic Party. LBJ and the Democrats were escalating the war. . . . The Dixiecrats were against the civil rights movement."[21] Thus the path of electoral politics was closed off as an option to SDS. And since campus issues no longer warranted the attendees' attention, by far the greatest share of discussion now went toward resistance to the war and the draft, with an emphasis on "direct action."

That year the issue of women's roles in the movement arose for the first time at an SDS convention, when discussion of women's liberation reached a critical level despite derision from many male attendees. A formal Women's Liberation Workshop offered a statement to the convention floor; it stimulated both greater turbulence and more long-term impact than any other topic on the agenda. The workshop statement was unambiguous. From today's perspective it reads as a clear declaration of the leftist women's independence from the male-dominated movement and would become known as a watershed in this phase of American feminism:

As we analyze the position of women in capitalist society and especially in the United States we find that women are in a colonial relationship to men and we recognize ourselves as part of the Third World. Women, because of their colonial relationship to men, have to fight for their own independence. This fight for our own independence will lead to the growth and development of the revolutionary movement in this country. Only the independent woman can be truly effective in the larger revolutionary struggle. We seek the liberation of all human beings. The struggle for liberation of women must be part of the larger fight for human freedom. We recognize the difficulty our brothers will have in dealing with male chauvinism and we will assume full responsibility in helping to resolve the contradiction. Freedom now! We love you![22]

Elsewhere in the statement was a critical phrase that especially drew the male attendees' ire, calling on activist women "to help relieve our brothers of the burden of male chauvinism," an indication that the women felt their male counterparts would require some assistance in the effort.[23] The proposal was finally approved on the floor of the convention, if with much rancor, and a committee was formed and directed "to study the problem." However, soon after the convention, *New Left Notes*, a newspaper published by SDS, reprinted the women's workshop statement, dismissively and derisively accompanied by a graphic of a young woman with "large eyelashes and earrings ... a polka-dotted waist-high miniskirt with matching bloomers and black stockings" holding a sign saying "We want our Rights & We want them NOW!"[24] The reaction to their proposal at the convention, the follow-on treatment in the SDS newspaper, and the insulting graphic would only further fuel the activist women's drive to affect the organization, the movement, and society at large. The coming women's liberation movement of the 1970s and '80s was clearly visible in the grievances of these pioneer activist women of the 1960s.

Attending SDS members from Illinois observed the convention events with eyes wide. Years later, Vern Fein remembered, "It was mind-blowing. It opened up ... a revolutionary view. Free speech was no longer a consideration—stopping the war was, as well as topics we had never really considered like women's lib, radical ecology, racial justice. The result was a radicalization of our [Illinois] leaders."[25] Joseph Hardin, a junior, especially recalled the furor over the women's issue, brought into focus for him with one incident. "There was a nice-looking young woman sitting outside on the grass ... talking about women's oppression. ... I stopped and listened to her. ... But the response [of other men] was pretty much dismissive. Her oppression was nothing like that of the Vietnamese people or American blacks. ... Some just laughed at her. It troubled me ... [but] I was told to get serious."[26] Looking back today on the treatment of women by the men of the movement, Vincent Wu would simply say, "We did them a disservice. We took them for granted."[27]

Though the convention provided some direction, the new issues provided as many questions as answers to the Illinois activists. The focus on antiwar, draft resistance, and "direct action" efforts so visible at the convention would drive the student movement at the University of Illinois in the next semester, where the war would take over center stage from the issue of free speech. But the women's issues that arose at the convention, noted by Hardin and Fein, and demonstrated at Illinois in the coming semester by Parker's ongoing conflicts with the male-dominated senate, would largely remain under the surface within the student movement, at times bubbling up, causing stress between the sexes, but not yet receiving the attention that it would in years to come.

George D. Stoddard, UI president, 1947–1953. Photo courtesy of the University of Illinois at Urbana-Champaign Archives, image 7804.tif.

David Dodds Henry, UI president 1955–1971, Jack W. Peltason, Chancellor, UI Urbana campus 1967–1977. Photo courtesy of U of I News Bureau.

Edward Yellin. Photo courtesy of the *Daily Illini*.

Leo Koch. Photo courtesy of the *Daily Illini*.

Free Speech Now. SFS Demonstrators. Photo courtesy of *Champaign-Urbana Courier*.

SFS Demonstrators. Photo courtesy of *Champaign-Urbana Courier*.

"No one has the right to revolt." Counter-protesters. Photo courtesy of the *Daily Illini*.

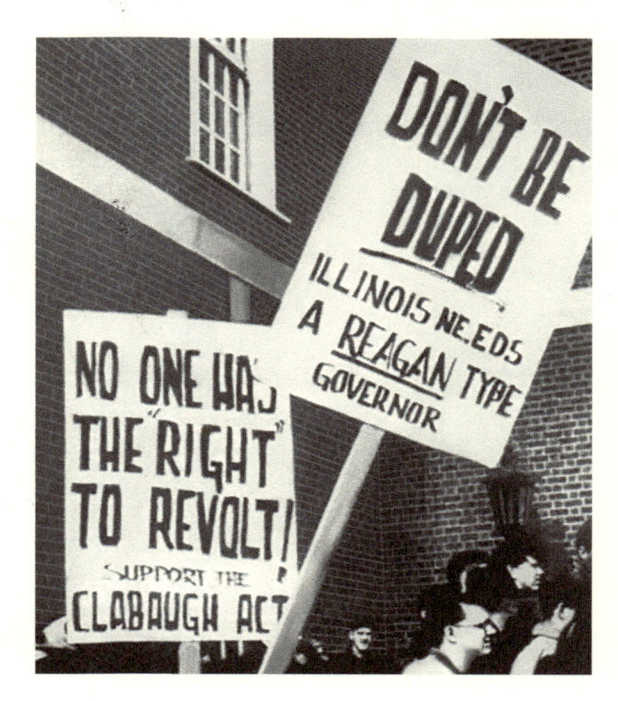

"Don't be duped." Counter-protesters. Photo courtesy of the *Daily Illini*.

Joe Allen and Vic Berkey. Photo courtesy of *Champaign-Urbana Courier*.

Louis Diskin speaks on the quad. Photo courtesy of *Champaign-Urbana Courier*.

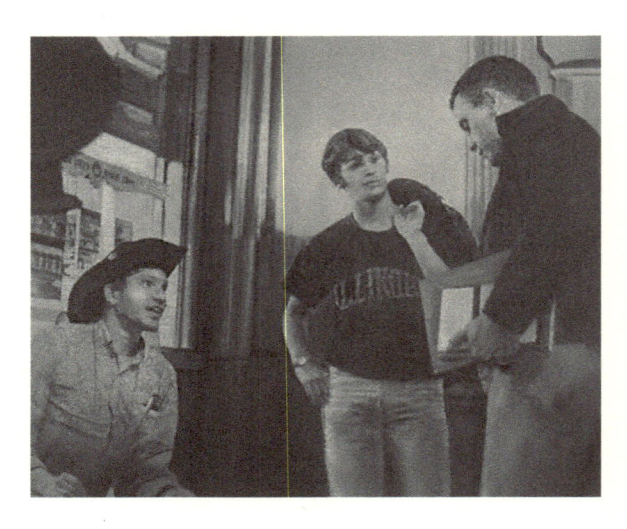

Steve Schmidt and Bernard Gershenson proselytizing. Photo courtesy of the *Daily Illini*.

Early antiwar protest on Union patio. Photo courtesy of the *Daily Illini*.

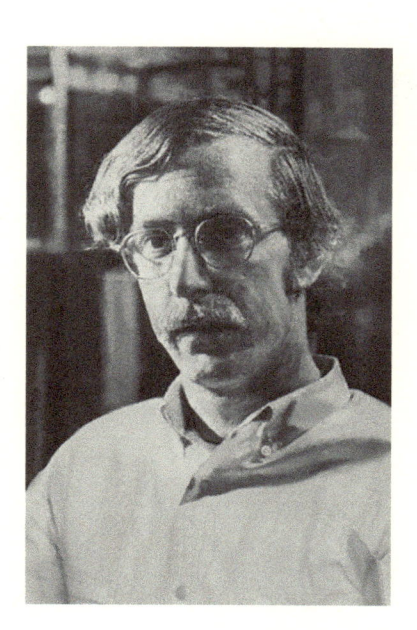

Phil Durrett. Photo courtesy of the *Daily Illini*.

Vern Fein. Photo courtesy of the *Daily Illini*.

Dow sit-in, October 25, 1967. Photo courtesy of the *Daily Illini*.

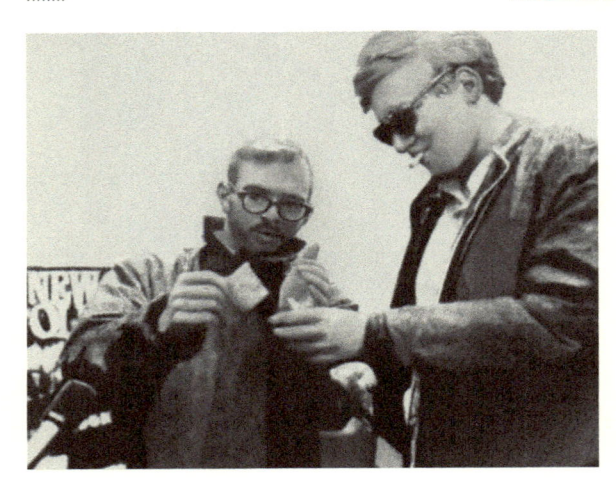

Rick Soderstrom and Steve Schmidt burning draft cards. Photo courtesy of *Champaign-Urbana Courier*.

Security Office. Steve Schmidt, Fred Landis, Vern Fein, Vic Berkey, and friends. Photo courtesy of the *Daily Illini*.

Keven Roth and Nancy Engelhard at Champaign draft board protest. Photo courtesy of the *Daily Illini*.

John Lee Johnson. Photo courtesy of the *Daily Illini*.

Patsy Parker. Photo courtesy of the *Daily Illini*.

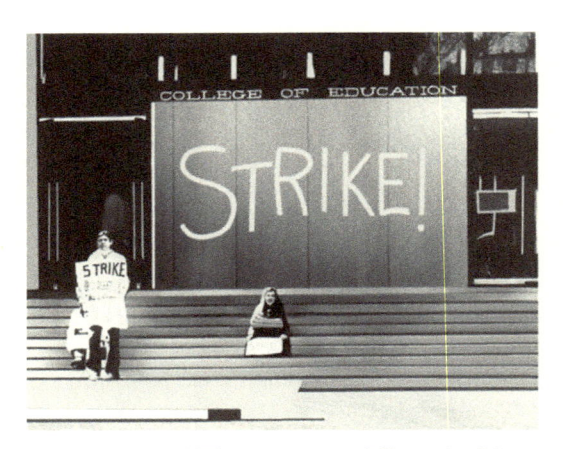

Student strike, May 1970. Photo courtesy of *Champaign-Urbana Courier*.

Picket line at the Administration Building. Photo courtesy of the University of Illinois Archives at Urbana-Champaign, *Walrus* vol. 1, no. 2, record series 41/66/869.

Students and troopers face off at the Illini Union. Photo courtesy of *Champaign-Urbana Courier*.

PART III

The Antiwar Movement, 1967–69

CHAPTER 19

Fall '67: A Hectic Beginning

The Illinois campus had gone through many changes in the twenty years leading up to 1967. From the rabid anticommunism of the George Stoddard era, through the threatened expulsion of former red Edward Yellin and the firing of the sexual revolutionary Leo Koch, to the crowd of thousands gathered on the quad exercising their right to hear a real communist, Louis Diskin, speak unfettered on the Illinois campus, the historically conservative university had evolved dramatically. The McCarthy era was past, opposition to the Clabaugh Act was now more the norm than not, expectations of free and open campus speech prevailed, the university's in loco parentis housing rules were under attack and held in general disdain, and antiwar feelings ran high on the campus.

On the national scene, racial strife raged, with summer riots in Newark, Detroit, and Minneapolis, all vying with the ever-escalating war for the lead on the evening news, with more troops, more bombings, more deaths, and no apparent end in sight. More than eleven thousand American military service members would die in Vietnam in 1967, nearly double the total of the year before. The campus had evolved considerably, both politically and socially, since the Stoddard era, but in the fall of 1967 the pace of change would dramatically accelerate, and an unprecedented surge in political energy would erupt on the campus, resulting in extraordinary student activism. The focus of that activism would undergo a shift from the earlier campus-related issues of free speech and academic freedom to a focus on the war, an issue that affected university students, as it affected all the youth of America, but especially the males, directly, personally, and existentially.

That fall would see protesting Illinois students move from verbal protests to nonviolent action, heeding the advice of Berkeley's radical student leader Mario Savio, who had preached, "There is a time when the operation of the machine becomes so odious, makes you so sick at heart, that you can't take part, you can't even tacitly take part, and you've got to put your bodies upon the gears and upon the wheels, upon the levers, upon all the apparatus, and you've got to make it stop."[1] The time had come for Illinois students to put their bodies upon the apparatus.

The new semester was the first with Jack Peltason as chancellor of the Urbana campus. In his early days he set up an advisory board of centrist student leaders, with representatives from student senate, the Pan Hellenic and Inter-fraternity Councils, and the independent housing groups. No activists from SDS or the SFS movement were invited to join the group. The new chancellor suggested the advisory board might act as a student cabinet of sorts, and he explained his choices this way: "I picked these people with an eye to their contact with the greatest number of students."[2] Dean of Students Millet made big news when he announced loosening of rules on women's visits to men's housing, even though the new rules strictly limited their presence to "public areas." Millet had been considering the change for more than a year, after a faculty committee on student governance had officially proposed it. The dean went so far as to suggest that twenty-one-year-old students might even someday be allowed liquor in their apartments. He also announced plans to upgrade the student rules handbook, pointing out antiquated prohibitions of student sunbathing on much of the campus. Millet certainly must have felt that under his guidance the rules for students were being greatly loosened.

On a topic of more interest to activist students, freshman Steve Schmidt, speaking for the Channing Murray Foundation, a Unitarian-Universalist community center a block off the main quad, one "celebrating and honoring a diversity of social identities and experiences," announced the opening of a coffeehouse in the basement of the building. In exchange for managing the facility, Schmidt was given a rent-free room off the basement; he remembers it as "a first venture into running a business." The Channing Murray facility would become the site of many years of activist student meetings, organizing efforts, and event planning sessions. The coffeehouse was called "The Red Herring," a name with several meanings. As a literary device, a red herring refers to a false clue or a distraction, such as a trail covered with a smelly fish to throw dogs off a scent. In the politics of the time, to accuse someone of being "soft on communism" was often a red herring, distracting attention from an individual's more substantive political positions.

The irony of the name for a gathering place of campus radicals was obvious, and it seemed to fit the subterranean coffeehouse well. The basement venue had been repainted in bright colors, adorned with Hare Krishna posters and suggestive quotations on the walls, such as "The disaffection of youth is the first malady suffered by decaying empires." In addition to becoming a favorite hangout for campus activists, the coffeehouse would be a staging area for local folk singers, with regular appearances by favorites Dan Fogelberg and Steve Goodman. The latter would often sing his hit song "The City of New Orleans" on the tiny Red Herring stage. Occasionally, the sweet scent of marijuana added to the low-light ambience of the musty basement. Schmidt's announcement also mentioned that a panel discussion with SFS leaders would be held in the new facility, to review the past year's activities and to discuss plans for the coming year.

Two weeks into the new semester, SDS held their first meeting of the school year. Vern Fein spoke and advocated for the group to continue to reach out to mainstream students, in the dormitories and fraternities and sororities, in order to effectively propagate the group's antiwar message. He proposed a continuation of the "gripe-ins" he had led the previous year in the south lounge of the Union; instead of focusing on the free-speech issues of the previous year, however, now everyone agreed the focus should be the war. Phil Durrett, perhaps harking back to his Air Force days in Georgia and the segregation he had seen there, advocated for the group's attention to the local racial situation, the need to build bridges with the "Negroes" of north Champaign, to pressure the university to increase minority hiring, and to work for improvement of conditions in the Champaign County jail. Rick Soderstrom and Vic Berkey announced a new effort, organized draft resistance, and the need to move beyond mere demonstrations to (unspecified but exciting-sounding) "action," and they invited the audience to attend a meeting on the subject the following week at Channing Murray. These three issues—the war, racial issues, and draft resistance—would take over center stage in the new school year, leaving the free-speech concerns and Clabaugh Act protests in the past.

These new areas would be formalized by the activists in the first and last meeting of SFS later that same week. On a Friday night in the first month of classes, the SFS organization, as little organized as it was, voted to disorganize itself in favor of several new, diverse projects. A "Radical Research Project," which Durrett championed, was one such effort; an antiwar dormitory education project led by Fein, was another; and Soderstrom's proposed draft-resistance effort yet one more. "There is the future of SFS," said Durrett, pointing to a blackboard with the various new projects listed, adding, "We need a lot of different groups for a lot of different issues."[3]

At the end of the planning session for the year, the group then settled into a philosophical discussion about the role of students in the modern "multiversity." Berkey declared that to understand the logic of the multiversity, students must "first realize that the University believes students are 'niggers,' second-class citizens to be treated as such." He continued with more metaphors: "The student [is] an empty can that the University fills up with the fruits of knowledge but does not allow you to fulfill your interest." Mike Warren, graduate student and history teaching assistant, seconded that thought, explaining, "The University is a training ground where students learn to conform. I teach a few history sections, and these kids know their social security number and their counselor's room, but they don't know about Brother Malcolm X." One woman in the audience asked why, if the speakers didn't like the university, they didn't just leave. Berkey explained, "I have no choice in the matter. If I don't have a certain number of credit hours I go into the army. I have a choice between this multiversity and another. If a slave chooses his master he's still a slave."[4] Given the conditions of the time, the nature of the audience, and their political inclinations, the group readily accepted his logic.

A week later, Peltason addressed a New Year Convocation audience at the Assembly Hall and presented a quite different point of view. He refuted the notion that "a university should be some kind of intellectual factory, or filling station for knowledge" and made it clear that he believed "in complete freedom for the students and faculty to express their views." The new chancellor metaphorically suspended the Clabaugh Act, though it was still the law of the land, (at least for the moment), declaring freedom of speech for all as a given on the campus. Peltason disparaged those "willing to concede that it is all right to let students think they are challenging important values provided care is taken to insure that the challenging takes place under controlled circumstances." Far from anything Charles Clabaugh would be comfortable with, Peltason claimed, "A university's mission is not the cultivation of manners ... [nor] to determine how students will act. Do not ask us to guarantee that our students will be attired in a manner that you approve. Do not ask us as a University to certify to the soundness of their political beliefs and behavior."[5] At least in his speech, Peltason presented a fresh approach to the challenges of the campus. His liberal attitude would soon be tested.

While Peltason was speaking in progressive tones to his audience, on the other side of campus the leaders of a newly formed group, the Draft Resisters Union (DRU), spoke a bit more radically to theirs. In their first meeting, the group agreed on a provocative founding statement, to be included in a petition for which they would soon be gathering signatures:

> We the undersigned men of draft age wish to announce that we refuse to be drafted into the U.S. Armed Forces. By withholding our participation we are saying "no" to the continuing barbarism of the Vietnam war. We are responsible for our actions. We openly say "no" to conscripted military service.
>
> Our refusal to participate in the madness of the Vietnam war in no way implies a renunciation of our country. Our act of refusal is in fact an act of loyalty because it aims at redeeming rather than smothering human potentiality here in the United States and around the world.

> We are taking this stand both to assert our personal integrity and self respect, and to stem the kind of assumptions and policies exemplified by the Vietnam war. We urge all young men of draft age who can conscientiously do so, to assume responsibility for their lives and to join us in this stand.[6]

The statement was easily voted through but was followed by a lengthy discussion of what behaviors would or would not constitute an acceptable level of resistance to the draft. Was simply handing out leaflets on the quad sufficient resistance? Would an acceptable level require civil disobedience? Did "sufficiently resistant" only describe those willing to burn their draft cards? Must an acceptable level of resistance mean willingness to go to jail for one's beliefs? Steve Schmidt, one of the new group's leaders, suggested, "Maybe if you're afraid of signing a piece of paper you shouldn't be here." The draft resister would later observe, "There was a lot of 'militance about the mouth' in our politics back then . . . a lot of people who could talk a militant speech but just weren't willing to do much. . . . When it came time to turn in a draft card, or burn a draft card, or sit in against a draft board, or sit in against Dow Chemical . . . even to take a bus to Washington for a march . . . they had other responsibilities or just really didn't want to get involved at that level."[7] After some debate it was agreed that any and all levels of resistance would be acceptable to the group, that the level chosen would be a matter of personal conscience, and that the organization was willing to support all those who resisted the draft, no matter their degree of radicalism. Schmidt, one of the more radical resisters, announced that he and a second DRU member, Goddard Graves, would soon publicly burn their draft cards.

This was a busy day on the campus, as President Henry also delivered a speech—much less provocative than Peltason's ringing endorsement of campus freedoms or the DRU meeting. Henry's speech was an annual event, titled simply "The Year Ahead." In addition to announcing continued growth in the physical plant, increased enrollment, and a new electronic computer network system, "Illinet," Henry lamented the lack of funding for a larger physical build-out of the campus and for badly needed new educational programs, blaming the shortfall in federal funding on the expense of the Vietnam War. Glaringly missing in Henry's speech was any reference to the difficult issues of the previous year. Not a word would be heard of academic freedom or of free speech on campus. If Peltason's speech had indicated that the university had moved beyond the previous year's issues, Henry's speech glossed over them as if they'd never been raised. Henry did make oblique reference to the difficult social clime nationally, describing the era as "a time of debate, public notice, unresolved issues," and perhaps with the previous year's protests in the back of his mind, he shared his concerns regarding the nation's growing student activism. "Student disorders, in many parts of the country, however unrepresentative of students generally, are disquieting, raising in the public mind questions of confidence in the system itself."[8]

The *DI* splashed reports of the DRU meeting and Peltason's speech on page 1, the former under the headline, "Draft Resistance Union 'Won't Go,'" the latter with "Peltason Supports Academic Freedom." The report on Henry's speech with the less-than-thrilling head "Henry Sees More Progress" did not make the front page, and the editorial staff panned the president's effort. "While Chancellor Peltason concentrated on . . . how he will try to run the Urbana campus, President Henry proceeded to reinforce the image he has built up during the last few years—that of a corporate executive, surrounded by computers and charts, worr[ied] about what people outside might think if his employees make too much noise."[9] Henry's lack of attention to the issues of the year before that had so gripped the campus irritated the editors: "Despite what is often said about President Henry—that he is quite concerned with student welfare and faculty problems; that he does, in fact, reject the need for such laws as the Clabaugh Act—he still fails to transmit this in his major statements to the public." They went on: "The University has just ended a year which saw more student activism than in past years. By treating the problem so briefly in his discussion of the year ahead, President Henry gives the impression that this is of little consequence to the future growth and direction of the University." The editors continued the criticism: "Instead of leading the University in its bid for shaking off all restraints on free inquiry, he has turned instead to the students, and in essence, has asked them to 'hold it down a little.'"

Apparently, the editorial staff had misunderstood the ramifications of Henry's decision to place the campus management on the shoulders of the new chancellor, Peltason. "We are not asking that President Henry stop his efforts at securing more and bigger grants for the University. . . . But we do ask him to spend a little more time in identifying with the students and faculty at the University." This seemed unlikely, as Henry had implemented the new governance structure specifically so that he would be able to focus less on the students and the faculty and more on the legislature, the trustees, and the general public. As his Assembly Hall speech indicated, it would now be Jack W. Peltason's role, no longer Henry's, to worry about campus hot-button issues like free speech, academic freedom, and "identifying with the students and faculty." The president's strategy would not work out quite as smoothly as he had hoped, but it was still only the first month of the semester, and issues and roles were still being clarified. However, what was already clear was that the fight for free speech at the university was yesterday's news. The student movement would be focused on other issues in the fall of 1967.

CHAPTER 20

A New Focus: The War

Toward the end of the first month of the new school year, Vern Fein hosted his first "gripe-in" in the south lounge of the Union, an area that would become a familiar indoor gathering place for the year's political discussions. Seventy-five students showed up for the session. Mike Warren spoke of the need to argue the antiwar cause not only intellectually but also emotionally, and urged students to join the CEWV. Phil Durrett revisited Eisenhower's warnings about the military-industrial complex, suggesting that the war was ultimately about economics, and spoke of the United Fruit Company's exploitation of South American peoples and countries. "Johnson is fighting to support U.S. investors in Vietnam. Although our investments are presently not great, the war is being used as a testing ground." Berkey backed up Durrett's economic analysis, suggesting the American definition of the "Free World" really meant "free access by American corporations." Warren, also an advocate of the economic case, noted, "For every man we kill in Vietnam, we give the family $34 in condolence money. Yet, for every rubber tree we destroy, we pay $87. There has to be something wrong with a system like that." The audience agreed. Such economic arguments would seem controversial at first but eventually would be commonly accepted by most in the movement. The discussion spoke directly to President Eisenhower's warnings about the power of American industry, now doing more and more of its business worldwide in the sixties, and the United States military supporting and protecting those corporations' global interests.[1]

CEWV announced a demonstration for the following day against an Armed Forces recruiting event to be held in the Union. Mike Hanagan, president of CEWV, said, "We have been outraged that a student union would grant space to these military people."[2] However, the demonstration would display less outrage and more the transitional state of the movement. Intending to focus on antiwar issues raised by the Armed Forces recruiting station, instead the activists reverted to the familiar issue of freedom of speech. After gathering on the south patio of the union, they moved into the building. But once inside, protesters began arguing with Union officials, complaining that the Marines were allowed space for recruiting but students could not reserve space for the DuBois Club, violating their right of free speech. Union director Earl Finder responded that the Marines were on campus at the invitation of the university's job-placement service, which only further aggravated the demonstrators. According to the *DI*, Finder blamed it on the university bureaucracy: "Finder said the University coordinating placement office requests the space 'just as the commerce department might invite General Electric or AT and T. There is no bending over backwards for one group or another.'" Soderstrom tried to pull the demonstration out of this administrative dead end by shifting to the intended antiwar focus, as he questioned the Marines on duty about their support for the war. The recruiter declined to join in such a discussion, saying, "I'll answer any of your questions on officer recruiting. That's what I'm here for. I'm not here to discuss anything else."[3]

Counterprotesters soon appeared in force and began arguing with the demonstrators. One, a Navy veteran, maintained, "I would say we were wrong to enter the war, but South Vietnam is worth saving. The South Vietnamese people realize they have a popularly elected government; the roots of democracy are being grown among a backward people."[4] Another, Henry Carlson, took a more libertarian viewpoint, stating, "I condemn you for not letting the Marines use this Union. I condemn you for the same reason I condemn the Clabaugh Act. You are denying a group the right of free speech." In reality the demonstrators were hardly preventing the Marines from using the Union and had little effect on the Marines' rights of free speech or their recruiting efforts and were, if anything, drawing more passersby attention to them. Hanagan was disappointed with the entire affair, suggesting the protest had badly missed its mark. "The main emphasis was supposed to be on questioning the Marines about the war and protesting University complicity in it. Instead, because of the Students for Free Speech background of many of the people here, it switched to a free speech movement."[5] The movement was having trouble finding its new direction, but on the positive side for the activists, it was only the first month of the semester, and already students were demonstrating. Sophomore Keven Roth and her friends found the experience exciting, and she wrote about it in a letter home to her mother:

> I was in a demonstration—not a very big or exciting one—but at least it was something. The Air Force has set up an exhibit in the union—so we picketed and had a

discussion in the lobby. Debby, Dee, Nance and I spent all last night calling people and telling them to come. We had about 80 students—and for the U. of I. that was pretty good. We're meeting a lot of people—really nice and interesting people.

We're the youngest ones in the group—and they kind of treat us that way—but they still respect us because we *are* so young and involved.[6]

Several outside speakers, sometimes referred to by supporters of the war as "outside agitators," visited the campus in the following weeks. The first, Gary Radar, former Green Beret turned draft resistance activist, was brought to campus by the DRU to speak at an evening event at the Red Herring. He shared his regrets about his Army life and urged the audience to resist conscription. He began philosophically: "Draft resistance is not concerned with protesting the draft but rather stopping it. A man who can stand up and say 'I am a free man' has control over his life. A man is as free as he thinks he is; this maintains his human dignity." He spoke of his personal experience. "The Army is the worst place in the world to be. . . . [Y]ou either will be killed or kill. The Army is about killing people." The Army, for him, was "completely dehumanizing": "I reached a point where I would rather go to jail than be in the Army. " He ended with a personal statement: "I want to go to jail, because if I'm not in jail I'm in the Army. At least I won't hurt people in jail, and my self-respect will be inside me."[7]

A second resister, Paul O'Brien, an organizer from the Chicago Area Draft Resisters, spoke with Radar. "O'Brien," the *DI* reported, "urged the audience to stop being a 'plaything of the war machine by carrying their cards. Some people carry their cards because they are afraid. . . . Draft resistance has got to be a radical movement. If we are going to be radical we must go beyond the question of what's going to happen to me.'" He had high hopes for the impact of the resistance. "We want to get to where when they (the Negroes) start tearing down American cities, the Army is going to have to bring troops back from Vietnam to stop it." But he acknowledged that things could quickly go south for the resistance movement. "We all could be busted immediately."[8]

Another outside speaker to visit the campus, Vernon Urban, an officer with the national SDS office in Chicago, also spoke at the Red Herring, which had quickly become a welcoming home away from home for the campus radicals. Urban argued that it was time for a fundamental shift of focus for SDS. "We need to change . . . the time has come for us to move our efforts into the streets. . . . making a commitment to spend the next 10 to 15 years building a U.S. liberation front. . . . going into these urban centers and organize the people towards the left." Urban had high hopes for his group's impact, likening the potential of SDS to that of students in the Cuban revolution. "Cuba started the same way, led by middle class student organizations." On a dark note, he suggested that the past summer's riots were only a taste of what was to come. "What happened in Newark and Detroit is duck soup compared with what is in store for this nation in the coming year." Urban ended by expressing concern over "the biggest problem confronting SDS," that after graduation, SDS students would forget revolution and become focused on finding jobs. "Most of them get caught up in the gray flannel suit bag and within six months after graduation won't even write nasty letters to the editor."[9] The speaker's prescient insight foreshadowed not simply the demise of SDS but the eventual end of the student movement, yet that time was still far off.

In early October the student senate announced that Staughton Lynd, a nationally known figure in the antiwar movement, had accepted their invitation to speak on the Illinois campus the evening of October 16, with the intention of stimulating student discussion of the war and the draft. Lynd was a former Yale professor, a long-time antinuclear activist and one of the most outspoken opponents of the United States' involvement in Vietnam. He had traveled to China and North Vietnam the previous year without a valid United States passport, had spoken out forcefully against his nation's aggression in Vietnam and advocated for civil disobedience to disrupt the "war machine." He was no stranger to the state of Illinois, having earlier in his career received an offer of a teaching position at Chicago State until it was withdrawn by the governing board overseeing the college. A resulting court case on that situation was still pending. At a meeting later in the week, SDS passed a resolution condemning the student senate for filing the required visiting-speaker paperwork around Lynd's visit, arguing that such documentation constituted "prior censorship." The group demanded that the senator who had submitted the form get it back from the university. The new senate president, Patsy Parker, agreed with SDS on the issue of prior restraint but suggested that the SDS request to take back the form and an SDS threat of "censure" against the senate was much ado about nothing. "I personally don't think that taking back the form would make any difference. The point was made with Diskin that the forms are irrelevant."[10] Again, free speech was last year's issue, one no longer worthy of attention.

With the back and forth between the senate and SDS over the Lynd visitor forms, no one was paying much attention to an SDS announcement that there would be a demonstration, details to come, against an upcoming Dow Chemical recruiting visit to campus. Berkey, chairing an SDS meeting, was quoted as saying, "We have a reception planned." They discussed leafleting on the quad along with burning of a dummy, symbolizing the effect of Dow's napalm on Vietnamese civilians. Rick Soderstrom, emphasizing once again the shift of the movement's focus, pointed out that Dow would not be attacked on free-speech grounds but, rather, more fundamentally: "because they don't have the right to kill people."[11]

CHAPTER 21

Draft Resisters Act

On Monday, October 9, the newly formed Draft Resisters Union met at Channing Murray and voted to "close down" the local draft board office, picking the date of October 16 for their action. That would be the day of Lynd's speech and also a day of scheduled antidraft activities across the country. The local action would consist of a sit-in inside the Champaign Selective Service office and a gathering of supporters outside. DRU members Steve Schmidt and Dennis Weeks announced they would burn their draft cards, a federal offense, on that day at noon at a rally on the south patio of the Illini Union.

The same day, Herbert Gutowsky, head of the university's Chemistry Department and host to the Dow recruiters scheduled to interview on campus, held a meeting with Vic Berkey, president of SDS, and Mike Hanagan, representing CEWV, regarding the two groups' plans to demonstrate during the upcoming Dow visit. Gutowsky justified the meeting this way: "I felt it would be constructive to meet with these leaders and make sure there was as good an understanding between us as possible. I believe students have the right to picket for free speech if they do so in a responsible manner." However, he continued, "There is a lot to be gained by defining what 'responsible' is," then went on to define the term as not interfering with the work of his department, and specifically not interfering with his department's recruiting and placement processes. Responding, Berkey said tactics for the demonstration were under discussion in SDS meetings that were, by necessity, closed to all but members, and added, "Personally the most important thing to me is talking to students. I am not concerned with astounding, scaring or alienating students. I don't want to be disruptive in a negative way." Keeping to the activists' line of the new semester, he said that this was not an issue of free speech but an issue of the war. Berkey questioned Gutosky about the morality of inviting the napalm manufacturer into his facilities. The department head replied, "As long as the war is national policy and not an illegal action, we will extend facilities to companies such as Dow. If an organization came to us that the government had declared illegal we would not participate with it. I have no recourse, as the head of chemistry, but to allow companies to send representatives." Berkey suggested that as a "free man," Gutowsky had the right to deny Dow access to his facilities. Gutowsky countered, "A man must wear many hats," claiming he did not have the option to deny Dow space, and he repeated that in his position he had certain responsibilities that simply must be carried out.[1]

October 16 was beginning to shape up as a day filled with activist events on the campus. CEWV announced they would be working with faculty to focus the day on the war, asking instructors to dedicate the day's classes to discussions of the conflict. A student senate committee voted to ask faculty to support the CEWV effort. As the day approached, the DRU attempted to clarify its intentions. "We might not be doing the right thing Monday. But people have heard noises and, right or wrong, we're going to explode into the consciousness of the good citizens of Champaign-Urbana," said undergraduate Goddard Graves, one of the planners of the DRU demonstration. Steve Schmidt affirmed his intent to burn his draft card as a demonstration of his refusal to cooperate with "an illegal, undemocratic, unconstitutional, inhumane system which builds armies for the putting down of national liberation movements throughout the world—not only in Vietnam—as well as within its own boundaries to depersonalize human beings to machines of destruction and killing." He added that he hoped others would be moved to join his act of defiance.[2]

Schmidt, a tall, thin, passionate freshman from the Chicago suburb of Naperville, would become a central figure in the Illinois student movement. He had been inspired by the southern civil rights movement, crediting that effort with his political awakening on the Illinois campus: "I was very much impressed with the courage and the moral character of the civil rights workers in the South."[3] Roger Simon, a *DI* staff writer at the time, interviewed Schmidt and fellow DRU member Dennis Weeks:

> You can usually see Steve, a cowboy hat on his head and a rawhide key chain around his neck, in the Commons of the Illini Union or joking with his friends at the Red Herring. But when Steve talks about the draft he grows serious. "I am against the draft—period. In all cases. The war in Vietnam precipitated the whole thing. It's just not the war though. It's the whole military-industrial complex." Schmidt recognizes

when he's using clichés and he'll put what he feels in simple terms for you. "The draft is the focal point of the whole war," he'll tell you. "Our fight isn't in Vietnam. It's here."[4]

David Ransel remembered Schmidt well. "He came from a very good family. . . . There were certain people," such as Steve, "who became very important in the protest movement . . . you can only attribute it to his very strong values, and he wouldn't give them up no matter what the cost. We thought of Steve as almost a Christ-like person."[5]

Weeks, a graduate student at the university, was a different case, in that his fight had been going on for some time. In 1963 he had mailed his draft card back to his Selective Service board, with a note saying he didn't want it. They sent it back with directions to keep it with him at all times. He tore it into pieces and mailed it back to them again. Simon told what happened next:

> The draft board classified him I-A and told him to report in October 1963 for induction. "I was on a peace march in Georgia at the time. . . . I wrote them and told them that instead of me going up to join the Army, they should come down and join the peace march." The FBI arrested Weeks in 1964 in Albany, Georgia. He pleaded guilty in June of that year and went to Chilicothe to begin his two year sentence. . . .
>
> Weeks' boyish face and offhand manner will fool you. You think that prison was kind of fun. But then you realize what two years out of your life can mean. But Weeks isn't going to be up there with Schmidt burning his draft card Monday as he had planned. Life holds certain priorities. Some things come before others. Weeks is engaged to be married. "It would be just too much," he said, "to take on marriage and the draft board, too."[6]

These young men were willing to endure great personal sacrifice in order to make a statement against the war, as the sentence for destruction of one's draft card could be as long as five years in a federal prison. Weeks had already been imprisoned for eighteen months. Eventually, Schmidt would also spend nine months in a federal facility for his actions.

As announced, October 16, 1967, turned out to be a day of draft-resistance actions across the country. Twenty-five cities saw demonstrations, and in ten of those, more than nine hundred young men surrendered or destroyed their draft cards. In Boston alone, 340 cards were turned over to Catholic, Jewish, and Protestant clergymen. In August 1965 the U.S. Congress had passed a law making it a crime to "knowingly" destroy a draft card. Two years later, on the University of Illinois campus, Steve Schmidt and Rick Soderstrom stood in a drizzling rain on the south patio of the Union and, despite the dampness (Schmidt remembers, "Rick had a butane lighter, as the weather was not very cooperative"), with some difficulty managed to light and burn their draft cards, marking the beginning of lengthy legal struggles with the government for both of them. Soderstrom read a letter to his draft board: "I will fight to destroy your system just as you are trying (unsuccessfully) to destroy the Vietnamese people."[7] Raised in the small northern Illinois town of Geneva—"no blacks, a few Catholics"—by loving, conservative parents, Soderstrom had been introduced to radical politics by the civil rights movement and was a veteran of SNCC-sponsored southern registration drives. The day after he and Schmidt destroyed their cards, a picture of the action would appear in the *Chicago Tribune*, and Soderstrom would be immediately reclassified by his local board and soon drafted. In response, he would hide out for a time, sleeping on Vincent Wu's sofa, in order to finish his university studies, then leave the country for Canada. Later, Rick's mother would answer the expected FBI knock at her door and respond to their queries with, "I am a Christian woman, and I will not lie to you. I know where my son is, but I will not tell you." His father joined her at the door, asking, "What's going on?" She replied, "It's the FBI, they want to know where Rick is," to which he shrugged and said, "Oh, he's in Canada, he says it's all right to tell you now."[8] Soderstrom would spend his entire adult life as an expat in Canada.

On the patio of the Union, Schmidt, too, read a letter he had sent his draft board in Wheaton, Illinois, calling the Vietnam War "a symptom of a terrible disease that perpetrates the mass repression of people all over the world.... The draft creates slave armies for the furtherance of the economic aims of an elite few."[9] Following this, the two resisters led a march of sixty to the Selective Service office in Champaign. Upon arriving at the office, the group formed a picket line outside, while a smaller number went into the office for a sit-in and to block traffic in an attempt to shut down the system, at least for the day.

Two Champaign police officers, alerted to the march, were waiting inside the office, and after some discussion with the protesters they arrested ten individuals, including Schmidt and Soderstrom. About a dozen faculty were among the supporters who waited outside, including blind English professor Gary Adelman, accompanied by his wife in the picket line, who said, "We want to commend those who have come to make this strong decision of conscience.... an act of conscience takes more courage than the willingness to kill." Champaign Mayor Virgil Wikoff also present, differed, responding, "As citizens they have the right to dissent but they also have the responsibility to serve their country." And if they didn't like the nation's policies, Wikoff had a suggestion: "They should get the hell out and find another country."[10] Dan'l McCollum, then an officer in the Army Reserves and years later elected mayor of Champaign himself, was among the protesters, and he overheard Wikoff's comments. Today he says, "I do not criticize Virgil for his sentiment—after all, had not the media bought the government line and helped to sell the public on what was being done in our name in Southeast Asia?"[11]

That evening on the campus, Vic Berkey introduced Staughton Lynd to an audience of more than seven hundred students and faculty, but he first asked that a collection be taken up for those jailed earlier in the day. Soon funds were collected to bail out all of the students, with Security Officer Tom Morgan, affecting a sort of gallantry, personally bailing out the two female students arrested.[12] The motivation of the eight men in the day's action is not difficult to comprehend; besides the issues of morality, their lives might well have been at risk in Vietnam. The motivation of the two women in this event, graduate student Nancy Goodwin and sophomore Maryon Gray, is more thought provoking. Again putting aside the questions of morality, might they have had a friend, a lover, or a brother threatened by the draft? The record tells us nothing on this count, and we are left to speculate. Steve Schmidt recalls, "Though they didn't get the press attention, as they didn't have draft cards to burn, they had the need to speak truth to power."[13] The *News-Gazette* reported that "deputy sheriffs and jailers were pleased when [the protesters] were gone, for they said some of the defendants were 'smelling up our clean jail.' Baths did not appear to be part of the protesters' regular daily routine." The conservative paper also noted, "Because of their hair, it was difficult to determine the sex of some of them."[14] When Lynd finally spoke, he commended the eight men and two women arrested, and he spoke about the day's events across the country. He mentioned that though he was no longer of draft age and in fact had already served time as a conscientious objector, he too had returned his draft card to his Selective Service board that day.

A *DI* editorial commented on the campus-wide conversations engendered by the day's events, noting the end of the free-speech-era and the now-dominant antiwar focus, and highlighted Dean Millet's comments that the draft-card-burning event was "outside the jurisdiction" of the university's regulations, clarifying for all that the administration had no intention of becoming involved in disciplining such activities:

> The draft card burnings south of the Illini Union on Monday have provoked widespread discussion about all issues of draft resistance. At places all over campus, people have been talking about the burnings, the sit-in, the arrests and what should or should not be done to the students involved.
>
> The University has made only one official statement, that by Dean of Students Stanton Millet, and it deserves special notice. In his statement Dean Millet said the draft card burnings and the sit-in appear to be outside the jurisdiction of the University. Millet went on to say that those involved would likely be subject to normal prosecution by the state, but that the University would only take action when the

protests on the campus threaten the physical safety of others or the destruction of property or when they interfere with the rights of other members of the academic community.[15]

William K. Williams wrote a report on the sit-in to Henry, Peltason, and Millet. In it he emphasized that the demonstration organizers had been in communication with his office, the campus police, and Champaign police prior to the demonstration. "This is the kind of thing we have encouraged the activists groups to do."[16] Williams, attempting to balance what would likely be negative press reports on the incident, went to some length to ensure that the recipients of his report received a balanced view:

> Because some of you will be responding to the public opinions on these activities, I think it is noteworthy that this, on the part of our students, was a protest action which was planned and executed with some care. Most of those involved seemed to have a sense of the seriousness of the circumstances, and proceeded out of personal convictions. They cannot be arbitrarily dismissed as either irresponsible or simply draft dodgers.[17]

The new administration of Jack Peltason would no longer be dealing with DuBois Club issues, or issues of academic freedom, or with what individual from what organization might speak on campus, what they might say or what law might be violated. For Peltason, the growing student protest against the Vietnam War would overshadow all else throughout his tenure.

CHAPTER 22

Then There Was Dow

The Dow Chemical Corporation was well known to sixties college students for two things: manufacturing napalm used in the Vietnam War and actively recruiting soon-to-be graduates on the nation's campuses. The national SDS organization had advocated for some time against Dow recruitment on college campuses, to little effect. However, localized demonstrations against the company had drawn student and faculty attention at many colleges. As of October 1967, no violence had resulted. That peace was to end in Madison, Wisconsin, on October 18. Dow recruiters were at the University of Wisconsin for a full day of interviews of potential employees. Just as activities at the Illinois Chicago Circle campus triggered a surge in political activity at Urbana in spring of that year, actions in the fall of '67 at Madison were to trigger another escalation of political activity on the Urbana campus.

On the morning of the scheduled Madison interviews, approximately two hundred University of Wisconsin students entered the old Commerce Building on the campus and engaged in a sit-in outside the office where the Dow recruiters were to conduct their interviews. A crowd of about a thousand gathered outside, some simply spectators, but most picketing in support of the sit-in. Inside, the students successfully blocked passage of the scheduled interviews and essentially took control of the building. "The students were as solid as a rock. They locked arms and wouldn't let anyone in for the interviews." Negotiators from the protesters' ranks were sent to the office of Dean of Students Josef Kaufmann, with an offer to end the sit-in if the interviews were stopped. Kaufmann bluntly refused, saying "There is nothing to negotiate about."[1]

Recently named chancellor, William Sewell headed the UW administration; until the sit-in, he was known as a liberal, antiwar, former sociology professor. However, and unfortunately for all concerned, Sewell had very little administrative experience, and that day he made a fateful decision to hand off responsibility for dealing with the protest to the Madison city police, asking them to intervene and remove the protesters from the building.[2] Left in charge of the situation, police, wearing helmets with face shields and carrying hefty riot sticks, broke windows and entered the building; violence erupted almost immediately. It was unclear who initiated the disturbance, but once started, it quickly escalated out of control, with police using tear gas and sticks to break up the protest, dragging students down the stairs of the Commerce Building and inciting further violent reactions from previously neutral bystanders. More than seventy people were injured, including ten police, with most treated for lacerations and bruises at the nearby university hospital. At day's end, Chancellor Sewell announced that the Dow interviews would be suspended until further notice. The students claimed a bloody victory for the day, and from Sewell's and the administration's point of view, the day was a public-relations disaster. In Urbana, Henry, Peltason and Millet watched reports of the day's events closely and learned from them.

On Thursday evening, one day after the Madison sit-in, the Illinois SDS group met and voted to hold a sit-in against Dow recruiters scheduled to visit their campus the following week, on October 25. Once again, issues of free speech threatened to split moderates and radicals in the group, as some argued a sit-in would interfere with Dow's fundamental rights. Fred Landis answered that claim vehemently: "This is not a free speech issue. I'm sure no one would object to Dow coming here and making a speech. What we object to is their doing business [on campus]." Gutowsky, somewhat courageously, if hopelessly, attended the SDS meeting in an attempt to dissuade the demonstration. "What you are saying is 'my view is right, yours is wrong, therefore I have free speech and you have to step over me.'" Sit-in supporters loudly responded that their right to stop Dow's atrocities in Vietnam trumped Dow Corporation's right of free speech. Gutowsky persevered with his arguments for the duration of the meeting but converted no one to his side.[3]

As the week progressed, plans expanded to include a teach-in and picket lines outside the building in support of the student demonstrators inside. Gutowsky, indefatigable, made offers to the planners that no police would interfere in their demonstration if the students agreed to stay out of the building—or, if inside, to not interfere with his department's business. His proposals were ignored. When asked if this meant police would be called in, he responded curtly, "Hell, how should I know?"[4]

During the week, a sizable contingent of Illinois students returned from the previous weekend's March on the Pentagon, in Washington, D.C. Organized by a new umbrella group, the National Mobilization Committee to End the War in Vietnam, the march attracted a throng of more than one hundred thousand—young and old, liberals, moderates, radicals, straights and hippies, all mostly white. Some in the group attempted to "levitate" the Pentagon building by chanting, others tried exorcism; some charged the soldiers guarding the building entrances, others settled for inserting flowers into soldiers' gun barrels. By the end of the weekend, police arrested more than seven hundred demonstrators; the Pentagon was neither levitated nor exorcised, and the war went on. Frustrations mounted. Keven Roth, one of the Illini marchers, said of the rising emotion: "We can't just sit around and demonstrate and hold rallies anymore. You've got to make people listen to you." Joanne Chester, who also marched, observed, "It was a big picnic, [though] scaling the walls of the Pentagon was absurd. I didn't want to go near the Pentagon and have my head bashed," but, she added, "I had to go. If I didn't I wouldn't have been able to live with myself."[5] Secretary of State Dean Rusk ridiculed the Pentagon marchers. "Our soldiers, sailors, marines and airmen in Vietnam are the ones speaking for the American people."[6] Roth, Chester, and the Dow protest planners would disagree.

The night before the Dow visit, a meeting was held at Channing Murray to finalize plans for the next day's confrontation, which would take place only a few short blocks from the meeting. Dan'l McCollum recalls:

The ultras were determined to shut down the whole building and angrily accused the moderates of being gutless. I recall [English professor] Gary Adelman standing up and defusing the situation with a short speech . . . something like: We are all here because we oppose this awful war. Each of us has his or her own way of wanting to express that opposition. Those of us who want to shut down the East Chem building can do that; those of us who just want to carry our placards outside and parade and bear witness can do that as well. There must be room for all of us.[7]

As the day of the Dow face-off arrived, the *DI* urged restraint on all sides. "Today representatives of Dow Chemical Co. will be on campus to interview students for positions with their organization, and sometime before noon other students will sit-in hoping to disrupt these interviews. It will be a tragedy if any violence occurs due to the predicted attempt at stopping the interviews."[8] Images of the Madison violence had been shown on national television and in the local papers and were vivid in students' and administrators' memories. The Pentagon demonstration over the weekend had only heightened the tension. On the morning of the protest, several hundred gathered at the now familiar location, the south patio of the Illini Union, and listened to speakers. The last to speak would be Air Force veteran Durrett. He would leave the campus the following semester for the more liberal atmosphere of Amherst College in Massachusetts, so the sit-in and its aftermath would represent the end of his political involvement at Illinois. Several of the younger students who were in the group that day remember him well:

> Smart, articulate, confident, and humble ... a persuasive speaker, and since he'd already been in the service his anti-war stance was selfless; he would never have to face the draft. He had the ability to distill complex issues into language that was easy to understand.... [He was] quiet, sincere and willing to talk to you.
>
> He clearly felt honestly about the horrors of American imperialism and was personally outraged by its history. He worked with the churches as well as black groups. Phil's sincerity was clear ... a mix of vulnerability, openness, strength, confidence and righteous indignation.[9]

That morning Durrett's wife Sandy had asked him not to participate in the sit-in, fearing violence. Fortunately for many of his anxious fellow protesters, he turned her request down, and his calm, confident demeanor would reassure many in the crowd. Durrett stood atop the union patio, reminded the crowd why they were there, urged them to remain nonviolent, then announced it was time to move out, and the group began what felt like a very long march of a block and a half to the eastern edge of the campus, to Gutowsky's East Chemistry Building. Somewhere between one hundred fifty and two hundred people entered the building, while outside another hundred set up a picket line in support, student president Patsy Parker among them. Later, despite snow flurries, Thomas Krueger, professor of history, would lead a teach-in with the group outside, with prowar and antiwar speakers.

Those inside took the stairs to the second floor and sat down in a long, crowded hallway leading to a room at the end, where the Dow recruiter had already settled in. Berkey, Fein, and Durrett positioned themselves at the head of the hallway, interacting with the recruiter and Gutowsky. The protesters would stay for five hours, allowing no Dow interviews to take place. Protesters linked arms and refused passage to any interviewee who showed up. One whose path was blocked said, "You are denying me my rights by not letting me in. You are breaking the law by being here," to which Berkey replied, "You are breaking a higher moral law."[10] Richard Bogartz, associate professor of psychology, went into the building to observe the sit-in, and later wrote to Peltason, describing what he saw.

> While I observed the sit-in, almost all the students were sitting on the floor. Many were reading.... Several times as I watched, the students were addressed by other students and by Dr. Gutowski [sic]. One announcement was that the students had offered to buy lunch for [Dow recruiter] Dr. VanDyke. A good-natured cheer was the result.... I observed Dr. Gutowski walking back and forth a number of times

through the hallway occupied by the sitters and at no time was his movement interfered with. Many people, including at least one who was carrying laboratory equipment, walked back and forth and were not obstructed, much less intimidated.[11]

Thoughts of the Madison violence were not far from anyone's minds throughout the day. John Saltiel, one of the sit-in leaders, repeatedly reminded the demonstrators that the sit-in was intended to be peaceful. "This is a nonviolent demonstration. Anyone who is seeking violence should not take part. Relax, be confident, you're committed to a high moral purpose." Durrett passed word that William K. Williams had told him that no arrests would occur. In fact, there was no police presence whatsoever, all day. The highest university authority present at any time during the day was Gutowsky, who, after five hours, at 3:15 P.M., finally announced to the demonstrators that, "in order to avoid possible bodily injury and destruction of property," the day's interviews would be canceled.[12]

The Illinois administration had viewed the decisions made by administrators at Madison and determined to follow a different path on their campus. According to the *Champaign-Urbana Courier*, unnamed "university sources" reported that Peltason, with Henry's approval, had made the decision the day before that there would be no intervention. "Calling in police had never been seriously considered, especially in light of last week's incident at the University of Wisconsin. . . . The chancellor felt . . . it would be foolish to go in and try to carry the demonstrators out . . . but with the disciplinary action to come it will be clear the university is not just looking the other way."[13] In a written statement the following month, Peltason confirmed that report: "Essentially, our choice was between using police to break through the crowd, or putting the burden on the mob for having brought the interviews to a halt. . . . After careful and agonizing deliberation, we chose the latter course."[14] The Illinois chancellor had determined that a compromise solution, with no immediate police action but disciplinary action to follow, would trump a Madison-style violent confrontation. An Illinois faculty member summed it up in a letter to a Wisconsin peer: "The explosion at your campus was probably responsible for the lack of one at Illinois."[15]

The day after the sit-in, the student senate passed a resolution commending the administration for its "reason, patience and self-restraint." Peltason announced that "appropriate disciplinary action, including preparation for the filing of formal charges, has been initiated against all those persons who have participated in this interference with the educational processes of the University."[16] By week's end the university had announced it would bring such charges against only eleven students, to which the activists responded by planning "a complicity statement" to demonstrate their shared responsibility for the demonstration. The *DI* complimented the administration's restraint:

The University could have used the legal means at its disposal to protect the rights of Dow Chemical and the students wishing to interview for a job and used force to evict the demonstrators. But with 200 students crammed into a passageway, this could have turned the demonstration into a violent melee, resulting in personal injury to both demonstrators and policemen. Instead the University made what we think was the wise choice to not exercise the least bit of control over the demonstration and allow the non-violent expression against Dow to continue.[17]

The protesters were in a less conciliatory mood, however, and came together later in the week to finalize the complicity statement, to ensure that everyone who participated in the affair would receive equal punishment, and that no one would be singled out. After much debate, a final statement was hammered out, and by the following Monday more than 350 signatures had been gathered, far exceeding the number of people who had actually participated in the sit-in. On Monday morning, thirty students showed up at Morgan's office to attest in person to their complicity. Morgan's reaction was to offer the students detailed written instructions on how to submit such claims of complicity:

> It has been indicated that a number of persons wish to establish that they participated in the "Dow Chemical Company Sit-in" Oct. 25, in the hallways and in room 216 of the East Chemistry Building, University of Illinois. If you are one of these individuals, it is recommended that you write a full, detailed individual statement in which you describe the extent of your participation in the blocking of the hallways adjacent to room 216 of the East Chemistry Building during the day of Oct. 25. The statement should also reflect the times of your involvement and your specific location in the building in relation to the doorway of room 216 East Chemistry Building. Finally, the statement should reflect that it is voluntary, unsolicited, and that it is true and correct. It should be signed by you with your full name, the date of the statement, and your local address.[18]

Somewhat taken aback by the detailed instructions, one student responded, "He wants a confession!" Vic Berkey characterized it as "a clear form of entrapment.... Nothing was required of those already charged." Nonetheless, the students dutifully wrote out their required statements; but Morgan, after a quick review, judged them imperfect, commenting, "I am disappointed that they are unable to follow directions on a simple little statement." When Vern Fein arrived an hour later, leading a second group of students claiming complicity, Morgan again passed out his instructions, observing that the previous group "hadn't followed directions very well," and implied that statements from Fein's group might be equally unsatisfactory. Fein, a rhetoric instructor, perhaps affronted, declared that if Morgan found the group's statements unacceptable, that they might have to take them directly to Peltason. "I am really disgusted in the way the University is disgracing civil disobedience. It is making a mockery of individual responsibility."[19] It was proving to be more difficult than expected for the students to receive the guilty sentences and associated punishment to which they felt entitled.

The president of the Dow Chemical Corporation sent a personal follow-up letter to Gutowsky, complimenting his management of the affair. "It's my understanding that you've had a rather hectic week. I'm told that a potentially damaging situation ... has been handled in the best manner possible, due largely to the extraordinary amount of time and effort you devoted to the problem." Understating the situation, he continued: "We were keenly aware of the gravity of the situation. We're aware too, that there are no easy or ready-made solutions.... The fact that you were able to handle the matter in such an efficient manner is a real tribute to your imagination and good judgment.... [We] look forward to many years of continued cordial relationship."[20]

Others were less complimentary. Persistent rumors that Gutowsky had arranged for the Dow interviews to be held "in secret," avoiding the demonstrators, were raised in the *DI*. Supposedly, the interviews had taken place on the day before or the day after the sit-in, or perhaps in another campus building, or even in the hotel room of the recruiter. Peltason denied the stories. English professor Daniel Curley suggested that if such had occurred, the university was guilty of "the vilest kind of entrapment of the students and owes them an apology rather than punishment." Demonstrating his familiarity with medieval English history, Curley analogized, "It now seems that Professor Gutowsky played the part of Richard II in placing himself at the head of Watt Tyler's rebels, promising them redress and sending them home and then arresting and executing them at his leisure."[21] In fact it was never ascertained that any such secret interviews took place, leaving Gutowsky cleared of Curley's charge of villainy.

Chancellor Peltason appeared at the Red Herring the following week, on the day of the fiftieth anniversary of the Russian Revolution, as was noted in his introduction, prompting some nervous laughter. The chancellor gave a short address, then for more than an hour he patiently took questions from the audience. The discussion was dominated by the issue of complicity and how students and faculty might be appropriately included in the offense. Peltason stated that he had instructed Morgan to forward all the complicity statements, regardless of their completeness, to the appropriate committee for possible disciplinary action. "I'm not trying to deprive anyone of their right to go before a disciplinary committee."[22] This seemed to appease the crowd, but the chancellor said he would decline to accept the 360 names published in a full-page statement of complicity in the *DI*. The audience seemed reasonably satisfied with this compromise. Professor John Werry, who earlier had sternly insisted to Peltason that he be included among the sit-in offenders, had the final word. "I think we owe a vote of thanks to Chancellor Peltason for having the courage to come here." The audience broke into a round of applause.

One week earlier, Carl Oglesby, national secretary for SDS, had visited the Illinois campus, speaking first at noon at an SDS gathering in the south lounge of the Union. Later in the evening, on the same Red Herring stage from which the chancellor would speak, he urged his audience to refute whatever compromises the liberal Peltason might offer. "You have to see the reality of America. Our society shapes you, molds you, and puts you into a slot. A slot that you have absolutely no control over. It has already been shaped by the ruling classes."[23] Oglesby distinguished between the radical, who "realizes the struggle has to be collective, social and for the freedom of all man," and the liberal, whom he disdained as those who "fight other people's battles. They attempt to raise everyone to their own position and are motivated by conscience and guilt." The true radical understood, Oglesby said, that "the 'new left' represents a struggle based not on guilt but on personal freedom." He praised the Black Power movement, as having "the most profound effect on the white radical movement. It forced Americans to see the total racism of themselves and their society" and required "white radicals to look at themselves and come to grips with the 'liberal conscience' versus the 'radical consciousness.'"[24] He encouraged the students to recognize their privileged and influential position in the social structure. "Student power contains within it not only the possibility of liberating students but of liberating all society. . . . [S]tudents could not free their universities without freeing all of society. . . . [F]ight for structural reform, for anything that weakens the existing system. . . . Anything you can do to destroy this system is a benefit."[25] Bringing to life all the fears represented by the Broyles Commission and the Clabaugh Act, Oglesby called for a revolution, one that would bring down the institutions of American government and society. For those in his audience who would return for Peltason's talk the following week, the distinction between the two men's ideas was as clear as could be.

The *Daily Illini* editors spoke to the contrast between Oglesby and Peltason, between the radical and liberal point of view:

> The mood of campus protesters has become increasingly more militant. . . . The rationale used by the protesters is that a university should have no right to participate in the military efforts of the country. . . . Protesters have become so frustrated by United States involvement in that war that they have decided the only way to help things is through strong, direct action. . . . A higher moral law is now used as a guideline for action, and when that moral law conflicts with a national law, the moral law prevails.

The editors presented their judgment:

> Those opposed to the sit-ins . . . say that protests should be used for protest, not to stop normal proceedings. . . . [T]hey do not believe the demonstrators have the

right to interfere with the freedom of others. It is this interference with the rights of others which is stigmatizing the protest movement across the country.... Dissent and protest are rights of everyone in society; preventing persons from engaging in their own affairs is not.[26]

Carl Oglesby would not have hesitated to label the newspaper's editors as liberals with a limited understanding of the dynamics of the establishment, and he would exhort students to reject the paper's advice and to develop a more radical perspective. But the editorial spoke to a central issue of that school year and the next, the growing tension among students who had responded positively to earlier issues of freedom of speech and academic freedom, but for whom Oglesby's call for radical consciousness and revolution would simply be a bridge too far.

CHAPTER 23

The Aftermath

The weeks following the Dow action saw the beginnings of a months-long bureaucratic, legalistic back-and-forth between the protesters, who, having successfully ensured their complicity, now worked just as hard to minimize their punishment, and the university, which, while navigating among concerned parents, a divided public, and the legislature, attempted to establish an approximation of "due process" for the offenders. Law school faculty leaped to the defense of the students, while university disciplinary mechanisms, traditionally geared toward dealing with violations of cheating on tests, theft in dorm rooms, or, at worst, panty raids, were stretched to find appropriate responses to the sit-in. Letters supporting both sides poured into Henry's and Peltason's mailboxes throughout the process.

Five graduate students—Robert Solomon, John Saltiel, Vern Fein, Howard Rothman, and Vic Berkey—were the first of the Dow protesters called to face a disciplinary hearing on November 10, in front of a graduate discipline committee. They were represented by law professor Herb Semmel, two other law faculty, and one law grad student. Semmel immediately moved that the meeting be made public, a change from all previous disciplinary hearings, citing the due process clause of the Fourteenth Amendment. When, after some debate, that idea was rejected, he presented a motion questioning the jurisdiction of the committee, also rejected, and then presented a third, claiming that the university had not been sufficiently explicit about which rules or statutes the students had violated. After lengthy debate, the chairman of the committee (a faculty member, not a lawyer) made the decision to recess the hearing until the committee had sufficient time to study Semmel's procedural moves.

The following week, on November 15, eight undergraduates were called in, one by one, to face a separate undergraduate disciplinary committee. The eight were Phil Durrett, Ray Couture, Brion Kerlin, Mike Irwin, Fred Landis, Phil Hardy, Mike Hanagan, Steve Schmidt, and Mark Whitney. Semmel responded to this hearing by submitting a petition to the faculty senate and separately to Dean of Students Millet, challenging the veracity of the evidence submitted to the committee. The senate and Millet each denied his petitions. Once the hearings began, Durrett reported, "We were told that we couldn't plead guilty or not-guilty as we wouldn't have been charged unless we were guilty."[1] Another defendant read aloud an unidentified passage from the Declaration of Independence, to which a committee member responded, "It sounded like a typical Marxist document."[2]

Despite all Semmel's creative maneuvering, the graduate committee declared later that week that all the graduate students would receive the relatively light sentence of conduct probation, a judgment with little impact other than a notation on the student's record, albeit with the threat of expulsion if the offense were repeated. The same day, however, apparently unaware of the graduate committee's already-announced decision, the undergraduate committee submitted their decision—that seven of the eight students they had heard would be expelled, creating an obvious and perplexing inconsistency in sentencing. The eighth undergraduate, Kerlin, when asked why he escaped expulsion, suggested he had cooperated with the committee: "I didn't take Semmel up there and raise hell."[3] A protest gathering on the quad the next day drew three hundred. Student Senate president Parker chaired the rally and threatened to resign her position, but only after withdrawing all students from their faculty-student committee assignments. An engineering professor, Walter Rose, announced his resignation in protest over the inconsistency of the verdicts as well as the lack of due process. Vic Berkey decried the administration as "the cutting edge of the state. The University didn't want to bring this to the civil courts because the civil courts would have given us due process," and warned ominously, "The next thing the University does after expelling you is to notify your draft board."[4] Following the angry speeches, many in the crowd joined the guilty undergraduates in a march to the Office of Student Discipline to file appeals.

The next two weeks saw a flurry of activity. First, the undergraduate disciplinary committee announced that charges would be heard next against an additional forty-seven students. Abner Mikva, the head of a prominent Chicago law firm, a former state assembly member, and personal friend of President Henry, announced in the Chicago newspapers his intention to file an injunction in federal court against the university, barring any further disciplinary action. With Mikva's threat hanging in the air, Chancellor Peltason recommended to the faculty senate that further disciplinary hearings be delayed until appeals for the original seven were heard, and revealed that he had been working with the student president, Parker, and other student-government representatives to create a student-faculty committee that would begin a comprehensive and rigorous review of all student judicial processes at the university. On December 9, Professor John Werry disclosed to the *DI* that he had received word from Peltason, in confidence, that Werry would receive nothing more than a written reprimand placed in his file. Numerous faculty communicated to Peltason and Millet their feelings regarding the basic unfairness and inconsistency of the sentencing and/or the lack of due process in the proceedings. A typical letter, this one signed by twenty of the twenty-four teaching faculty of the Political Science Department, advised reconsideration: "We urge a full and searching review of the equity of the punishment so that a decision can be reached that better serves the interests of the students and of the entire university."[5]

Three days later, with little explanation, the seven expelled undergraduates were notified by a higher faculty committee that they had been reinstated and that they, too, would receive conduct probation, just as the graduate students had. Within a week, the hearings of the first ten of the additional forty-seven students were conducted, "in a very cut and dried manner," according to one student, as most of the group refused to answer any of the committee's questions on the grounds that they were being denied due process. The ten were identified in the *DI* as Martha Blomme, freshman in agriculture; Lester Wall, senior in commerce; Richard Blackwell, senior in liberal arts; Joanne Chester, freshman in liberal arts; Steve Cochran, sophomore in fine arts; Robert Baillee, sophomore in liberal arts; William Bernstein, senior in liberal arts; Alice Maynard, sophomore in liberal arts; Michael Metz (the author), junior in liberal arts; and Gloria Landsman, senior in fine arts. All were given conduct probation and advised that with good behavior the probation could be lifted by the end of the school year. A week later, eighteen more undergraduate conduct probations were handed out. By the end of Semmel and Mikva's legal machinations and all the university's committee hearings, a total of forty-one students had been disciplined, rather moderately, for the Dow affair. However, with decisions announced and letters mailed to students at their campus addresses as well as to parents at the students' home addresses only days prior to winter break, it's likely that some tension marred the students' holidays.

Sophomore Keven Roth received a typical letter:[6]

Dear Miss Roth,

On December 15, 1967, Subcommittee A on Undergraduate Student Discipline placed you on conduct probation to Dean Roland Homes, 294 Lincoln Hall, for your participation in the mass demonstration of October 25, 1967, in the East Chemistry

Building on the Champaign-Urbana campus without approval of University officials which did disturb and interrupt the normal activities of the University and students, faculty, and staff in and about said building, and found that you were a knowing participant in the demonstration and should be held accountable for your participation. You were also denied a motor vehicle permit. . . . You will remain on this status until your petition for removal therefrom is approved by this Subcommittee.

> Very Truly yours,
> Arno Hill,
> Chairman,
> Subcommittee A on Undergraduate Student Discipline

cc: Parent, Dean of Student Personnel, Recorder, Dean of LAS, Dean Holmes, DMV Division

As in the spring, letters from the public flowed in to the administration; the samples below, addressed to President Henry, are found among his papers in the university archives.[7] From Jack Hall, member of the Champaign Chamber of Commerce: "I hope that the ringleaders are dismissed from the university and the action sticks—as it is in my mind, intolerable to permit the students to tell the University officials and the trustees how they should run the University." From "A worried and disappointed member of Class of 57": "It is time for you to take a stand. . . . We do not want this Hippie crowd to take over as they have done in California. . . . The fact that faculty members are now joining in and urging students to burn their draft cards is just too much. . . . Do something about it before it is too late." From State Senator Robert Mitchler, a regular champion of the school's budget in Springfield: "I am very disturbed, as many other citizens are disturbed, over the attitudes of students on campuses throughout the United States, including the University of Illinois. . . . I am told the University of Illinois has rescinded the authorization for recruiters from Dow Chemical Company to come on campus. Is this true?"

But not all were opposed to the demonstrators. An alumnus, a New York dentist, wrote, "The ousting of the seven students leaves a black mark upon the name of the University of Illinois. These students should be the pride of the university." A friendly but concerned letter—signed, "Kindest personal regards"—from the Chicago lawyer Abner Mikva: "I was very shocked to read that some eight [sic] students had been expelled. . . . Experience tells us that many of the 'campus radicals' turn out to be responsible, concerned citizens. . . . It is refreshing to see students who are concerned about the problems of the day. . . . It is better than swallowing goldfish." A Unitarian pastor from Chicago had this to say: "It would be a mistake to take disciplinary action against those students who recently took part in protesting nonviolently, the presence of Dow Chemical.... To expel students would tend to create... a new era of self-imposed McCarthyism.... [T]hat I shudder to imagine sir." The pastor ended with a line from Illinois poet Vachel Lindsay: "Let not young souls be smothered out before they do quaint deeds and fully flaunt their pride."

Found in President Henry's archived private papers of the period is this ditty, likely sent by some sympathetic person, noting the stress of Henry's position:

> It's not my job to run the train, the whistle I can't blow,
> It's not for me to say how far the train is allowed to go,
> I'm not allowed to blow the steam, nor even clang the bell,
> But let the damn thing jump the tracks and see who catches hell.

As the letters were filling administrators' mailboxes and as the legalistic, disciplinary machinations were progressing for the Dow protesters, the campus draft resisters were not standing still; in fact, they were ramping up their activities. On December 1, DRU member Ray Couture, one of the original seven undergrads charged in the Dow sit-in, announced a twenty-four-hour "Fast for Peace" on the quad. Fifteen students planned to pitch tents and spend the period abstaining from all food as a protest against the war. Couture claimed he had received "tacit approval" from the university for the event.[8] During the night of their campout the campers were attacked by individuals who were soon apprehended by campus police. If that wasn't discouraging enough for the protesters, a light drizzle soon turned into a driving snow, and the campers soon abandoned their site, moving to the Channing Murray building for the remainder of the night. They refused to press charges against their attackers, not wanting to cooperate with police.

The next week Couture, an Air Force veteran, joined four other resisters—Mark Whitney, Mike Irwin, Robert Bailee, and Ron Lucas—in burning their draft cards at a three-hundred-person rally on the south patio of the Union. Steve Schmidt, having already burned his card, burned a delinquency notice from his board. Following speeches, a segment of the crowd, Patsy Parker among them, marched to the Champaign Selective Service office, where several of the resisters attempted to present the ashes of their draft cards. Otis Stanley, working the desk at the office, at first refused to accept the burned cards, but then changed his mind, deciding he would send them on to state headquarters, and characterized the demonstrators as "a nuisance."[9] Stanley told reporters that the standard procedure was to reclassify such individuals as 1-A. They would then be ordered to appear for induction, with noncompliance likely resulting in a two-year sentence in federal prison. A small band of counterprotesters from a group that called themselves United Students for America (USA) followed the resisters to the draft board and picketed across the street. Champaign police kept the groups apart, limiting the interactions to shouting and chanting.

On December 21, at a board of trustees meeting on the second floor of the Illini Union, trustee Ray Page was delivering a speech suggesting draft-card burners be expelled from the university. Fifteen feet from the trustees' conference table, Ray Pollack, a DRU member recently withdrawn from the university, stood and held up his draft card as Steve Schmidt, next to him, set it aflame. The trustees, focused on Page, at first were unaware of the action until the group accompanying Pollack began cheering. Finally grasping what was happening, trustee Earl Hughes immediately called for disciplinary action against the entire group and called the draft-card burning "an act of harassment . . . an attempt to discredit Page's proposal."[10] Page agreed, adding, "It is an honor and a privilege to attend the University of Illinois, but any privilege is accompanied by responsibility to abide by the rules," arguing his proposal would prevent such actions, with a threat of expulsion. However, since Pollack was no longer a student, expulsion would not likely be a deterrent in this case. Pollack, seeing the world quite differently from the trustees, told reporters he had dropped out of school because "he found it irrelevant to life," adding, "Burning the draft card was an act of moral commitment."

And so the tumultuous year of 1967 came to an end on the campus. Draft resisters like Pollack and Schmidt mentally began preparing themselves for prison, while the Dow protesters who'd been disciplined headed home to explain the newly arrived probation letters to worried parents. It had been a year of unprecedented student activism on the Illinois campus, but the next year, 1968, would make the previous one seem calm in comparison.

CHAPTER 24

1968: The Wildest Year

Some years in history are particularly momentous: 1789, 1848, and 1914 come to mind, as does 1968. A military reversal in Vietnam, assassinations, nationwide riots, the Democratic convention in Chicago, an eventful presidential campaign, and worldwide student rebellions all vied for the year's headlines. Cascading events proved larger than any one individual, any one event, or any one group; hence, it is not surprising that on the Illinois campus, the tumult of events seemed to overwhelm the student movement, and memories of the previous semester's successful Dow sit-in quickly receded. To student activists, as well as to the citizenry at large, it felt that every new week might bring another shattering event. Nineteen sixty-eight would become a pivotal year for Illinois student activists, as the element of violence that had dominated the era—military violence, police violence, racial violence—finally caught up with them and, in time, became a major factor in the movement's development. The turmoil in the world outside the campus, along with a strategic decision by Illinois movement leaders to deemphasize confrontational protests and demonstrations in favor of outreach and education, left the campus movement in a more subdued, thoughtful, and less dramatic place than in the previous year, with the local movement appearing more influenced by outside events than a dominant actor on its own.

The political events of the year began at the end of January with the Tet offensive in Vietnam, when combined Viet Cong and North Vietnamese forces—the same forces assessed by Johnson and his generals to be near defeat—simultaneously attacked more than one hundred government-held villages and towns throughout the South. The effort would fail militarily but would prove to be a dramatic public-relations victory, shattering Johnson's illusionary claim that victory was in sight. Largely as a result of Tet, within a month, for the first time in U.S. history, a sitting president was challenged for re-election from within his own party. The rebellious candidacy announcement by Senator Eugene McCarthy would soon force Johnson to withdraw from the race.

In March dissident black students took over buildings at Howard University in the nation's capital, a scene repeated in April with radical white and black students in New York City at Columbia University, and in May with Sorbonne students, soon joined by French workers, fighting gendarmes in the streets of Paris, bringing their nation to a standstill. In April, Martin Luther King Jr. was assassinated on a hotel balcony in Memphis, Tennessee, triggering riots in towns and cities across the United States. Before the nation could begin to absorb King's death, Senator Robert Kennedy was murdered in June in a Los Angeles hotel kitchen. Steve Schmidt remembers, "Students and faculty were really energized by Kennedy.... He was going to be the knight on the white horse. When he was murdered, that was the end ... the wind went out of the sails of the ship of the left opposition.... It was clear that the convention in Chicago was just going to be a done deal. Humphrey was the guy."[1] In early August, Republicans in Miami nominated Richard Nixon for president; later that month at their convention in Chicago, in the "done deal" that Schmidt spoke of, Democrats settled on Johnson's vice president, Hubert Humphrey, as what a federal study would later term a "police riot" raged on the streets outside.

As these explosive events played out nationally and internationally, on the Illinois campus the year lacked the dramatic actions of 1967, but memories of the previous year's activism still figured large with the administration. Chancellor Peltason, with understatement, reported to the trustees that today's students were different, that their demonstrations of excess energy had shifted from the panty raids of previous years and were now channeled toward issues of major social and political import, while at the same time he emphasized that even in the largest demonstration of the previous year, the Dow sit-in, less than 1 percent of the student population participated. Attempting to prepare for more of what he had seen the previous year, the chancellor presented to the board what he hoped was a less cumbersome, streamlined set of disciplinary procedures that would better prepare the administration to deal with future activism.

Campus SDS leaders, overcome with the same larger events as the rest of the nation, planned a more local focus for the new year, announcing they would run a slate of candidates for student offices, while also preparing for a presence at the summer's Democratic convention in nearby Chicago. By now the Red Herring had become the unofficial headquarters for campus radicals, though both the coffeehouse managers and their Unitarian sponsors billed the dank basement venue as open to all lines of thought. In the midst of the Tet offensive of January-February 1968, the basement facility became the birthplace of *The Walrus*, a campus underground newspaper that sold for "fifteen cents next time." The paper's first issue listed a nonhierarchical "Ed Staff" of Joe Hardin, Vic Berkey, Don Mayer, Vern Fein, Bern Gershenson, Les Wall, and Mike Metz (author), though Hardin was the driving force behind the effort.

Joseph Hardin was raised in the small southern Illinois town of Lebanon and came to college with no higher goal than "setting the curve in [his] intro chemistry class." But by his sophomore year politics was calling. "I was checking out groups on campus talking about the war and civil rights. I had been called to take my physical by my draft board the previous summer, and I decided I should look into this Vietnam war business." He found his way to an SDS meeting, "understood half of what was said," then attended some meetings on fair housing and related discrimination issues, growing his political awareness. "By the beginning of my junior year I was convinced something had to be done and became active in the anti-war movement." That year, with the help of friends, he started *The Walrus* to provide a voice for people on campus like himself, the "young, disenchanted, often angry, occasionally stoned viewers of the disturbing, evolving scene in our country and halfway across the world."[2]

The *Walrus* masthead quoted Lewis Carroll: "'The time has come,' the Walrus said, 'to speak of many things.'" And of many things the publication did speak over its five years of existence, with "articles, cartoons, poetry, movie and book reviews, editorials, and advertisements about Vietnam, racism, the University, Champaign-Urbana, middle-class values, police, drugs, sex, pollution, the Armed Services, and government and political affairs."[3] Through its many incarnations, with varying quality and differing names on the staff list, *The Walrus* was always close to the heart of the campus counterculture and student movement during its short life. What it lacked in professionalism it more than made up for in enthusiasm and passion.

Characterized by the *DI* as "anti-war, anti-draft and anti-establishment," the founders, self-described "rads" (short for radicals), explained themselves in a page 1 editorial in the first issue that indicated the enlarging scope of the movement, from straightforward antiwar feelings to wholesale dissatisfaction with the university, with the government, and with American society as a whole:

> The war in Vietnam continues in the face of the greatest protest against American foreign policy in the history of the U.S. From the protest has come an increasing dissatisfaction with the "American Way" and with American society.... The universities have been the target of much of the current dissent.... [They] channel young people into institutions and jobs which, instead of correcting the glaring social ills of America, simply perpetuate the unjust system to which these students object....

The university is not simply complicit in the war and discrimination. It is in fact an integral part of the machinery and structure which prosecutes the war and continues racial and political discrimination.... We hope to delineate our society's functions, to whose advantage and disadvantage, and further, how the university fits neatly into the present American system.... Our society is sick.... Ghettos threaten to go up in flames. An inhuman war costing two billion dollars per month is going on. American soldiers are dying half way around the world. People are starving in America. Little is changing. The time has come. Eds.[4]

Included in the first edition were articles attacking the university's "Plastic Education," the Selective Service system ("The New Draft Law and You"), and the government's war policies ("Bringing the War Home NOW"). The basement of the Red Herring would be a busy spot in 1968.

Meanwhile, the local Draft Resisters Union, meeting regularly in the same Red Herring basement and now led by Schmidt, kept up pressure on the university by repeatedly distributing literature, unsanctioned, on university property—in the Union, the Armory (home of ROTC programs), and other campus locations—while the administration repeatedly moved them away. During registration at the Armory, however, Schmidt and his fellow DRU member Mark Cooper refused to leave, which eventually led to formal charges of criminal trespass and a sentence of five days in the Champaign County jail.

On February 7 Fred Halstead, presidential candidate of the far-left Socialist Workers Party, spoke at Channing Murray. "There's only one way to support our boys in Vietnam, and that's to join the antiwar movement and get them the hell out of there."[5] The avowed Marxist criticized the McCarthy candidacy as too limited in its objectives, ensuring the continuation of the country's two-party system. He urged the audience to understand that the war was only one example of U.S. imperialism, an updated version of Kipling's nineteenth-century idea of the white man's burden. Though Halstead's campaign message was primarily "Bring the boys home now" and left aside his socialist ideology, his larger message of socialism as an alternative system piqued the curiosity of many students. Halsted had been invited to Channing Murray to speak by the local Socialist Workers group, a small group of old-left types on campus, derisively referred to as "Trots" by many in the student movement, after their ideological guru, the assassinated Russian revolutionary Leon Trotsky.

The day after Halstead's appearance, Vivien Rothstein, another "outside agitator," as supporters of the war might say, also spoke at Channing Murray. Rothstein, recently returned from a visit to North Vietnam, was on campus at the invitation of the CEWV. She talked about the history of the Vietnamese people, their oppression under the French, and the vital role women now played in Vietnam, "taking care of the defense of the villages and of agriculture." She described the Vietnamese

"Women's Union," which worked to ensure that women were taking full advantage of their rights and privileges as prescribed in the Vietnamese constitution, and passed around a protective, heavy straw hat that all Vietnamese children were required to have with them at all times, for protection (however minimal) during periods of American bombing. Attendees for Rothstein's talk, like Halstead's, filled the room at the Unitarian facility.

Rothstein applauded the antiwar sentiment on the Illinois campus and reminded the students that the Vietnamese were very aware of the American students' antiwar movement. "Everywhere we went [in North Vietnam] they said they knew the distinction between the peace-loving Americans and the American government."[6] The report of Rothstein's speech appeared on the front page of the *DI*, directly above a report of three black students shot to death by police on the campus of South Carolina State College in Orangeburg, where the state's governor blamed black power advocates at the school for "sparking violence."

Later in the month a less political program was held at the Red Herring, perhaps not by chance on Valentine's Day, as a local doctor spoke to a large student audience on the efficacy of "the pill" as a method of preventing pregnancy. Reassuring the students of the pill's safety, he vowed, "The only effect of prolonged usage of the pill for ten years, is—no kids for ten years."[7] The doctor also emphasized, to both female and male students, that contrary to what they might have heard, there was no such thing as a "day after" pill for men. The next evening, Dr. Timothy Leary, LSD advocate and "guru of the turned-on love generation," appeared to a large crowd in the Assembly Hall, proclaiming "This is the first generation that could turn the world on to peace." He announced that "love is where it's at, but we've lost the love thread temporarily." He ridiculed President Johnson and warned ominously about the coming summer Democratic convention. "Soon, within the next six months, you're going to have to cop out or drop out. By cop out I mean jail. If we don't talk and dance and sing now, we'll be talking in a concentration camp." Leary predicted that several million people would come together for a summer love-in at Chicago, preventing Johnson and the Democrats from holding their convention. "We'll laugh him out of the White House," Leary said, and endorsed the black comedian Dick Gregory for president. "We won't be able to hold our heads up high among the nations of the world until we pick a black man to be president."[8]

In March, Rothstein returned to campus, this time to speak on the topic of women and community organizing at an open forum at the Lincoln Hall women's dormitory, hosted by the newly formed Women's Union.[9] The new group would run a half-page ad in the *DI* in April proclaiming, "War is not healthy for Children and other living things. We demand Peace in Vietnam—NOW," signed by three hundred campus women.[10] Later in the year, a founder of the group, Gail Reed, would explain the group's position to a reporter:

The union was formed as an outgrowth to the committee to end the war. The women do not feel free to voice their opinions within the mixed political group so decided to find out how they could improve their situation.

Miss Reed said during the initial meeting of the Women's Union the women found they shared common feelings about speaking out in the presence of men. Some of the women accepted this as a natural phenomenon, while others felt it is a trait peculiar to themselves as individuals.

The group then expanded itself to holding sessions in dormitories, attracting a diverse audience of women. Miss Reed said discussions centered mostly around "myths" of the female role concerning family relations, passivity and marriage.

The discussion groups revealed that most families fail to initiate a sense of independence within their daughters, as they do with their sons. Most girls do not feel they must learn to think and speak on their own because they consider this more of the man's role in society.

Other topics of discussion explored the institutions of marriage and subservience taught by the Catholic Church. Philosophies of raising children were debated and the benefits of communal living where several adults act as parents to a child were raised.

Individual response within the group, Miss Reed said, has been directed to defining a role for oneself, first as a human being. The benefit of group discussions has encouraged feelings of confidence among individuals by knowing they all share similar feelings and emotions.... Miss Reed said the union will be inviting persons to speak and also will open discussions to male participants.[11]

Reed herself is not remembered by her peers of the time as someone reluctant to speak out in the presence of men; SDS faculty advisor David Ransel mentions her as the exception in that organization, a woman who spoke up regularly, "[She was] a very together woman ... able to stand up and talk at meetings."[12] Bernard Gershenson, a friend since junior high recalled, "She came from a Republican family that supported Nixon in the 1960 election, so following the lead of her parents, she did too. Her father, I believe, was on the school board. She had a warm, generous mother who unfortunately died of a massive heart attack when we were freshmen in high school. She was an excellent student, obviously bright." In their junior year they began to lose touch: "We drifted apart when she went on to more radical activities than I was engaged in."[13] Reed would join the newly formed *Venceremos Brigade*, a group of SDS members who traveled to Cuba to show support for the Cuban revolution in the face of a punishing United States trade embargo and worked side by side with Cubans to harvest that year's sugar crop. Neither Reed's conservative Republican father nor her very conservative Republican grandfather, Illinois state senator Arthur R. Gottschalk of the Chicago suburb of Flossmoor, would approve of such actions.

In Vietnam the Tet fighting continued through February with Marines still working to regain control of the northernmost provincial capital, Hue, and in the same month on the Illinois campus, SDS members debated the right response to the pending return of Dow recruiters. As memories of disciplinary procedures still lingered from October's sit-in, few of the radicals had appetite for a repeat performance. Eventually, Vic Berkey, now unofficial head of the local SDS, announced a series of teach-in activities, with movies and discussion groups in the Union lounges. The goal was to bring people together for dialogue, to educate rather than to alienate. "This time we're offering a chance for discussion, whereas last time we were accused of impeding free speech," added a spokesperson for the group. Invitations to join the teach-in were extended to Dow representatives as well as to Chemistry Department head Gutowsky, administrative point man during the October sit-in. There were no reports that either took up the invitations.

The teach-in activities indicated a new strategy of the activists for the spring semester, with fewer actions to antagonize the public and more outreach in the dorms, fraternities, and sororities, intended to help build up the movement's base. "There will be a de-emphasis on meetings and demonstrations so it will look like nothing's happening," said Vern Fein, now president of the Committee to End the War in Vietnam. "More and more people are coming out against the war. . . . We want to get to as many of these people as possible and give [them] an understanding of why not only the war policy but our entire foreign policy must be changed." Berkey voiced similar thoughts, remarking on the unanticipated growth of the campus movement at Illinois. "Last spring [1967] there was no anti-war or anti-establishment movement, it just began this fall. It was really a surprise to me to see how many people would come out and demonstrate." But now he felt the situation called for a change of tactics. "People are realizing that's inadequate," referring to the demonstrations. Much of the student and faculty population "did not understand *why* the demonstrations." But at this point, he said, "It's important to broaden our base rather than take part in emotional confrontation." Even the Draft Resisters Union, probably the most radical and action-oriented of the left-wing campus groups, called for an increased focus on education. Ron Lucas, speaking for the group, agreed with the strategy of reaching out to the dormitories and the community at large. "We're going to talk to people, work on our 1-A program for guys who have just been told to report for induction and continue our work in the high schools." Lucas acknowledged that the demonstrations of the previous semester had failed to attract large numbers of new people, and at times the resistance had alienated the public. But, he cautioned, "If something comes up where direct action is needed then we will take it."[14]

CHAPTER 25

Race Returns to Center Stage

Early in the spring semester, foreshadowing the widespread racial conflicts that would soon erupt in the nation's cities, north Champaign resident and community organizer John Lee Johnson spoke at a McKinley Center YMCA/YWCA faculty forum on race relations and declared himself an unapologetic black revolutionary. Speaking to a largely white audience of attentive if somewhat taken aback faculty and students, he declared, "Since I want to be free, I will do what I must. If we, as blacks, must kill you, then we will because as it stands now I can not, nor can my black brothers, see any freedom." Johnson suggested that the black revolutionary's "best tool" was his hatred of whites. He told the somewhat cowed whites gathered in front of him, "It is so easy for the black man to hate you. . . . All the problems we live with are telling us to hate you. You have killed us before and you still hold genocide over our heads."[1]

John Lee Johnson was born in the north end of Champaign, the seventh of twelve children, a product of the Champaign public schools, and would remain a lifelong resident of the town. He would spend his entire life working as a community organizer, displaying "a compelling drive to see his community become a better place to work and thrive."[2] He would host a radio show, serve on the city council for ten years, and either found or be associated with countless local organizations that advocated for people of the lower socioeconomic class. But in the spring of 1968 Johnson became best known to student activists on campus as a fearsome and angry black man who had no reticence at sharing that anger with anyone—privileged white students, university faculty, administrators, or police—while maintaining a large presence on the campus throughout the duration of the movement.

Johnson returned to his theme a week later, as an invited group of both liberal and conservative faculty members, radical student leaders, and nationally prominent educators gathered in the south lounge of the Union to discuss the topic of student power on campus, for a program to be broadcast on the local public television station. The meeting host opened the discussion by comparing and contrasting the rights of the previous semester's sit-in participants with the Dow recruits' rights of free speech, but Johnson interrupted, taking the opportunity to harangue the group about the moral and psychological damage done to blacks by the racism of the university community. When the meeting facilitator turned the discussion back toward his intended topic, Johnson and his supporters angrily stormed out of the meeting.

In March, Eugene McCarthy nearly defeated his party's incumbent president in the New Hampshire primary, sending a blow to Johnson's chances for reelection. Robert Kennedy, emboldened by McCarthy's showing, reneged on his promise not to challenge the president and announced his candidacy. Friction arose on campus between student groups supporting each of the Democratic senators, with McCarthy backers characterizing Kennedy as an opportunist, and Kennedy's countering that McCarthy realistically just couldn't win. McCarthy's support on the campus was quite strong, and several hundred students signed up for bus rides to Milwaukee to canvas for him in the upcoming Wisconsin primary. Female students were asked to wear skirts, while males were advised to cut their hair, shave their beards, and "Come clean for Gene." In the final weekend before the primary, Illini students working for McCarthy in Milwaukee gathered around a hotel television on the last Sunday night of the campaign were stunned to hear Lyndon Johnson announce to the nation that he would not be a candidate for reelection. So the Vietnamese enemy would not mistake this for weakness on his part, the next day the president ordered intensified bombing raids over North Vietnam.

Unappeased by Johnson's decision to withdraw, five draft resisters and four hundred of their supporters gathered on the back patio of the Illini Union the following day. The meeting began with two Park Forest, Illinois, brothers, Mark and Rob Cooper, leading the crowd in a rendition of Bob Dylan's "Blowing in the Wind." Two local pastors and student president Patsy Parker spoke in support of the resisters. Parker called for a national system of alternate service and a draft system that treated everyone equally, one not focused primarily on the poor or only on men. Five draft cards were passed to Parker, from a mix of students, non-students, and university employees—Don Mayer, Jim Starkey, Charles Cox, Richard Blackwell, and Dan McCollum. After the speeches, loaves of bread were passed through the crowd and shared, then about two hundred of the demonstrators hiked to the

Champaign draft board, where, when officials refused to accept them, Parker left the five cards on the office counter. The group then serenaded the office workers with several folk songs before marching back to campus. No violence nor any attempt at disruption was reported.

Later in the month, as warm spring weather bloomed on campus, the chancellor's declaration to the board that panty raids were a thing of the past proved false, as four hundred male students surrounded several women's dorms, chanting "We want panties." Six campus police cars responded to break up the crowd, their work stymied by female students tossing underwear out the windows. The following night seventy-five women students, in a show of revenge, marched on men's dorms chanting for underwear. One explained, "We just wanted to get even. It's a success. We got some shorts and disrupted their studying."[3] No one was injured and no arrests were reported.

These traditional rites of spring ended abruptly in the first week of April with the murder of Martin Luther King in Memphis, Tennessee. Before the minister's body was cold, predictions of violence were heard far and wide, and proved accurate. On the Illinois campus, Rodney Hammond, a psychology undergrad from Chicago, campus YMCA officer, Liberal Arts Council member, and founder of the campus Black Students Association (BSA), called the murder a testament to Malcolm X's words. "We can only find justice at the mouth of a gun. There is no doubt in my mind now that violence is the only way to get anything." Hammond spoke of "naïve white Americans" who believed a peaceful racial resolution could be found; he warned, "They kept saying that peace is the way of life here and something like King's death could never happen. Yet in the tide that is to come, some of them will be sucked up." He claimed to speak for his black brothers and sisters: "I say … the white man [is] more than ever a monster to be distrusted and feared. [He] has lost the only black friend he had." The angry student leader warned, "From now on [the white man] will have to deal with us black militants." Paul Brady, another BSA spokesperson, predicted "open rebellion and a complete destruction of society.... King's death will convince more people not to die like he did, kneeling, but to die in a violent way for the black cause."[4]

As one would expect, John Lee Johnson also spoke out, saying he'd be "disappointed if there were no violence in reaction to King's death." He warned his fellow blacks, "If they killed Martin Luther King, they will kill you," and notified them they must be willing to fight to survive. "Trust in God and the belief that man is a fair animal and that when man cries out for freedom, it will be given—this hope is gone. Martin Luther King held great hope for people who didn't want to shed their blood for the black cause. Trust in God and belief in human goodness will not do any good."[5] In Memphis, violence had erupted immediately when word of the shooting spread. Black youths threw firebombs and snipers opened fire on police and national guardsmen. A black seventeen-year-old Memphis youth was the first casualty of the riots that would erupt in more than one hundred American towns and cities in the following week.

Within days of King's death, a new group was formed on the Illinois campus, Citizens for Racial Justice (CRJ), composed largely of white faculty members. On the Saturday after the assassination, following a gathering on the quad, a CRJ group proceeded to President Henry's residence in Urbana but found only his wife at home. Confusing the marchers for yet one more antiwar group, she asked plaintively, "What do you want from my husband? He can't end the war in Vietnam."[6] Dean Stanton Millet, demonstrating uncharacteristic responsiveness, arranged for an afternoon meeting with CRJ leaders and the president at Henry's office in the Administration Building. CRJ asked for three things: that the university commit to increased hiring of local blacks, publicly declare support for an open housing ordinance then before the Champaign City Council, and open campus recreational facilities to community blacks. After an hour-long meeting, Henry came outside to speak to the demonstrators and promised complete support for their requests. The group repeatedly cheered his remarks, and in return Henry expressed support for their efforts. Speaking of his meeting with the CRJ leaders, he told reporters, "There was a meeting of minds on all the fundamental things. . . . We have been involved in many aspects of this problem for a very long time, so I respect the work you [CRJ] are doing." Philip Meranto, assistant professor of political science and CRJ spokesperson, praised Henry in return. "He in good faith met the demands that we put forth and demonstrated his willingness to work on these problems."[7]

In the Champaign-Urbana area, blacks made up between 15 and 20 percent of the population, but the university workforce included fewer than 3 percent blacks, and most of those in the "unskilled" category. Even fewer clerical positions were filled with blacks, and the percentage in the academic ranks was worse. The group asked the university for a requirement of nondiscriminatory hiring by all contractors and unions and to work toward a goal of a workforce that fairly represented the local population. In the twin cities, CRJ and the NAACP pushed for city governments to increase their hiring of blacks. At a Champaign City Council meeting, when Clarence Davidson, president of the local NAACP, asked how many Negro firemen were employed by the city, City Manager Warren Browning reluctantly admitted, "There are 56 commissioned firemen and none are Negro because none have passed the civil service examination."[8]

There was better employment news for blacks in Memphis, as city garbage collectors, whose strike had brought King to their town initially, returned to work two weeks after his death with a settlement nearly identical to what they had sought and been refused only weeks before the murder. Black Councilman J. O. Patterson Jr. blamed that city's council for the prolonged work stoppage and the resulting violence. "Seven weeks ago we agreed to the main issues almost identical to those before us today and then a majority of the council changes its mind . . . [they] refused to take any action on this matter and a lot of hell broke out across the city and across the nation. We could have avoided all this, including the death of Dr. King."[9]

On the Illinois campus antiwar activists also went back to work after King's death. Sticking with their new strategy of education and outreach, activists joined a national SDS-sponsored "Ten Days of Protest" taking place on campuses across the country. They scheduled pray-ins on the quad, led by local ministers and priests, teach-ins in the Union lounges, a day of draft-resistance education in the dormitories, guerrilla theater and antiwar poems recited by English professor Gary Adelman on the south patio of the Union. A "Gentle Thursday" was planned, modeled on a University of Texas event where activists showed their softer side, "a celebration of our belief that there is nothing wrong with having fun," with music, Frisbees, soap bubbles, and colored chalk.[10] That same week the CRJ group proposed a program of "recruitment and retention" of promising but disadvantaged students, urging the administration "to attack the racial problem by possibly waiving the admission requirements for Negroes," while providing such students with additional support resources to ensure their success.[11]

Thinking along similar lines, even before the King assassination, Peltason had created an ad hoc "equal education opportunity" committee to offer recommendations; the committee's report called "for broad changes in admissions policies to enable students who normally would not qualify to enter the University, as well as changes in curricula and normal progress regulations to lower the failure rate among culturally deprived students while maintaining equal quality of education for all University students." Their proposal called for a gradual increase in the number of black students at the university, with "admission of 100 additional culturally deprived Negro students each year for the next five years."[12]

Once the committee's report and recommendations were made public, CRJ members quickly judged it "totally insufficient," and proposed instead that a larger number of students be admitted in a shorter time frame. Soon, the BSA, equally critical of faculty and CRJ proposals, submitted their own plan with an even more aggressive goal of five hundred new students who would be enrolled not over five years but within a few short months, by the beginning of the upcoming fall semester. Dan Dixon, BSA president, pointed out that "of the 30,000 students enrolled here, only one per cent is Negro. Total Negro population for the state of Illinois is 14 per cent."[13]

Illinois wasn't the only university struggling with such issues as racial tensions on primarily white campuses arose across the country. In late April, black and white students at Columbia, eschewing the Illinois strategy of outreach and education, voted with their feet for a dramatic confrontation, occupying five buildings on their campus and refusing administration and police demands to leave. African American militants H. Rap Brown and Stokely Carmichael visited on the second day, providing the students with symbolic support in front of network television cameras, only increasing the pressure on the administration. That same week on the Ohio State campus in Columbus, 150 students, blacks and whites, took over the Administration Building until the university president agreed to establish an office of black student affairs. In May, on the campus of Southern Illinois University at Carbondale, "a bomb caused $50,000 worth of damage to the Agriculture Building," presumably due to the facility's use by the campus ROTC. This caused cancellation of a scheduled speech by Carmichael, which led to a two-hundred-person (mostly black) takeover of the president's office. Security personnel cleared the office, arresting eight. SIU president Dwight Morris brusquely announced, "Some are in jail. Some are in the hospital. And all are expelled."[14]

President of the National Urban League (NUL) Whitney Young spoke in Champaign that week. The league, a historic civil rights organization headquartered in New York City, was founded in 1910 and focused on the economic improvement of black communities across America. Asked why so many of the country's youth, black and white, seemed in open rebellion against society, Young answered with an echo of the *Walrus* editorial. "America's young people have become increasingly frustrated and disenchanted with what they see in America . . . they can see social and economic conditions haven't changed in the last 100 years, and they see a morally bankrupt society."[15]

After the Columbia building occupation had gone on for a week, with most classes cancelled and the campus virtually paralyzed, university president Grayson Kirk called in New York City police to clear the buildings, in the dead of night. Arrests totaled 628; many students charged police brutality. Following the arrests, the administration declared all would now return to normal. "We anticipate a full schedule of classes today."[16] This overly optimistic outlook was contradicted by an immediate student strike that received support from 60 percent of the students and many faculty who chose to cancel classes for the remainder of the semester. The same week, in Washington, Selective Service director Lewis Hershey announced an upward revision of the draft call for 1969 to 345,000, an increase of one hundred thousand over that of 1968. It was a turbulent time, with widespread national tension over both the war and race, with growing student frustration toward the seemingly intractable, unresponsive attitudes of university and government authorities. Meanwhile, the war just continued to grind on.

Back at Illinois, on Tuesday, April 30, 1968, less than one month after the death of Martin Luther King Jr., Chancellor Jack W. Peltason, having reviewed suggestions from his own committee, from the CRJ, and from the BSA, announced the program that would be associated with his name through his tenure at Illinois and, in fact, throughout his career. The aggressive goal of the new program would be to enroll five hundred black students at the university—not over five years, as his faculty committee had recommended, or even over two years, as the CRJ group had urged—but for the upcoming fall semester, less than four months away, just as BSA had demanded in their response to the faculty report. The chancellor's office announced the hiring of Clarence Shelley, graduate of Wayne State University, as a new dean (in what must have been an extremely accelerated recruitment process) to lead what would officially be named the University of Illinois Special Education Opportunities Program but would become popularly known at the university as "Project 500." Some, including Rodney Hammond of the BSA, were not mollified by Peltason's announcement. "The chancellor's press release doesn't say much. We want to see tangible results."[17] The program, which was to become one of the most significant and best-known efforts at confronting a social problem in the university's history, was announced to the world in a small article on page seven of the *DI*, alongside a report of a white student boycott of Chicago schools, protesting the busing of Negro children to the white schools.

The day following Peltason's announcement, one hundred black students at Northwestern University in Evanston, Illinois, occupied the school's business office, barricaded the doors with chairs and desks, prohibited all entrance to the building except for other black students, and presented the administration with a list of demands, one of which called for an immediate increase in black student recruitment at Northwestern. The Illinois chancellor, a progressive liberal at heart, was working hard and fast to stay ahead of events.

CHAPTER 26

Spring Sputters to an End

In the final month of the spring semester, Jim Kornibe, a housemate of Vern Fein's, was elected student president for the following year, succeeding Patsy Parker. Kornibe, an army veteran a few years older than most undergrads, was associated with the activist sector of the student population but ran his campaign on a moderate platform of reform and reorganization of student government, with goals such as increased student control over rules of visitation and on-campus drinking, more pass/fail classes, and looser foreign-language requirements. Once elected, Kornibe would appear less moderate, as when he responded to a student's query about the Office of Security by saying, "We don't have any need for a security office at all. People don't need to be watched that way."[1] Such comments would reveal his more radical leanings and gladden the hearts of student leftists, but in the spring of 1968 a more restrained campaign, one acceptable to a still largely apolitical student body, was called for; it worked—the junior won by several hundred votes.

Despite all the turbulent national and international events, at Illinois, with the activists focused on education and outreach, and the campus headlines dominated by the politics of McCarthy, Kennedy, and Kornibe, the semester wound down to a quiet close with the student election. Student leaders Fein and Berkey had successfully steered the semester's antiwar movement away from dramatic sit-ins and demonstrations, albeit with mixed results. The relative low energy of teach-ins, gripe-ins, pray-ins, and educational "Days of Protest" generated neither the excitement nor the press coverage of the previous semester's campus sit-in. Linda Picone, veteran staff writer for the *DI*, in an end-of-semester analysis, suggested that the New Left was perhaps losing steam, at least on the Illinois campus, and described the semester's political events as "unexciting and unattended," with speakers receiving "neither the audience nor the attention they deserved." Though agreeing that they might have long-term effect, "teach-ins and lectures do not have the emotional impact, or the press coverage, that a sit-in does."[2] Blaming part of the loss of passion on the presidential campaign and the candidacies of McCarthy and Kennedy, Picone questioned whether the campus movement's leaders had lost their way or perhaps had simply been overwhelmed by the torrent of larger events.

By semester's end both Berkey and Fein had moved away from their respective bases in SDS and CEWV and were now involved with CRJ and issues of race. In the new organization the two pushed the university hard to improve relations with the black community and increase black hiring, while at the same time arguing strenuously with more conservative CRJ faculty, whom they considered part of the very establishment that was at the root of the problems. The result was, again, less drama, little excitement, and some small improvements in minority hiring by the university—yet overall not that much to show for their efforts. Meanwhile, the war raged on, announcements of draft numbers continued to rise, and in the summer, ghettos continued to burn. To many members of the student movement, nothing seemed to be changing. Picone expressed the growing frustration felt by many: "The griping, demonstrations and commiserations of many Left groups have led to nothing but more griping, demonstrations and commiserations."

Many in the movement began questioning the way forward, as dramatic events erupted elsewhere, across the Atlantic in France, where students occupied buildings in nearly all of the country's universities, flying red and black flags of rebellion and anarchy. The French premier called it "a trial of our civilization" and compared it to "the hopeless period of the 15th century, where the structures of the Middle Ages were collapsing."[3] In contrast, for Illinois students, not only were the structures of authority not collapsing, those structures seemed largely unaffected despite all their efforts.

Some end-of-year excitement arose with the election of an aggressive new BSA president, David Addison, who advocated a "no holds barred" approach to achieving the group's demands. When asked about the use of force, he responded, "If BSA wants it, we will get it by any means necessary.... [W]e can get the administration building in 48 hours."[4] Campus Young Republicans responded to such threats by unanimously passing a resolution condemning any Illinois students, black or white, who would deny access to university buildings by other students. At the same meeting they voted for recruitment of a black Republican candidate to oppose Chicago Mayor Richard Daley in the upcoming November election, preferably someone from a Chicago ghetto.[5]

David Eisenman, a physics grad student at Illinois with a bachelor's degree from Harvard who was now working in the UIUC Graduate College, would become an outspoken champion of the Project 500 program. In May he announced a fundraising campaign for the new students arriving in the fall, with a somewhat overly optimistic target of $500,000. The energetic and dedicated young man, easy to spot in his trademark bow tie, proposed a mere ten dollars from each student and twenty-five from each faculty member to provide financial assistance to the disadvantaged students. Unfortunately for the program, Eisenman's efforts did not come close to meeting the goal, but certainly not for lack of enthusiasm or hard work on his part, as he managed to generate coverage of his campaign and donation announcements on a regular basis in the media throughout the remainder of the school year.

As the semester quietly entered finals week in Urbana, on the south side of Chicago seventy black students at the University of Chicago took over their administration building, demanding increased black student enrollment. North of Chicago, at Northwestern, the trustees approved the administration's decision to accept the demands of the previous month's sit-in. At Carbondale, black student leaders announced that all black students there would withdraw from Southern Illinois University if the administration failed to meet their demands for greater black enrollment. Parker and Kornibe sent a joint telegram of support to the SIU students.

The trauma was not confined to this country. In France, with rebellious students now on strike at nearly every university in the nation, workers in nearly all the country's ninety-five departments went on a general strike, in parallel with the students, with their own set of demands—higher wages, reduced hours, and better benefits. Though the workers claimed their actions were independent of the students,' it was hard not to see a connection. The Paris stock exchange dropped 5 percent.

While it now seemed that students everywhere were in rebellion, Chancellor Peltason in Urbana must have felt he had succeeded in dodging the worldwide wave of disruption. He spoke proudly of his project to bring the disadvantaged five hundred to campus, claiming, "We are on the verge of a very exciting period of educational reform. . . . Our job is to provide people an education. We are trying to seek people who otherwise might not have this opportunity." Talking up Eisenman's fundraising drive, he explained, "We're appealing to human beings to help other human beings get an education. I think it's a worthwhile cause." The chancellor likened the incoming underprivileged students to disabled students at Illinois's nationally known physical rehabilitation center. "This University is worldly famous—and justly so—for its programs for the physically handicapped. We did not lower the standards for the physically handicapped to attend the University." He continued the metaphor: "So it is with persons society has handicapped primarily because of color. We're trying to build the ramp—to help them get the education they need and deserve. We're not lowering standards any more than having therapists work with the physically handicapped."[6] The chancellor, his administration, and the university displayed the most admirable of intentions.

However, in 1968 noble intentions alone were not sufficient to dampen student unrest. At a Centennial Convocation held that year in the Assembly Hall to celebrate the one-hundredth anniversary of the university's founding, educational reform champion and graduating senior Paul Schroeder, the only student representative on the agenda, was only allocated four and a half minutes but made the most of his time. When introduced, he rose to speak and dramatically unzipped and removed his academic gown (which all speakers wore) and laid it on the chair next to him, distinguishing himself from previous dignitaries who all praised the university. He took a different tack, declaring to President Henry, Governor Otto Kerner, and the four thousand other celebrants in the crowd, "Our university is simply not listening to critical questions of our age. . . . Our society is distressed. I, and thousands of other students, question the priorities of a nation that devotes to a senseless war resources badly needed to cure the disease at home." He identified himself as "a student who has spent four disappointing years at the university" and judged that "this university has failed us. . . . We cry out to you in our need. And we see no one listening. . . . Someone today must accept personal responsibility to build a more sensible society." He quoted the French philosopher and revolutionary Regis Debray: "To judge an intellectual it is not enough to examine his ideas, it is the relation between his ideas and his acts which count." Then Schroeder challenged his fellow students to walk out of the hall and join him "to build education for a new century."[7] Today Schroeder suggests he misspoke badly about those "disappointing four years," and now feels differently. "All of us found the place coming up short when measured against what it really needed to be or what it could be. And yet my years there weren't really disappointing. If anybody had fulfilling, enriching, growth-inspiring years at Illinois, I would have to say that I had them." He added, "I probably more regret saying I had four disappointing years than I regret taking off my academic gown."[8]

Within days of Schroeder's speech, Robert Kennedy would lie dead on the floor of a Los Angeles hotel kitchen and, with him, much of the hope for an electoral solution to the nation's turmoil. President David Dodds Henry returned to Wayne State to deliver that school's convocation address, where he bemoaned "the epidemic of student convulsion on our campuses" and called for "reason in debate and discussion, . . . respect for the views of others and their right to express them, and intellectual humility." Henry argued that the modern university must "reflect the ideals of an orderly society" and criticized "those who would alter its corporate character from one of neutrality in community conflict to one of social activism." Passionately disagreeing with that logic, the students of the sixties movement wholly rejected the president's concept of university neutrality when faced with injustice, felt no intellectual humility when confronted with the failings of their disorderly society, and rebelled in reaction to what they considered an immoral war, a complicit university, and an unjust, unequal society. Contrary to Henry's hopes, summer 1968 would only raise the level of disorder.

CHAPTER 27

Summer '68: The Turning Begins

The decade of the sixties was a violent time, marked by assassinations, domestic riots, and a disastrous foreign war. But in 1968, for the first time, such violence would finally, directly touch the privileged, white, middle-class youth who made up the student-protest movement. A period of innocence would end, illusions would shatter, and the issue of violence would move to the forefront in the consciousness of students in the movement.

These youth had come of age surrounded with violent images, from the assassination of John F. Kennedy to police using billy clubs, fire hoses, and dogs, to the innocent child victims of a church bombing. Throughout the years of the decade, network cameramen transmitted Southeast Asian battles into America's living rooms nightly, with images of the fire fights, dead soldiers, napalm victims, body bags, and returning coffins. Images of the Martin Luther King and Robert Kennedy murders were run and rerun in the media. In summer there were the burning, rioting ghettos, always televised, habituating America to ongoing human tragedy. In the decade's early years violent speech poured from white segregationists, in the later years from black revolutionaries, and all the while there was the war. Violence was ubiquitous in the era.

So to many Americans the televised violence that would come with the Democratic convention in the summer of 1968 would seem just one more chapter of the decade, but to the country's college students, this time it was different. This time the mayhem on the nightly news was not directed at civil rights marchers, Viet Cong prisoners, or revolutionary blacks, but at people who looked like them—white, privileged, and middle class. This firsthand confrontation with establishment violence would mark a watershed for the movement and begin the turn from the exhilarating and exciting adventure of making a better world, to a dangerous, frightening, and, at times, life-threatening experience.

Mark Rudd, Columbia student-protest leader and later a principal figure in the violent Weatherman faction of SDS, would refer to the pre-1968 period in near-ethereal terms, as a time of "beautiful hallucination . . . the world was about to be remade; that this monster of militarism and injustice was about to fall; that young people in this country would join with people all over the world to end imperialism and make a new world."[1] But such beautiful hallucinations would come to an end in 1968. Activist Joseph Hardin described the rollercoaster emotions this way:

> I was frightened and exhilarated and excited, all at the same time. Things seemed to be breaking out of their old mold, even if some of the breaking was dangerous and scary. . . . I felt that something was coming and we were a big part of it.
>
> We were affecting things. We were defining our views and refining our understandings of what was going on in the world and what was right and wrong. Much of the time, including demonstrations where we got our fair share of abuse, it was kind of thrilling.
>
> This was reinforced by the national news that thought what we did was important, and the culture that legitimized our anger and valorized our efforts. We were all heroes. The doubt, pain and loss would come later. But during this period, we were peaking.[2]

The violence of 1968 would change students' outlook, but the violence that was to come at the summer convention would not be without precedent. Earlier in that year, on April 27, Chicago police staged a rehearsal for the summer convention at an anti-war march in the Chicago Loop, as protesters walked from the lakefront at Grant Park to the Civic Center. Cars filled with Illinois students made the drive north to join in the march. Bernard Gershenson remembered it well:

> A bunch of us drove up from Urbana, . . . Just as the first wave of marchers were approaching the Civic Center, a phalanx of cops, dressed in riot gear and swinging their batons, charged. . . . All hell broke loose. Another phalanx joined the first so there were cops everywhere. We, and everyone else, took off running.
>
> The downtown stores all locked their doors so no one could take refuge among the shoppers. I lost track of everyone as I ran, up Washington street, then toward the lake on Randolph. Had to sprint several blocks to lose the cops. I remember seeing people who couldn't run squatting in the doorways of stores, their arms crossed over their heads.
>
> I ran down into the Randolph Street station, which turned out to be a safe place. I stayed there for I don't know how long until the coast was clear. Emerging, I bumped

into the sister of one of my good friends from Park Forest. I remember she was crying uncontrollably.³

Patricia Engelhard also remembered the event:

> We did not have cell phones or computers. How did we know where we needed to be? . . . I think we existed in a true grass roots world, without leaders. We did what we thought we should. We believed that if we showed up, eventually the war would end. Why else would we do it? And most of us—certainly the ones in our world—went in peace.
>
> Indeed, I was on crutches . . . inept on crutches. We assumed the march would be peaceful. We may not have fully understood Mayor Daley's anger. . . . To Daley we were a profound threat. I do not think that possibility had yet occurred to any of us. We were not even certain anyone was really listening.
>
> It started as any other march, peacefully moving through the streets of downtown. . . . The police moved us along but what we did not know until later is that they were splitting up the crowds into smaller groups. While we were being turned down one street, others were broken off in other directions . . . but what did we know?
>
> And then they started attacking. We were under the el tracks in the Loop. I was unable to move easily. People were running. [We moved] into a Marshall Field's doorway to get out of harm's way. But the doors were locked so none of us could find refuge in the store.
>
> We were stunned, shocked, terrified and exhausted. What we understood later was that the police response was training for what was to come in August. Daley was consumed with the fear that the convention would be disrupted by protest and he would look weak.⁴

One Illinois marcher, Kackie Berkey, spouse of Vic, was injured in the melee. "The cops came up swinging batons, hitting and pushing people. Kackie was pushed right through a storefront window. I don't know how we got out of there."⁵

The conservative *Tribune* reported their version of the events this way:

> The march to the Civic Center was noisy but peaceful. . . . When the marchers reached the Civic Center, they found the plaza around the Picasso statue roped off. . . . As the marchers circled the Civic center, some . . . broke the ropes and others followed into the plaza. Police . . . attempted to restore order. Unable to do so, they began moving the marchers off the plaza and into Washington and Clark Streets. About 250 of the demonstrators attempted to stage a sit-down in the plaza and the first of the mass arrests occurred.
>
> As the police moved the marchers across the streets and broke them into small groups, some resisted police. At the southwest corner of Dearborn and Washington Streets, police had to use MACE, which was used often before the battle ended.

Later, in the central district lockup, army intelligence agents in plain clothes, FBI agents, and the police subversive unit, looked over those arrested, seeking soldiers absent without leave and known Communists and Communist sympathizers. In the pocket of one man arrested, police found a book on ways to sabotage.[6]

Gershenson and Engelhard were high school classmates, both from liberal Democratic households in the mostly Republican suburb of Park Forest, Illinois, south of Chicago. One of Gershenson's earliest memories was of his parents watching the McCarthy hearings on television, remembered mainly because, he said, "I couldn't watch what I wanted to watch." "My first politically active moment happened when some of my eighth grade friends and I held Kennedy signs while Nixon was speaking in front of Goldblatt's department store." Much to his shock, he said, "Some adult ripped the signs out of our hands. I was dumbfounded. I didn't know adults did things like that." By 1965 his political consciousness was raised significantly: "I registered for the draft in early August. I knew that there was no reason for me to fight and possibly die in Vietnam." Once on campus at Illinois, he remembered, "I attended an SDS meeting sometime during freshman year . . . Keenan Sheedy seemed to be in charge. . . . They were talking variations of Marxist politics and I didn't understand a thing. I didn't go back," but, "As the war escalated, so did my knowledge of what was going on and so did my opposition to it."[7]

Engelhard's parents met in Washington, D.C., in the aftermath of World War II, her father "a German Jew whose parents had lived in the U.S. for generations," her mother "barely a first generation Orthodox Jew whose parents escaped pre-Revolutionary Russia." Both were "liberal in their DNA and passed on their views of the world and humanity and our responsibility to take care of each other." She entered the university in 1965 but dropped out and moved to Berkeley, California, returning a year later. "I was an activist from my freshman year and so was everyone I knew. We did not see any other way to cope with the world we faced."[8]

The April march, begun in peace and ending in a soon-to-be repeated police riot, was frightening for the Illini participants and would prove to be a harbinger of the rising wave of violence that would threaten and eventually engulf the movement. As anti-war sentiment and even mainstream opposition to the war began to grow, so too did students' frustration with their inability to affect uncompromising government policies. Commensurately, the determination of authorities to restrain the opposition grew with rising disapproval of the war and the proliferating marches and demonstrations. On both sides, positions hardened and emotions intensified. As students tried to understand the issues with which they were confronted, some turned toward more radical positions. Only a few years removed from the McCarthy era, authorities saw such student radicalization as proof of their worst fears, clear evidence of that direst of threats, the familiar boogeyman of godless, international, communist revolution.

SDS played a key role in stimulating these establishment fears, for after years of peaceful protest, and the war that seemed to have no end, many of its members began to turn toward violence, first in speech, later in action. A defining, critical rupture would develop in the student movement in 1968, between those willing to make such a shift and those not. This split would become dramatically apparent to Illinois students attending national SDS meetings in that year. In the first half of 1968 there were two such meetings, both in mid-America, and at each the growing tendency toward violence was evident. Both meetings were attended by Illinois students who would return to campus and spread word of the new temperament. In March, at a National Council meeting in Lexington, Kentucky, with close to five hundred attendees, short tempers and growing anger was readily apparent. Some of the Illinois attendees were taken aback at the extreme emotions, the unruliness, and the infighting, as well as the calls for and against violence. One Illini, Lester Wall, recalls:

> It was like my family getting together at Passover, people yelling and screaming at each other, and nobody listening. It was really discouraging. Everyone knew the FBI was there [undercover] and heard people inciting violence. This was serious rhetoric, and remember, J. Edgar Hoover was still around then.
>
> People in the government started taking us seriously. They thought we were a real threat. And maybe we were. It wasn't everybody, but there was a significant radical segment. We [SDS] were part of the escalation of violence of the time. Mayor Daley sure took us seriously.
>
> We were pushed into answering "Which side are you on, boy, which side are you on" . . . to say whether you're in or you're out, and the powers that be were just as determined to stop us. And of course, eventually, they did.[9]

Wall had grown up on the south side of Chicago, attending a high school whose population was three-fourths Jewish. His parents were Democrats in a predominantly Democratic neighborhood, and for him, "The Holocaust in Germany was the biggest determinate of my political beliefs." From his first year at Illinois he "was a strong supporter of the civil rights movement, the free speech movement, and freedom and equality issues in general." He credited "the lies of the Johnson administration" for his feelings on Vietnam, radicalized in part because of the U.S. military's treatment of Vietnamese civilians, which to him "made America seem the oppressor."[10]

The Lexington SDS meeting marked an additional shift, from a focus on the war to an increased emphasis on race. National SDS officer Carl Oglesby told the attendees, "The job of SDS now is to turn from the issue of war to that of racism."[11] The group passed a unanimous resolution to give top priority to the "black struggle for liberation." The Lexington meeting adjourned on a Sunday afternoon, and it was that evening, on national television, when Lyndon Johnson withdrew from the campaign. Any feelings of triumph that members of the student movement might have felt were short lived though, as a week later Martin Luther King Jr. was assassinated and the ghettos exploded.

Three months later, in June, a crowd of more than one thousand activists and an unknown number of undercover agents gathered for the annual SDS National Convention in East Lansing, Michigan, where the radical evolution of the organization was visibly displayed. Posters of Bolshevik revolutionaries Vladimir Lenin and Leon Trotsky hung on the meeting-room walls, red and black flags of revolution and anarchy adorned the stage, and Chairman Mao's little red books were circulated around the conference. From the podium, national officers Bernadine Dohrn and Mike Klonsky bluntly declared themselves revolutionary ("small *c*") communists.

Dohrn, one of the few nationally known women leaders in the student movement, had evolved to become one of the more extreme of SDS leaders. She had graduated with a degree in political science from the University of Chicago, with honors, and was also a graduate of Chicago's law school. By 1968 though, Dohrn's life had changed dramatically from her years as National Honor Society member, cheerleader, and editor of the newspaper at her upper-middle-class Wisconsin high school.[12] Klonsky, often seen sporting a hip-length black leather jacket popular among Black Panthers, came from a more radical family background, his father a veteran of the Spanish Civil War, later prosecuted but cleared under 1950s McCarthy-era antisubversion laws. At the convention Dohrn, Klonsky, and Rudd would head up an "action faction," a subset favoring active confrontation over outreach and education; they would soon give themselves the label "The Revolutionary Youth Movement" (RYM), later evolving into the infamous Weatherman group. A workshop on sabotage and explosives offered a flavor of the convention's mood, though many suspected that undercover police and informants had arranged the session and then made up the bulk of the session's attendees. Some estimated that as many as three hundred of the convention attendees were undercover agents.[13]

For the first time at an SDS convention, traditional old-left-style Marxist-Leninists were a significant presence, representing the Communist Party, the Socialist Workers Party, and, the largest faction, the Progressive Labor Party (PLP). The PLP, considered Maoists by others on the left, believed in social revolution led not by idealistic students but by the "industrial proletariat," causing them to eschew the counterculture with its long hair, marijuana, and rock music, attributes then largely repugnant to working-class Americans. The PLs, as they were known, worked the conference as a well-organized unit and clashed fiercely with the RYM group, portending a major conflict that would eventually cause the implosion of the entire organization. Convention attendees from Illinois had rubbed shoulders with a few such old-left Marxists on the Urbana campus, followers of Trotsky or

Mao or even Stalin, but those were viewed as curiosities or even cranks, and in East Lansing, such an old-school communist presence and influence simply added to the confusion. For the first time at an SDS convention, talk of violence and revolution strongly permeated the air. To other, less radical convention participants, still focused on an antiwar agenda, such talk sounded simply crazy.

With an apparent split developing in the organization, these 1968 national SDS meetings failed to provide any coherent sense of direction to the Illinois attendees and only added to a growing sense of uncertainty about the local movement's direction. However, it was obvious to Illinois activists that, by early summer of 1968, the movement had changed dramatically. In a transition from the simpler demands of the previous year—free speech for all, including the right of communists to speak on campus, protests against university regulations—many were now converted to radical political thinking, Marxist revolutionary ideas, vaguely stimulated by romantic Third World heroes in Cuba, Vietnam, China, and elsewhere. Some others, looking askance at the new extreme direction, would begin to drift away from politics toward pronounced pacifist positions or immersion in counterculture mixtures of music, drugs, Eastern religions, or back-to-the-land efforts. Even the Beatles looked to be struggling with uncertainty as they released a new single, "Revolution," that summer. Referring to violent change, on one version John Lennon sang "count me out"; on another he vacillated, "count me out—in."

In this dramatic summer, after the assassinations, the violence of the Chicago march in April, the conflicting messages from the national SDS meetings, and the apparent failure of electoral politics after Kennedy's death and Humphrey's likely nomination, the situation seemed to offer Illinois students of the movement—and the Beatles—only unattractive choices, either a turning away from politics entirely or turning toward a radical path of increased confrontation. Middle-path options were fading. The summer's Democratic Party convention would only further harden, and limit, the options.

Many University of Illinois students participated in the demonstrations at the Chicago convention. Again, Patricia Engelhard remembers it well:

> We went to Grant Park every day . . . came home every evening to watch ourselves on Walter Cronkite (*CBS Nightly News*). He reported the events of the day, including what was happening in the streets. . . . He became our voice. . . . Back in those olden days there were only three TV stations. That meant that ALL of America watched the same news—everything we knew came from that source. We saw Dan Rather pushed to the floor by police. We saw Mayor Daley losing his little mind in front of the whole country.
>
> Things got increasingly tense every day. . . . Remember that Daley had given a "shoot to kill" order [during the riots following King's assassination] and that the April demonstrations had embarrassed him further. . . . One night, as the police

tried to push us back from the Conrad Hilton hotel with national cameras rolling, someone began the chant that became our anthem: "The Whole World Is Watching." It was exhilarating and empowering.

Dick Gregory arrived one day.... He told the crowd (tens of thousands) that although we were not being allowed near the Convention Center, we could walk to his home. As luck would have it, his home was just blocks beyond the Center. Of course, the tanks rolled in and stopped us from moving down Michigan Avenue.

I believe that is what prompted the tear gas. People with gas masks [actually helmets] were asked to go to the front of the crowd. Joe [Hardin] had a mask [a helmet]. We encouraged him to move to the front. He was not so sure! So we went with him!!! Solidarity is admirable but not always smart. Indeed we were all gassed. My eyes were filled and I fell to my knees—it really hurts! A medic came and doused me with water to rinse out my eyes. It was most dramatic.

We were so sure of ourselves and certain that we would make a difference. My recollection is that this week was most definitely a turning point. Suddenly everyone saw young middle-class kids being beat up and gassed on an American street because we wanted the war to end.[14]

And a memory from Joseph Hardin, he with the helmet:

We headed up to Chicago in a caravan of cars from Champaign... I brought my motorcycle helmet in case the demonstrations got serious; seemed like a good idea at the time. The one time I remember wearing it was the evening when someone said we were going to march to the black part of town.... [The march] started around the park, in front of the hotel where the delegates were... I was marching down the sidewalk/street with a bunch of people and a call came from the front: "Everyone with helmets up to the front." I said to myself, "Shit. This helmet thing may not have been such a good idea."

I looked around for a minute thinking, "Well, what should we do here?" and then started weaving through the crowd, heading toward the front. I think that some friends came up with me, but I'm not sure. I think my perceptions narrowed a bit in those moments. As I walked up to the head of the march, pretty much scared shitless, with people letting me through as I had a helmet, I came to the place where the National Guard had stopped everyone by parking their jeeps, the ones with the barbed wire strung on 2x4 frames attached to the front bumpers, across the road. There were guards with their rifles by the jeeps, and cops. Didn't look good to me.

Those of us bright enough to have helmets were pretty much in the very front, just where you didn't really want to be. There was some milling around and chanting and looking around wondering what to do now, and then the guard or the cops solved the problem by shooting tear gas over our heads and spraying it directly at us and moving forward to push the crowd back, all at the same time. There was no way to get away from the cops and gas coming at us other than to run through the tear gas behind us.

I got a bunch of gas and my eyes were flooded with tears and I was coughing. A news motorcycle courier guy from a local CBS news station was carrying film from reporters' cameras covering the demonstrations, and we tried to help him get through the crowd ... a bunch of people running and yelling and wheezing from the gas ... not too sympathetic to a guy on a big motorcycle in our midst, with us shouting "Go tell them what's happening here, what they're doing to us."

That and wrapping my face with a bandanna to try and protect against the gas, and debating whether it should be wetted or not, is about all I remember.[15]

Thousands of students were in Chicago, but exponentially more across America watched film like that the motorcyclist carried, on their television screens in the safety of their homes. To many, the scenes of convention violence shattered what hope they still harbored in the establishment, frightened them personally, and further increased their confusion about a path forward.

The level of violence that was loosed on the protesters by Chicago police was unlike anything the students had experienced in their lives—thousands of demonstrators, the great majority peaceful, set upon by tens of thousands of Chicago police, Illinois National Guardsmen and federal troops. To be present at the affair was dramatic and impactful (in the most literal sense of the word), but it was equally as affecting for the hundreds of thousands, perhaps millions, watching on television. In response to the violent behavior of the police and guardsmen, the demonstrators chanted, "The whole world is watching," thinking that would matter. But their words had little effect on the aggressors, and as this realization sunk in, a frightening and demoralizing reality dawned. Suddenly, these privileged college students, the elite of their generation, recognized how little power they truly had. The disproportionately aggressive establishment behavior, violating civil norms the students had taken for granted their entire lives, shattered their illusions with overwhelming finality. They learned a significant political lesson from the establishment violence in Chicago—that finally, when sufficiently challenged, the political establishment would respond with overwhelming force, and that force could prevail, at least in the short term, over idealistic students marching in the streets, no matter how many they were or how just their cause. Illinois students, along with their peers across the country, learned the lesson well, a lesson delivered with a harsh message. David Ransel remembers his moment of realization: "I saw the level of power that was arrayed against us. It wasn't just the police who were beating the shit out of everyone ... behind them were the National Guard, and behind them jeeps with barbed wire, then up on the buildings they had snipers.... I realized that they could just slaughter us all ... I began to sour on confrontational politics; it just wasn't going to work."[16]

Even the usually liberal *Sun-Times* published a conservative columnist's suggestion that the convention violence was a lesson the students needed to be taught.

"Militant groups will have to learn that nothing is gained by 'demonstrations' that incite to violence."[17] The convention was by no means the end of the protest movement, as the aggressiveness of the Chicago police and the incoming Nixon administration would provide ongoing fuel to the movement, and national moratoriums and marches on Washington would grow in strength, but with the convention, hopes for a peaceful middle path were diminished. From this point forward, a stark choice faced student activists; either let go of hopes for wide-scale political change and thus escape establishment retaliation, or continue the struggle by fighting violence with like violence. As one activist put it many years later, "We came to a river called violence, and I could not cross it."[18] It took some time for this lesson of overwhelming establishment violence to be fully internalized and for the choice to become clear, but when that happened, the great majority of students would choose the former path, and only a very small number would choose the latter.

CHAPTER 28

Fall '68: Project 500

Nearly lost in the news in the summer of '68 was a decision by a three-judge panel of the United States Federal Court for the Northern District of Illinois permanently striking down that seed of the Illinois student movement, the infamous Clabaugh Act. Said District Judge Alexander J. Napoli:

> We hold that the Act, both on its face and as applied to these plaintiffs, has denied them due process of law, because it lacks the precision of language required for a statute regulating an area so closely intertwined with First Amendment liberties; because it is an unjustifiable prior restraint to speech; and because it lacks the procedural safeguards required for a form of regulation amounting to censorship.[1]

But to many, the law now seemed an anachronism, a marker of a distant past, when the world was simpler and activist victories still possible. By the beginning of the fall semester of 1968, the violence of the Democratic convention had changed the conversation entirely. After the convention, establishment violence was now an accepted factor, a new norm in the minds of many students, along with the norms of ghettos burning in the summer, soldiers returning home in body bags, out-of-control police rampaging where and when they liked, and angry black revolutionaries carrying guns and threatening death to whites.

At Illinois, as the semester began, new, young, black faces, the chancellor's privileged, underprivileged five hundred, were on campus, and it quickly became clear that they were not happy with the state of their affairs. The accelerated recruitment program, largely carried out by BSA students, had been more aggressive than the administration had planned or expected, and in the first week of school the real number of Project 500 students was revealed as 640. With less money to go around, individual financial packages fell short of expectations. In addition, due to the higher number of students and typical beginning-of-year dorm room assignment problems, some black students were left temporarily housed in dormitory lounges, with those students assuming discrimination the cause. David Eisenman noted that the program had problems baked into it from the beginning: "In the first place the Black Student Association recruited many more people than we had room for, so there were problems with accommodations. They also made promises about financial aid that were far in excess of what they were authorized to promise, so Jack [Peltason] was struggling." In addition, the chancellor's "staff never believed [BSA] would recruit even 500 students, so the kids over-recruited, the staff expected under-recruitment, and he was stabbed in the back by his own people who never really thought they'd have to do anything." Eisenman claims to have seen the troubles as they developed: "[Peltason] didn't know this yet, but I knew it, because John Lee Johnson, the black activist from the north end [of Champaign] really knew what was going on around campus, and he talked to me."[2]

In response to their issues with dormitory accommodations and the financial shortfalls, the black students gathered in the south lounge of the Illini Union in the first week of school to air their grievances. They sent an emissary to ask the chancellor to join them. After much back-and-forth among his staff, Peltason declined. Dean Millet, never the most skilled of diplomats, did appear and attempted to address the crowd, but he was shouted down by Steve Jackson, a local resident and now one of the five hundred. Millet gave up and left, the union closed, and the students voted to remain, again asking the chancellor to come listen to their grievances. Instead, he, who in the previous year had wisely chosen not to send police into the Dow sit-in, avoiding a reoccurrence of the Madison melee, on this night chose to call in an overwhelming show of force, a combined 133 officers, from both cities' and the university's police forces.

Looking back, Eisenman suggests that "if Jack had gone to the Union and talked to them, he might have stopped the whole thing in its tracks, but his advisors said there was too great a chance he'd be personally assaulted, and then we'd really have trouble." Later, Peltason confided to Eisenman, "It wasn't my choice. My instinct was to go but when the head of your police department and all your advisors are telling you not to, what are you going to do?" In the end, Eisenman judged Peltason "too cautious . . . his instinct was to stand back, to allow things to happen, always to keep the lid on, to keep the worst escalation from occurring"—but still, "he believed in discussion, and free speech . . . I would have had him be much more activist than he was, [but] in the long run, I think he [and his choices] may have been right."[3]

By night's end 244 arrests were made, a few pieces of furniture were damaged and several paintings slashed. Damages were later estimated at between three thousand and five thousand dollars; the most serious harm may have been inflicted on a white student, John Hackman, a member of student government present at the affair, who was hit by a chair (and subsequently hospitalized) when he declined the group's direction to leave. Grossly inaccurate stories in the influential *Chicago Tribune* described the situation as a "black student riot" on the campus. Weeks later Eisenman would publish an article in the *Columbia Journalism Review* analyzing and critiquing the distortions of the *Tribune's* reporting. More accurate reporting by *DI* editors, in a front-page article, referred to it simply as another example of "An Old Problem":

> The Blacks who met at the Union Monday night had legitimate grievances. . . . They tried talking to housing division officials . . . they tried to take their problems to someone in a position to help them. They ran into a problem which students have run into time and time again: administrators will not act when students merely talk. It usually takes some show of student power to force administrators into action.
>
> Realizing this sooner than most other students have, the Blacks took over the south lounge of the Illini Union and said they would not move until the Chancellor came to speak to them. . . . We hope the administration will open its eyes and recognize students as ordinary human beings with basic rights.[4]

The indefatigable Charles Clabaugh, still representing the central Illinois area in the General Assembly and always good for an indignant quote, responded to the incident in his inimitable style. "If the University doesn't clean its house and put an end to this sort of thing, the legislature will be forced to step in and take greater control," proclaiming: "We as legislators just aren't going to put up with all this damn foolishness and continue to pour hundreds of millions of dollars into a University that can't maintain law and order." His Democratic peer in the district, Paul Stone, displayed a calmer demeanor. "The legislature has no business getting involved in anything as complicated as higher education. We are involved in enough issues without entering one we know little about." Stone continued, "Personally, I have great confidence in the administration. The legislature can do nothing to help the situation."[5]

The BSA placed responsibility for the incident entirely on the administration for not responding earlier to the students' needs. "The attitude of apathy and arrogance by the University administration in the face of innumerable demonstrations of bad faith and willful failure to live up to its commitments to students in the 500 Project," was to blame.[6] Eisenman published the best overall analysis of the incident in the *DI*, accurately describing the situation's complexities and cautioning his readers about the many issues that warranted consideration:

It would have to recognize the heightened degree of insecurity characterizing these students, who come here knowing that it is uphill all the way for them . . . administrators must realize—and some of them do already—that the students in this special program came here to make it by themselves despite handicaps, and that therefore they will react more desperately when their way to progress seems impeded.

Conversely, the black students will have to de-escalate their tactics. A university community willing to stick its neck out as this one has done, cooperating closely with the BSA in floating a major program for deprived students in a few months, cannot in fairness be treated like certain big city machines. [The university] may bumble, but it has shown an ability to adapt and to learn. . . . The greater reality is that our University is trying to do a very hard but a very important thing, in which properly we all have a part.[7]

The local NAACP threatened a lawsuit against the university, and SDS passed a resolution demanding the university drop all charges against the students—and if not, to provide due process for the accused, including trial by a jury of peers. CRJ also quickly came to the students' support, sponsoring a rally on the quad and asking that all charges be dropped. Chancellor Peltason published his thoughts with a statement in the *DI*:

A university community cannot long exist in an atmosphere of crisis, confrontation and confusion, demands and counter-demands, threats of force and fears of violence. Such an atmosphere of discord not only undermines public confidence and support for the university, but it leads to internal division, suspicion, and tensions that make difficult the performance of our major responsibility—the pursuit of advanced learning.

However, showing that he was not without some flexibility, he added:

I do not consider any of our existing rules or regulations sacrosanct and welcome the active and vigorous participation by all segments of the academic community to work for their improvement through orderly procedures for change. Where modifications are necessary to better enable previously unrecognized concerns to be voiced, we shall endeavor to make such modifications. But change must be brought about by the procedures appropriate to an academic community, that is by persuasion, debate, consensus and cooperation.[8]

After several weeks filled with legislators posturing, the NAACP threatening, BSA and SDS demanding, the *Tribune* editorializing, and the faculty senate passing motions alternately supporting and condemning the students, eventually the calmer heads prevailed. Law professors came forward to defend the students in disciplinary hearings, and the student senate passed a resolution recommending all charges be dropped. The board of trustees issued a statement expressing support for Peltason and Project 500, unanimously declaring the program "worthy of support." Formal charges of mob violence against the students were dropped, and 204 of those arrested received letters of reprimand. Those housed in dormitory lounges were soon relocated to acceptable housing, additional financial support was secured; the students completed their registration and began their college careers.

Clabaugh once again offered an outraged (and outrageous) opinion, declaring the offending students "kooks, nuts, rebels, and anarchists. . . . The admissions policy they used for the project, if any, is dragging the standard of the University down. I'm as compassionate as the next person, but I'm tired of sympathy for the 500." Asked how they might respond to his words, he responded, "Oh, I imagine they'll riot." If anyone harbored any doubts, he added, "I was against it from the minute I heard about it."[9] Disciplinary hearings for the remaining black students dragged on for months before most of them also received reprimands, with one receiving conduct probation and four acquitted entirely. By the end of the affair, in his never-ending attempts to stay ahead of protesters' actions, Peltason announced plans to form yet one more committee to review and streamline the university's disciplinary procedures. The affair of the rebellious black students, the extended disciplinary procedures, the hearings, protests, appeals, the eventual resolution of the incident, and other racial issues all became the central focus of campus activists for much of the school year. Race was again front and center at the university.[10]

PART IV

The Violent Time, 1969–70

CHAPTER 29

Spring '69: Heating Up, but Not Boiling Over

In spring the campus political landscape continued to be dominated by issues of race. White radicals scrambled to show support for the Project 500 students, driven by a mixture of frustration at their ineffectiveness at stopping the war, deep feelings of righteousness for the blacks' cause, and admiration mixed with unease at the level of black anger. BSA and Project 500 students led various protests, usually disdaining white radicals' support, and antiwar activities took second place on campus. But to some 1969 felt like a letdown, like the morning after a raucous party—subdued, with headaches.

Early in the semester SDS and BSA together brought one such headache on themselves by inviting Chicagoans Bobby Rush and Fred Hampton, leaders of the radical, revolutionary Black Panthers organization to speak on campus. Their appearance generated more excitement than expected, as Hampton spoke while other Panthers closed and blocked the doors, guarding the room's entrances and preventing any exit. Hampton urged the black students in the audience to arm themselves. Such actions on university property may or may not have violated campus rules and/or state laws, but that did not bother the Panthers. Hampton reminded his mixed audience of the words of Eldridge Cleaver, a celebrated author and early leader of the Black Panther Party. "If you're not part of the solution, you're part of the problem." Then the whites in the room were told to leave, violating university regulations a second time—but again, not a nicety that would bother black revolutionaries. The evening was further enlivened by the Panthers' announced expectation that they would be paid $1,000 by SDS for their appearance, a commitment made, so it was said, by the Chicago SDS office, though no one had so informed the local SDS group.

A report of the meeting appeared in the *DI* the following day and included a firm denial from Vic Berkey of rumors that he had been held captive until a satisfactory speaking fee was negotiated. The veteran SDS leader had spent several hours in a closed-door session discussing the issue with the Panthers, with the aforementioned guards blocking any whites from entering, but, as Berkey explained, "At no time was my life in danger.... Things were happening on a lot of different levels and people got pretty confused." He attributed the rumors of his abduction to "latent racism."[1] It was widely rumored that student-government funds were secured to resolve the issue of the Panthers' speaking fee, but despite an investigation by *DI* reporters, no such impropriety was ever confirmed. In the same week, Peltason revealed yet another new set of campus disciplinary procedures to the board of trustees, tougher this time, with automatic penalties and no appeals "for any action that substantially impedes University operations, substantially interferes with the rights of others or takes place on premises or at times where students are not authorized to be." Since the black revolutionaries from Chicago were not students, their interference with Vic Berkey's rights did not seem covered by the new measures.

Though issues of race were now dominant, the war was not forgotten. In February Vern Fein and junior Mickey Hogan, a star Illini football player, led a crowd of one hundred in protest against the presence of military on campus at a Marine recruiting station in the Union, engaging the officers manning the station in argument over the war, to little effect. Eventually, a group of about twenty broke off from the protest to march to Peltason's office in the English Building, demanding an end to all campus activities in support of the military. The chancellor willingly met with the students and offered them a choice: he could either send their demands to a faculty senate committee for discussion, or the students could elect a small group to schedule an appointment with Peltason at a more convenient time. The group chose the second option and, feeling somewhat victorious, left the building with fists held high, chanting "Death to the ruling class."[2]

That evening, Ekkehart Krippendorff, a visiting professor of political science from West Germany, debated several Illinois faculty on the justifiability of protest violence at an event forum titled "The New Left in Europe and America: Transitional or Revolutionary Phenomenon?" The question presented to the audience was, "Is the New Left justified in using violence to achieve social change?" Krippendorff took the affirmative position; Illinois faculty members of law and political science were opposed. He argued that at times, social destruction can have long-term productive results and that "the violation of due process, law, and order can have some justification in order to correct injustices, and is inevitable at times."[3]

The Illinois law professor, Rubin Cohn, argued vehemently against the idea of attacking institutions of higher learning in order to eliminate injustice and oppression in the larger society. The second Illinois professor, political scientist Norton Long, agreed, suggesting that such institutions do much to move society forward on issues of social justice. Cohn accepted that blacks and other minorities might at times have no alternative to violence in order to successfully bring about social change, but he distrusted the justification of such behavior by white college students, who in his opinion were experiencing little societal oppression. Vic Berkey rose in the audience to take issue with this point, suggesting that white activists, especially those targeted by the government, should be placed in the same category as minorities. The evening, rich in discussion, did not end with any final conclusion, nor was it likely that any minds were changed as a result.

In mid-February, Hogan announced he would be quitting the Illinois football team to "gain more time to address myself to other educational opportunities at the University." A standout defensive tackle on a less-than-standout team (the Illini compiled a 1-9 record and finished eighth in the Big Ten that year), Hogan had become increasingly involved with radical politics during the year. The *DI* reported that the junior might be considering a run for student-body president, and Hogan admitted he was meeting with student leaders to explore the possibility. Fighting Illini coach Jim Valek suggested Hogan's decision had nothing to do with the football program and admitted, "We don't control the players' lives outside the program." Hogan supported the coach, saying, "Quitting had nothing to do with the coaches or the program," and called his football experience "enjoyable and fulfilling," adding that "there was nothing intrinsically wrong with the program except for the time."[4]

The star athlete, whom the Illini Quarterback Club had just days before named lineman of the year, was a psychology major with a 4.7 grade point average and seemed to be looking for meaning in his life somewhere other than on the gridiron. Explaining his decision and his search for additional interests, Hogan said, "It could have been anything from drama to band to sensory training. As it turned out it was student politics—which I guess I should have expected all along." He admitted an interest in the student senate: "I want to learn about it, the structure of it, and I have some ideas about changing it." Speaking of his involvement with left-wing campus politics, he said, "If you're going to understand the campus political scene, you have to understand the stuff that's happening in that faction." He explained his involvement at the recent Marine recruiting station protest by saying, "Something like that action brings facts to the attention of others. I don't support demonstrations as a way to coerce people, but as a means of getting attention to problems just so people will stop and ask themselves, why are these people protesting?" Hogan's action marked him as a one-of-a-kind figure on the campus, a star athlete and member of the Alpha Tau Omega fraternity, now converted to radical politics.[5]

On the same Wednesday that Hogan made his announcement, two hundred white students gathered in the Illini Union south lounge to discuss how to support the BSA's claims of institutional racism, which they felt permeated both the university and the surrounding community. The issue had manifested itself most recently with weekend arrests of nine visiting Chicago Black Panthers by Champaign County police for allegedly not paying their bill at a Rantoul Holiday Inn and the arrest of two other Panthers in the Illini Union for disorderly conduct. In response, BSA had issued a series of demands to the administration, including the removal of Chief Security Officer Tom Morgan from his office and the elimination of civil-service hiring procedures at the university. However, the black students had notably voted against a sit-in to reinforce their point with the university.

Wednesday night, the white students also debated the tactic of a sit-in, with even less enthusiasm than black students had shown the night before. "Sit-ins are really getting to be a stale tactic," judged Michael Rossman, a new face on the campus political scene whom the *DI* described as "a leader in the educational reform movement" at the University of California Berkeley. While briefly enrolled as a grad student at Illinois, Rossman would become a bit of a rival to the established new-left leadership on campus. He suggested that instead of a sit-in, the group could carry out a series of tactics intended to "tie up certain University functions through legal means, by getting administrators to spend a lot of their time talking to individuals about various complaints." Rossman's plan involved students setting up individual meetings with administrators, making repeated phone calls to university offices, and presenting ongoing complaints to their departments. The idea was that these tactics would interfere with the functioning of the university to such a degree that frustrated administrators would finally pay attention to students' issues. The tactic would prove less than effective, as administrators largely ignored the calls and complaints, but the Berkeley veteran managed to convince his audience, claiming "This is simple, clean, humane, honest, and it's legal." Not surprisingly, the unusual idea was not universally applauded, one calling it "the worst form of liberal cop-out . . . [institutional racism] is not an ed reform issue, you can't use ed reform tactics." Another argued, "People want some kind of mass action. Nothing will get done without a sit-in. . . . A sit-in stimulates discussion." One student, claiming to be in contact with black student leaders, announced that the blacks were expecting the white students to sit-in; he suggested, "Whatever you do, it better be good."[6]

The sit-in was voted down 328–32, at which point Vic Berkey proposed an alternative, a march to President David Dodds Henry's home that night, a distance of about a mile from the Union. "We can just take a stroll . . . down Florida

Avenue... get on our knees and tell him our demands." Berkey added, facetiously, "If some of you want to crawl around and say 'grovel, grovel, who are we to ask for power?' that's okay too." Rossman, responding to the laughter at the idea, judged such guerrilla theater brilliant, and said "You all laugh at this, but you don't see what a serious tactic it can be.... [T]here is a whole new beautiful plan in front of you that you don't recognize."[7]

The *DI* reported on the orderly march to the president's home, with the first "grovel-in" on the campus, likely the first and perhaps only time such a tactic would be used in the nation:

> Ten feet from the door of the house, the group fell to its knees. "We are groveling in humility before the president," one protestor said. While the demonstrators remained on their knees, one of the students read a list of demands. Six helmeted University patrolmen, poised at both ends of the driveway and at the door, allowed the protest to progress without interference.
>
> A police spokesman told representatives of the marchers they would be allowed to gather at the president's door as long as traffic was not obstructed, no damage was done, and so long as they remained orderly and confined themselves to the driveway.[8]

After reading their demands, the students stood, gathered in a tight group, and, with fists raised, chanted "Power to the people, fight racism."

The movement for educational reform, which Rossman represented at Berkeley, also had its advocates on the Illinois campus. To its leaders the effort was part of the larger student movement, if more inwardly focused, working within the university system for change, but still perceived by some as every bit as antiestablishment as the outwardly focused, antiwar movement. The leaders of the Illinois education reform group—Patsy Parker, Robert Goldstein, John Hackman, and Marty Shupak, among others—had drawn up a dramatic manifesto, proclaiming, "We the students refuse to be prostituted any longer to the demands of a sick society." They called for "a more flexible University of the future," with "no required courses and no specified curricula," suggesting that "grades also will be abolished" because "grades are responsible for the authoritarian atmosphere in the classroom." The reformers called for students "to have a meaningful role in the decision-making aspects of the university," with "a voice in matters of curricula, admission policies, teacher hiring and criteria, and election of administrators," adding that such participation should be encouraged, and even that students should "receive credits for engaging in expressing that voice."[9] Their manifesto called for:

> Freedom from authoritarian relationships by implementation of an educational style based on dialogue... [that] presents a flexible, ever-changing conception of the University, requiring partnership and dialogue between students and faculty.

This dialogical approach assumes no one can forecast the directions in which a person should grow. An educational style centered on dialogue, rather, prepares a student to act effectively in a wide variety of situations which neither student nor professor can foresee. Most important... this approach to education assumes equality of all participants, students and faculty. This view maintains that a student's curiosity and interest should be as much a determinant of curriculum as the professor's biases about his field.[10]

The Illinois educational reform movement would, over time, have significant influence on the university, with tangible results such as published student evaluations of courses and instructors, an "experimental university" effort with pass/fail classes, and eventually a "Free University," with nearly a thousand students and community members attending classes completely outside the oversight of the administration.

But such positive institutional change was off in the future, and while the Illini students were groveling at the president's home, more direct action was taking place at other schools across the country. Students called a strike at the University of California at Berkeley; police arrested thirty demonstrators, and Governor Ronald Reagan declared a state of emergency on the campus. At Duke, guardsmen were called out after a building takeover, and police shot tear gas canisters into a milling crowd following the twelve-hour occupation of the campus administration building by black students. At the University of Chicago students continued a fifteen-day occupation of a campus building, and the administration announced the suspension of eighty students. At City College of New York, one hundred students occupied their administration building demanding Negro and Puerto Rican studies programs. At the University of Wisconsin at Madison, the governor sent in nine hundred national guardsmen in the midst of a three day boycott of classes called by black students and supported by white radicals. Marshall Colston, a Wisconsin black faculty member, condemned the ongoing Madison strike, saying, "Black demands have become secondary, and the university is being threatened by those who want to destroy it."[11]

The situation continued to heat up at Illinois, but for a variety of reasons it did not boil over. On a Friday afternoon in mid-February, 150 black students marched on Peltason's office in the English Building with a list of sixteen demands intended to end institutional racism at the university. They milled around the office peacefully, careful not to cause damage, break any laws, or even interfere with the secretaries at work. A representative from the chancellor's office made them an offer: if they would leave the building by closing time, 5:00 P.M., he would arrange for their leaders to attend a previously scheduled 5:30 meeting with the Faculty Senate Committee on Student Discipline to present their grievances. The black students accepted the offer, as their primary demand was the removal of all reprimands for the September Illini Union incident, which was under consideration by that very same committee. Additional demands included a larger budget for the BSA, increased black hiring at the university, wage hikes for janitorial and food service staff, establishment of a black culture center, and the creation of a black studies program.

At 5:00 P.M., the black students, now joined by about seventy-five white students, walked in an orderly, single-file column up Wright Street, through the university library, down Sixth Street, and into the Law Building, where the leaders met with the faculty committee and read out their list of demands. They then left the meeting and trekked back to the Union, where they gathered in the south lounge to await the committee's verdict. In time, they received word that the committee, after listening politely to the demands, spent an hour debating and then rejected all the demands, voting to leave the student reprimands in place. The black students were furious. Paul Chandler, newly elected BSA president, announced to the group, "They still think we're bullshitting. They say they cannot agree to the demand, not because they don't have the authority, but because they feel they shouldn't." Doris Whalen, graduate student in law and another BSA leader, said, "This afternoon we tried a rational approach in attaining our demands. We even cleaned up after we left Peltason's office. They had their minds made up.... We are going to show what we want, what we demand and what we are going to get."[12] Another protester pointed out, "A damn thing hasn't happened to the Greeks in over a hundred years and yet the university has a Greek department... The Man is not going to give up easily. Our action is going to extend until we get the things we want."[13]

Tensions festered over the weekend, but Peltason, sensing an opportunity, put the time to good use, conferring with colleagues and developing a plan. On the following Monday he issued an announcement that the university would immediately move to establish a Black Cultural Center under the new dean, Clarence Shelley, and would create a new faculty committee on black student affairs, made up of five white and five black faculty. The chancellor went out of his way to praise the black students for not being coercive with their demands, with an eye to the increasingly violent black student protests spreading across the country. In addition, by the middle of the week he had named a faculty-student committee to make recommendations on a black studies program. But Peltason's proposals fell on deaf ears among the rebellious black students. His ideas were rejected out of hand by former BSA president David Addison, who issued a statement calling the offer of the cultural center especially unacceptable, as the student demand had specifically stipulated that BSA, not the administration, be in charge of the new center. Addison ended his announcement by issuing a new set of demands, upping their list from the original sixteen to forty-one.

Late in February, nine hundred student activists from the United States and Latin America, gathered in Chicago by the Student Mobilization Committee (planners of the previous October's Pentagon demonstration), called for a "world-wide student strike against the war in Vietnam and racism."[14] A black contingent at the convocation, caucusing separately, voted to support the strike. The planned action would correspond with ten days of national antiwar activities scheduled by SDS, labeled "Ten Days to Shake the Empire."

CHAPTER 30

Black and White Together

Illinois legislators did not stand still in the face of such threats to "shake the empire," and most of them did not differentiate between white and black student unrest. The week following the Illinois black students' new demands, the State Senate Education Committee recommended passage of a bill calling for revocation of state scholarships from "student rioters." With a grim tone, "members of the committee cited the threat of communism sweeping across college campuses and said the bill was the first step toward controlling 'revolution, anarchy and chaos.'" In language evocative of the 1950s Red Scare, Senator Dennis Collins of DeKalb declared, "There is a Communist conspiracy going on in our nation today. The leaders are misleading good, well-intentioned students. This is the way they started in foreign nations, and this is the procedure we see on our campuses now." Senator Broyles, rarely outdone in anticommunist sentiment, doubled down on the fear-provoking rhetoric: "We're not dealing with the average, good student, but with students who have been brain-washed, coddled and appeased by the Communist Party. These Communists have a long range plan—and I've been watching it the last 30 years—to obstruct, corrupt and brainwash the minds of our youths."[1] Weeks later the bill would be quashed in committee after four state university presidents, including President Henry, testified against it. Though Illinois's white and black student activists might feel distinctly separated by their race, in the minds of Illinois's conservative legislators, they were all part of the same dire threat to the way of life of central Illinois.

In March, in the last significant campus political event of the spring, a gathering of more than two hundred white student activists, led by a new campus organization formed to educate students on issues of race, Students Against Racism (SAR), gathered in a "student congress" and voted for a campus strike as a demonstration of opposition against institutionalized racism, to coincide with a board of trustees meeting the following day, March 19. SDS members were prominent in the new group, and one, Vic Berkey, realistically admitted, "We are not going to be successful in terms of closing the place down," but at least it would be a signal to the administration that some students "refuse to go to the factory and be molded." Vern Fein added optimistically that the Black Student Association and perhaps even some faculty might be convinced to support the strike.[2]

When the day came, the strike was largely ineffective, but a sizeable group, somewhere between five hundred and seven hundred students, met the trustees' bus at the front doors of the Union with boos, placards, and a few obscene gestures. The crowd then marched around the building, chanting "Power to the people" as the board met inside. The next day, perhaps only coincidentally, the chancellor took the occasion of the board meeting to declare his great satisfaction with the success of Project 500 and announced that the program would be expanded to include seven hundred students the following year. Changes would limit the program to Illinois residents, and the university would take over all recruitment responsibilities from the BSA. When asked about the student success rate, he replied, "They did better than most people thought they would do," and returning to a comparison he had used previously, he likened the five hundred students to disabled students at the university. "We have programs for the physically handicapped. Everybody understands that services for the paraplegics are intended to equalize. That's analogous to what Project 500 is trying to do."[3]

In the final month of the semester, several events occurred that would foreshadow the coming period of increasing frustration and, eventually, campus violence. In the last week of April, the chancellor used his emergency powers to suspend Paul Chandler, BSA president, for involvement in a brawl with white students in a campus dormitory that left three injured. When, in the first week of May, a disciplinary committee expelled Chandler, a new generation of younger SDS radicals, even less interested in negotiating with the administration, took up Chandler's cause. They staged a three-hour sit-in at the president's office, leaving only when threatened with expulsion; they then crossed the street to interrupt a forum headed by Henry himself at the McKinley Foundation, focused on improving the success rate for blacks in higher education. The SDS group stood in unison as their leader read out a list of demands, causing Henry to walk out of the gathering as his audience jeered the protesters. Faculty committees repeatedly turned down Chandler's appeals, and he would later plead guilty in court to a charge of disorderly conduct. Much to the student protesters' frustration, their actions had no effect on Chandler's situation.

In the final week of the term, widespread violence broke out away from campus, as the death of a black prisoner in the Champaign County jail led to several days of arson, firebombing, and shooting on the north sides of Champaign and Urbana; the troubles soon spread to the campus, where unidentified persons set several fires in dormitories and threw Molotov cocktails at fraternity houses. On the second day of the disturbances, a university student, a sophomore in business, was seriously injured when a bomb he was building with a friend in the basement of their fraternity house exploded in his hands. The student lost his left hand and suffered serious damage to both eyes. The bomb makers' motives were never made clear. In response to the general chaos, the university announced a rumor hotline and ordered an early-evening lockdown of all dormitories; the chancellor urged all "members of the University community to remain calm, await the development of facts and avoid hasty judgments or actions." He also strongly suggested that students remain in the dorms whenever possible.[4]

The fearful atmosphere subsided within a few days but was not entirely forgotten as the *DI* editors bid farewell to the school year:

> As a whole, it hasn't been a bad year. . . . [M]any accomplishments . . . many shortcomings, too. But as the year ends, one almost gets the expectation that the future may hold more regression than advancement, and this worries us. . . . [T]he University took a small step toward alleviating social problems . . . Project 500, which has been a learning experience for the University . . . as well as for the students enrolled under the program. . . . [V]isitation was approved, and freshmen women's hours were abolished . . . discrimination was attacked, ineffective systems were thrown out . . . of course, there remain areas that have not progressed. . . . [T]he past year has been neither the best of times nor the worst . . . but . . . generally progressive times, and we are optimistic that next year can be much the same.[5]

The editors' worries would be justified but their optimism would not, as the next school term, the last of the sixties decade, would most resemble the last month of the semester just ended.

Governor Richard Ogilvie spoke at the year's graduation ceremonies and issued a warning that would be relevant to the following year. Though expressing "support for students and their ideals," the *DI* reported, "he warned the graduates that student radicals' actions 'evoke before many of the older generation the haunting memory of Hitler's youthful supporters.'" Then he expressed the threat that reflected both the previous summer's Chicago convention violence and the incoming administration's attitude toward the student movement: "We face quite a different possibility—of action against extremists that becomes repression. What we must seek is not the suppression of dissent but the preservation of the system of law and fair play." President Henry carried on the same theme of support for the Western liberal tradition, emphasizing the role of the university as a constructive social force and adding his own admonition:

> Many students see the university as a mirror of the established order of things, an order which they would like to have changed. But the critics of society's failures, even those whose frustrations over those failures have led them into violence and disruption, have not perceived that the university is also society's means for change and renewal.[6]

Late in the summer, following the Democratic convention, Steve Schmidt was arrested. He relates how it went down:

> By that time they weren't prosecuting people for burning draft cards much, because there was a likelihood the Supreme Court was going to find that to be protected under first amendment freedom of speech, symbolic speech. . . . [Instead,] they decided that what they would do is take away your student deferments and speed up your place in line to be called for induction. That's what they did with me. . . . They sped up my induction, ordered me to induction, I did not go in for induction . . . and then they arrested me. . . . I was out on bail till early summer of '69, then Judge Parsons, presiding, decided I should be sentenced to five years in the slam, the maximum allowable. . . . I was trundled off to Cook County Jail, held for a while . . . till federal marshals took me up to prison in Sandstone, Minnesota, up north of the Twin Cities.[7]

Parsons, an African American, showed no mercy to Schmidt, declaring an acquittal would have been a "tragedy," adding, "His sentence was a message to radical students and to the men in Vietnam who believe in the war to say that their government is not going in with those radicals."[8] For Schmidt, a prime example of a nonviolent critic of society's errors, the government repression that Governor Ogilvie warned of was already quite real.

CHAPTER 31

A Sign of the End: Weathermen Come to Town

In the summer of 1969, SDS, as it had been constituted through the sixties, held its ninth, last, and maddest national convention at the Chicago Coliseum, with more than two thousand attendees. At this rancorous meeting, the conflict that had been festering between the old-left PL types (Progressive Labor) and the self-described action-oriented RYM (Revolutionary Youth Movement) came to a final and chaotic end, as RYM leaders Jeff Jones, Bernardine Dohrn, and Mark Rudd walked off the convention floor with their followers to an adjoining meeting room, where they voted to expel PL and its allies, the Worker Student Alliance (WSA), from SDS, leaving themselves with a smaller, rump organization. Now there were two SDS groups; the rebel group, RYM-SDS, would soon rename itself the Weathermen, taking its name from a line in a Bob Dylan song, "You don't need a weatherman to know which way the wind blows."

In late September, Jones, Dohrn, and Rudd, ostensibly in charge of RYM-SDS and ensconced in the national SDS offices in Chicago, visited the Urbana campus to speak to a large gathering of Illini activists in the Gregory Hall auditorium on the quad. The purpose of the meeting was to recruit students to a "revolutionary action" the Weathermen would call "Days of Rage," scheduled for Chicago, from October 8 to 11. The large lecture hall was packed with people standing in the doorways and sitting in the aisles, and tension filled the air. The trio took the stage together, the guys unkempt, grungy, with long hair and faded jeans, Dohrn, a bit better presented, with longer hair, short skirt, and high leather boots. The three had no prepared remarks and took turns speaking spontaneously, tensely, moving back and forth across the stage, in turn challenging and provoking their audience, declaring that the time had come for revolutionary action. They set out a stark choice to their listeners—either join with them or be labeled part of the problem. "Come to Chicago . . . bring the war home," demanded Jones. "We must take a stand, not by resolutions and long theoretical meetings." He predicted, "There's going to be an armed struggle. . . . That's the way imperialism is going to be defeated: by taking up the gun." After October, prophesied Jones, "the revolution will begin to push onto the campuses and into the communities with the kind of power that we'll learn in Chicago." He envisioned that "people returning from Chicago will push others to take the revolution seriously. . . . If American imperialism has to be destroyed, we have to end it right here: at home." Dohrn and Rudd echoed Jones with more incitement to revolution.[1]

To a few in the audience the speakers' words were exciting, but to others the speakers seemed badly mistaken in their assessment of the movement and the society's readiness for armed struggle. Joseph Hardin, in the audience that night, thinks back on it now: "Their message was way over the top and full of revolutionary guilt, which they tried to use on the audience. . . . A deep sense of revolutionary dread began to steal over me. . . . These guys were harbingers . . . of the desperation that would tear people and the movement up."[2] Vern Fein said: "It was disturbing . . . I had no sense politically that the country wanted a revolution. I had bought into the 'Bring the War Home' slogan . . . but a violent uprising was absurd."[3]

The Weathermen positioned themselves as the vanguard of a new American revolution, in solidarity with fellow revolutionaries in Cuba, Vietnam, and Europe, and with people of color everywhere, oppressed by the villain of U.S. imperialism. The three had not come to the campus for political discussion; they were making a straightforward statement of their plans and demanding support from their fellow activists. It was hard not to be enthralled by the spectacle they presented, and one or two in the audience shouted encouragement, but few seriously considered the Weathermen's challenge, and some scrunched low in their seats, exchanging nervous glances. "The time has come to take back the streets," Jones shouted from the stage. Though many of the campus activists might theoretically have favored some sort of revolutionary change in American society, most had higher priorities at the moment, such as graduating from college. Some thought back to the violence of the convention, Chicago police and the guardsmen, and the overwhelming show of force unleashed on them and their peers; they slumped lower in the seats. As the evening ended and the students filed out, many shook their heads, their eyes downcast.

To many of the Illinois activists who had challenged the university administration two years earlier for the right of a communist to speak on campus and only a year earlier had placed their college careers in jeopardy by sitting in against

Dow, the folks on stage, talking violent revolution the very next month in Chicago, were out of touch with reality. Even if the students might agree with the revolutionaries' analysis, few could embrace the proposed path forward. The Weathermen had drawn a line and asked others to cross it, but most would not. A few weeks later Dohrn issued a public "declaration of war" against the United States government, in the name of the Weathermen, who would, in October, create disturbances on the streets of Chicago for a few days, then get themselves arrested and released before going underground. A few Illini would choose to follow the Weathermen into the October debacle and would be arrested, or injured or disillusioned as a result. Today it is difficult to understand what drove these extremists to such tactics, but in a 2002 documentary, *The Weather Underground*, Rudd attempted an explanation:

> The part of the Weatherman phenomenon that was right was our understanding of what the position of the United States [was and] is in the world. It was this knowledge that we just couldn't handle; it was too big. We didn't know what to do. In a way I still don't know what to do with this knowledge. I don't know what needs to be done now, and it's still eating away at me just as it did thirty years ago.

A week following the Days of Rage, the Illinois campus SDS (or what was left of it, as membership had been dwindling) voted to withdraw from the national organization and form a new "issue-oriented" group to be known as the Radical Union (RU). A spokesperson for the new group, Ted Byers, claimed between twenty-five and forty members and said the decision to dissociate from the national was based on two criticisms: "Its 'adventuristic politics' and its 'absolute orders.' . . . They lay out a political ideology and if you don't conform, you're a pig, a fascist. . . . You either go along with the national office or you get out. We decided to get out," he said, adding, "It shouldn't be like that, but it is." He mentioned that the RU would be supporting a nationwide moratorium against the war in mid-October and suggested that such an effort, in sharp contrast to the extremism of RYM-SDS, would be "not a radical thing," but a peaceful effort "in hopes of getting mass support . . . a broad-based coalition."[4] Two days after the RU announcement, the faculty senate voted down a motion to suspend classes on the day of the moratorium, with Chemistry Department head Herbert Gutowsky speaking out forcefully against the idea, claiming such a move would be a violation of his and others' academic freedom and grounds for an AAUP censure. Instead, the senate agreed on a symbolic thirty-minute suspension of classes on the day, a measure quickly approved by the chancellor. Peltason had also opposed the full-day cancellation, taking the by-now-familiar position, "It was not appropriate for the university to take a stand on the war issue."[5]

On the day of the moratorium (October 15, 1969), the *DI* published a blank front page with the headline "DI Halts Business as Usual in Support of Moratorium."

The inside pages were dedicated to the antiwar events scheduled for the day, a detailed history of the movement on the Illinois campus, articles and editorials condemning the war, and a large photo from the previous year of Steve Schmidt and Rick Soderstrom burning their draft cards on the back patio of the Union. City police estimated that nine thousand people marched from the Illini Union to Westside Park in Champaign, eight to ten across, in a crowd that stretched for fifteen blocks. There they heard Lee Weiner, a member of the Chicago Eight (antiwar activists facing trial in Chicago on charges of conspiracy to incite violence at the Democratic convention), among others, speak against the war. The crowd gave a standing ovation for Schmidt, in absentia, as he was then residing in federal custody in Sandstone, Minnesota.

The Champaign marchers were part of more than one million people who marched worldwide that day in opposition to the war. Richard Nixon's response came at the end of the month when, in a primetime broadcast from the Oval Office, he announced to the nation that, in consultation with the South Vietnamese government, he had prepared a secret plan for ending the war in Vietnam, including an equally secret timetable for withdrawal of American troops. The president addressed his remarks not to the moratorium marchers but to the nation's "silent majority," and he thanked them for their ongoing support of his policies. "Let us be united for peace," he said. "Let us also be united against defeat. Because let us understand: North Vietnam cannot defeat or humiliate the United States. Only Americans can do that."[6] The next day a *DI* editorial condemned the speech, calling it "little more than an attempt to keep [the president's] own popularity through organizing a repressive, reactionary atmosphere at home against those who would force him to stop his immoral war-waging abroad."[7] As the DI editorial showed, antiwar sentiment was no longer a radical position, either in the United States or on the Illinois campus. The previous year, Walter Cronkite, television's most popular evening news broadcaster, had come out against the war. By fall 1969, a majority of Americans felt the war was a mistake, including nearly two-thirds of those over age fifty.[8] Questioning the rectitude of the war by now was a mainstream position. But Vern Fein saw the moratorium as "the last gasp of the peacenik faction," and labeled it a definite turning point on the Illinois campus toward a more violent approach by some students.[9]

On November 13 the national moratorium organizers responded to Nixon's "secret plan," first with a "March of Death," a single-file, silent walk of forty thousand people in the nation's capital, each carrying a placard with the name of a dead American soldier or a destroyed Vietnamese village. The silent march lasted all day Thursday and late into the night Friday, down Pennsylvania Avenue, past the White House, and ending at the Capitol, where protesters deposited the placards in makeshift coffins. The next day, November 15, saw the largest protest march in the nation's history to that point, with more than half a million participants. Three hundred students and faculty from the University of Illinois rode eight buses to the march, while others traveled on their own, some in Volkswagen buses caravanning across the country. Nixon said of the march, "Now, I understand that there has been, and continues to be, opposition to the war in Vietnam on the campuses and also in the nation. As far as this kind of activity is concerned, we expect it; however, under no circumstances will I be affected whatever by it." Comedian Dick Gregory responded aptly to Nixon: "The President of the United States said nothing you young kids would do would have any effect on him. Well, I suggest . . . if he wants to know how much effect you youngsters can have on the President, he should make one long distance phone call to the LBJ ranch and ask that boy how much effect you can have."[10]

In Chicago, in the first week of December, Black Panther leader Fred Hampton was murdered by officers of the Cook County State's Attorney, with two shots fired point-blank to the head as he slept in his bed in an apartment on the west side of Chicago alongside his pregnant fiancée. A second Panther, Mark Clark, was also slain. Police officers claimed the Panthers had shot first, engaging them in a shootout, but years of civil lawsuits would reveal that only one shot was fired by the victims of what could more accurately be described as a massacre by police. On campus, the BSA organized a one-day boycott of classes and a memorial march in Hampton's honor, walking from the quad through the north end of Champaign and back to campus. The march was made up of blacks only, three hundred strong, and was orderly, but tempers were short, with chants of "No more brothers in jail. . . . The revolution has come, time to pick up your gun."[11]

In the third week of December, the Champaign FBI office announced the arrests of graduate student and DRU leader Ron Lucas; twenty-two-year-old senior Laurie McCarthy, partner of Steve Schmidt; and thirty-nine-year-old Jocelyn Werry, wife of university professor John Werry, charging them with aiding, abetting, and harboring a deserter, Lynn Ellington, from the U.S. Marines. Schmidt, then serving his own sentence in a federal prison, was also named in the indictment. McCarthy and Werry were arrested at their homes in the morning by federal agents; Lucas was picked up later in the day at the Illini Union. Arraigned in federal court in Danville, the three had bonds set at one thousand dollars each; students and faculty quickly gathered contributions and rushed the money to Danville in time to free the accused the same day. Later, the charges would be quietly dropped after the government determined there were insufficient grounds to prosecute Ellington on the desertion charge. But at the time, the threat of charges against McCarthy, Werry, and Lucas, punishable by fines and a prison term, felt ominous.

This incident was not the only campus action in support of deserters. The presence of an Air Force base in nearby Rantoul, Illinois, provided numerous opportunities. David Ransel related one such action:

> This activity had to be kept quiet as you can imagine. . . . We had a safe house in C-U where deserters from Rantoul would be kept until we could arrange transport to Canada. A husband and wife from New Zealand provided one of the safe houses (I don't know if there were others but there probably were). I recall taking two of these deserters in the dead of winter, along with Steve [Schmidt] and Laurie [McCarthy], in my car up to Toronto. We had Canadians on the other side who would alert us to the times and places for safe border crossings. Some of the Canadian border guards were not friendly, others were. So, we had to be careful for the deserters and for ourselves.[12]

Ransel remembers the courage of Laurie McCarthy with particular irony: "Her dad was on the Red Squad in Chicago," an infamous unit of the Chicago police force that for much of the twentieth century unlawfully targeted alleged subversives in the Windy City. "Her brother had been a football player at Illinois, then got into the Secret Service and was shot when Reagan was shot" during the 1981 presidential assassination attempt that left Press Secretary James Brady permanently disabled. "And she was dating Steve," Ransel recalls, shaking his head. "Explain her—she comes from a family like that yet she ends up becoming a really important part of the movement."[13]

The day following their release, McCarthy and Werry marched with three hundred demonstrators to the Champaign Federal Building, demanding an end to the war, an end to the draft, and an end to university complicity with the military. The day after that, two hundred Illinois students traveled to Springfield to join an antiwar march to the State Capitol Building, demanding, yet again, an end to the war. The students were joined by hundreds of Springfield residents. Such antiwar sentiment in Illinois's conservative capital city indicated how widespread the antiwar movement had become. Growth in the movement was stimulated at the time by widespread publication of the investigative reporting of Seymour Hersh and grisly pictures in *Time* and *Life* magazines of a shocking massacre of hundreds of unarmed Vietnamese civilians, including men, women, children, and infants, perpetrated by American troops at a small village called My Lai. It seemed to those in the movement that an end to the war must surely come soon. But although an end of sorts would appear shortly, it would not be the end anyone expected.

CHAPTER 32

Spring '70: The Final Semester

The beginning of the end of the sixties student protest movement was to come not with a whimper but with a bang—many bangs—when Ohio National Guardsmen shot and killed four peaceful protesters at Kent State University; a cathartic, violent, nationwide cry of protest ensued, and soon after the movement effectively came to an end. But as the 1969–70 spring semester began, there was no hint that such a dramatic finish was at hand, as the new year felt much like the old, with no particular significance attached to the close of a decade. In Vietnam the combat raged on, in Washington Nixon still promised to "end the war with honor," in Urbana protesters still protested, and not very much seemed to have changed.

Many of the students who had entered college in the mid-1960s, as the antiwar movement took center stage, began to ponder life after graduation with a certain apprehension. None of the soon-to-be graduates could expect that their college careers and the student movement would come to a close together, much less in the unprecedented confluence of mayhem that was soon to materialize—an invasion, dead students, widespread rioting, and a serious right-wing political reaction. The invasion would be in faraway Cambodia, the riots would be on campuses across the country, and the coming right-wing wave, in part a reaction to the radical sixties, would last for decades. This is how their movement would end.

In early January a new issue arose for the students to consider, as the university announced the Illiac IV project, a new, powerful supercomputer to be installed on the campus, paid for by the Department of Defense (DoD) and operated "approximately two-thirds of the time" for DoD purposes, one-third for university research. Of greatest concern to antiwar students, the new machine would "play a vital role in the development of more sophisticated nuclear weaponry." The words "nuclear weaponry" figured prominently in large type headlining the front-page *DI* story, adding to the article's ominous tone. Such an announcement, at the time of virulent antiwar feelings on the campus, would not be accepted lightly, and a more blatant example of university complicity with the nation's military-industrial complex was hard to imagine.[1]

Hinting at today's internet, Daniel Slotnick, professor of computer science and director of the project, said the new computer would be tied into the Defense Department's Advanced Research Project Agency (ARPA) computer network, connecting Illinois researchers with peers at MIT, Stanford, and UCLA. Slotnick admitted that the new machine could well "make possible vastly more horrible and powerful weapons systems. . . . But . . . the project was justified in spite of these factors." The professor added sarcastically, "If I could have gotten $30 million from the Red Cross I would not have messed with the DOD," and emphasized that the new computer would, in the university's share of time, "be used for solving problems of ecology and economic and agricultural planning."[2]

Within days, a new group of younger faculty, Faculty for University Reform (FUR), formed to publicly condemn the project. They passed an aggressive resolution, which Phillip Meranto, assistant professor of political science had proposed; it stated, "FUR is opposed to (the presence of Illiac IV on campus) as long as it is funded by the Department of Defense in any way, and will take any means to keep it from operating." Defenders of the project replied, "The name of our game is to make a better world. . . . [R]ight now the DOD is the only one with that much money. . . . Either they set it up here and we get one-third of the computer time for our purposes, or they set it up somewhere else and the military gets three-thirds."[3]

The Radical Union was only a day behind FUR in issuing equally aggressive demands for the immediate cancellation of Illiac IV and, for good measure, an end to the university's ROTC program as well. The RU statement, delivered to the offices of both the president and chancellor, threatened, as had FUR, that "any means necessary will be used to accomplish the demands," though RU members admitted that "the 'means' haven't been worked out yet" and that "tactics are in a state of evolving."[4] Henry's office ignored the demands, while Peltason, acknowledging he had received them, had no response.

The following day, two youths—Larry Allan Voss, a sophomore university student in a wheelchair, and a high school student—were arrested after two firebombs were tossed through the window of the Champaign Police Department, causing first-degree burns to the arm and face of one officer. Voss was one of a group of ten who had recently split off from the RU, forming a campus faction in support of the SDS Weathermen. The two were apprehended less than a block from the station and identified as the perpetrators by eyewitnesses. Though no one offered an official motive for the attack, the incident demonstrated the rising level of violence some activists advocated. When contacted, Voss's mother claimed that her son was "an excellent student... never been in trouble before." She added that in a call to her he had denied any involvement in the incident, and that to her knowledge, "he belonged to no radical groups."[5] The Champaign Police Department soon began work to permanently brick up windows on the first floor of their downtown office facing busy University Avenue.

In other signs of the times, the Chicago-based RYM-SDS/Weathermen, reported they had held "War Councils" in Flint, Michigan, and Atlanta, Georgia, that each had drawn crowds of more than three hundred; the group now claimed a national membership of more than one thousand. The other SDS, East Coast–based PL-SDS (the faction dominated by the Progressive Labor party), not to be outdone, announced attendance at their national council meeting in New Haven, Connecticut, as more than seven hundred. Claiming that membership in their faction had soared during the previous months since the SDS split, a spokesperson added, "The organization is stronger now than ever before."[6] These competing SDS units disagreed intensely about timing, tactics, and strategy, but both believed that a violent American revolution was necessary and inevitable. The political space for a middle path of peaceful protest continued to wither, squeezed between increasingly dug-in establishment authorities and progressively violent, youthful revolutionaries.

In the final week of February, a firebomb was thrown into the ROTC lounge in the university Armory, though it caused no damage to property or persons. That same night, Dr. Benjamin Spock, nationally known pediatrician and author of the nation's perennially bestselling baby and child care book, now turned civil rights and antiwar advocate, spoke on campus. Jocelyn Werry, of the recent aiding-and-abetting charges, introduced him. Spock, frequently interrupted by applause, told the crowd, "We have to stick together in these terrible times," warning, "Things will get worse before they get better." The famous baby doctor/author reminded his audience that "the Declaration of Independence states that if people cannot get justice through legal means, they are entitled to cause a revolution. I have no philosophical objection to revolution if other methods have been tried." However, quickly raining on the parade of his cheering audience, he added, "Anybody who tries to start a revolution today would be reduced to a grease spot in two or three days."[7] Others disagreed; in the United States between January 1969 and April 1970, "radicals bombed five thousand police stations, corporate offices, military facilities, and campus buildings set aside for the Reserve Officers' Training Corp."[8] As even baby doctors were now contemplating the possibility of violent revolution, at Illinois and across the nation, hopes for a peaceful middle path continued to diminish.

CHAPTER 33

March: Patience Spent, the Storms Begin

The spring outbreak of violence on the nation's campuses that would mark the end of the movement began early at Illinois. In the first week of March the campus experienced three days of rioting, beginning on Monday, March 3, when representatives of General Electric (GE), perhaps the largest Vietnam War defense contractor, arrived on campus for employee recruiting. This time there was no talk of a peaceful sit-in, though the tactic had successfully stopped the Dow interviews only a year before. The sit-in now seemed a relic of a quite distant past. On Sunday night before the planned Monday demonstrations, the movie *Battle of Algiers*, documenting the violent struggle of Algerians fighting against French colonialism, was shown in the Auditorium to a large audience, adding to the intense feelings on campus. Disorganized mayhem would be the students' primary strategy with this military supplier, and by end of day Monday, the first of three days of riotous demonstrations, police would have nineteen students and two nonstudents behind bars, charged with various counts of mob action, resisting arrest, disorderly conduct, fleeing police, illegal entry, and criminal damage to state-owned property.[1]

Monday's turmoil began after a noon gathering called by the Radical Union to rail against GE's presence. The rally led to a loose march on the Electrical Engineering Building (EEB), where the recruiting interviews were to take place. Police attempted to seal the building, but protesters managed to find a way in via a second-floor fire escape. Once inside, the crowd broke office windows; police chased down protesters and made arrests as scuffles erupted throughout the building. The crowd then moved on to the chancellor's office, where more windows were broken before

John Scouffas, associate dean of students, and Lloyd Berry, assistant to the chancellor, came out to talk. The protesters demanded that those arrested be released immediately and that GE be banned from campus. Berry only irritated the crowd by reiterating the university's standard policy of open recruitment. The crowd, growing larger and angrier, then marched off into the middle of Green Street, stopping traffic and confronting police, who arrived quickly. A street-theater showdown between police and students followed, lasting two hours, with more arrests and ongoing scuffles, until the group finally dispersed.

Monday evening, at 7:30, the RU held another rally, followed by another march on the now-dark-and-empty EEB, where a few more windows were broken; then the crowd moved into Green Street and marched through Campustown. Here, storefronts up and down the street suffered broken windows, with Follett's Bookstore and McBride's Drug Store particularly favorite targets, as popular sentiment held these the worst of the price-gouging Campustown businesses. The crowd repeatedly clashed with Champaign police, who eventually forced the marchers back into the general area of the quad, where more windows were broken, trashcans overturned, and parking meters destroyed. The mob roamed the campus until nearly 10:30, when an emergency curfew, agreed upon by the university and both cities, was declared and announced with bullhorns, bringing quiet to the area.

Earlier in the afternoon the board of trustees had played a not insignificant role in stoking the students' anger. Against the recommendations of President Henry, Chancellor Peltason, and Vice Chancellor George Frampton, the trustees had voted to cancel a scheduled appearance on campus by William Kunstler, the lead defense attorney for the Chicago Eight. Kunstler, a radical lawyer and devoted civil rights campaigner, was well respected on the left for defending many of the nation's best-known activists and had been characterized by the *New York Times* as "the country's most controversial and, perhaps, its best-known lawyer."[2] Adding such a controversial figure to the already tense campus seemed to the trustees imprudent at best, incendiary at worst. In response to the previous day's violence, they had hastily pulled together an unprecedented emergency meeting at the LaSalle Hotel in Chicago that lasted for three hours, with attendees receiving regular updates by telephone of the afternoon's incidents. Even Governor Ogilvie announced he would join the meeting, but his plane was unable to leave the Springfield airport due to heavy fog. After lengthy discussion, the trustees finally voted that Kunstler's presence on the campus would present "a clear and present danger" to the safety of the campus and moved to cancel the appearance. Henry, at first opposed to the move, by end of day had come around to support the trustees' decision as the disturbances of the evening ground on. "Naturally I am an optimist and thought things might get better. But in view of the actions tonight, I am less convinced about that than I was this afternoon."[3] As if to validate Henry's qualms, two firebombs, glass bottles filled with flammable liquid, with cigarette fuses, were found in Altgeld Hall.

Tuesday showed little improvement. An afternoon demonstration at a U.S. Navy recruiting station in the Union led to an order to clear the building, and impatient state troopers, newly arrived on campus for the first time ever, moved in, shoving and clubbing resisting students. The Union was closed for two hours. That evening, a rally on the quad led to a peaceful march of what the DI reported as an "enormous line of demonstrators . . . approximately 4,500" that moved from the quad down the middle of Urbana city streets to President Henry's house on Florida Avenue.[4] Unusual for him, Vic Berkey, not known for dispersing protest groups, urged the crowd to go home for the evening, likely sensing another night of rioting and police reaction, but the march proceeded. After spending a relatively calm hour listening to speakers outside Henry's home, between two thousand and three thousand broke away and began a march toward the Armory but were intercepted by local police and state troopers on the way. The crowd then separated into smaller groups and spread through the campus, breaking windows, with McBride's again a target and several other campus stores also hit; police made another eight arrests.

Three hundred members of the Illinois National Guard appeared on the streets at 10:00 P.M. to enforce the continuing curfew. The guardsmen carried gas masks, tear gas, and unloaded rifles. Bayonets were fixed to the rifles, though the guard commander, Brigadier General Richard T. Dunn, blithely told reporters, "I do not foresee use of them." Dunn did express some concern about his troops: "A lot of recruits are here, and we don't know how effective they'll be," words that would be recalled with some dread later, following the Kent State killings.[5] This was the first of several nights of tense face-offs between the students and the guardsmen during a nearly week-long occupation of the campus. David Ransel remembers a shrewd gesture by Belden Fields, a professor in political science, who intervened between the students and the equally young guardsmen during one of the confrontations:

> A few of us professors got out to the street and placed ourselves between the line of armed guardsmen and the mass of students. Belden had the presence of mind to realize that the young guardsmen, who were largely rural youngsters, were probably as fearful of the students as the students may have been of them. Belden asked us to go up to the lines of guardsmen, identify ourselves and assure them that the students meant them no harm and that they could relax and calmly observe the protest. The students would not attack them. This was smart and courageous on Belden's part and helped prevent nervous recruits from accidentally drawing the wrong conclusions and firing.[6]

Ransel recollected another example of Fields's influence in that hectic week. At a demonstration at the chancellor's office, "some of the protesters got unruly and threatened to break the windows and glass doors. Belden had the courage to call out to them that if anyone tried that, he was out of there. Things calmed down.... Belden was not a radical. He was more of a liberal but very much opposed to our foreign policy" and, at the same time, quite rightly "concerned that the protests could get out of hand and cause injury."[7]

Chancellor Peltason published a letter in the *DI* on Wednesday, strongly condemning events of the week. "I am appalled at the destructive turn of events... and the irresponsible behavior of a small group of our students protesting the appearance of General Electric recruiters on the Urbana-Champaign campus." Peltason commended law enforcement authorities and asked everyone to assist "to restore normalcy to the campus." He ended cryptically: "We are all aware of the seriousness of the situation and are exploring every alternative in alleviating the crisis."[8] The paper's editorial for the day, published next to the chancellor's letter, hit closer to the mark with its assessment: "The incidents of the past two days drive home even harder here, where no one ever thought violence would come, that change, if it is to ever come through peaceful means, must come quickly, for both left and right are quickly becoming polarized to a point where violence will become commonplace."

On Wednesday, a third night of campus rioting brought out the entire assigned contingent of 750 Illinois National Guardsmen, with gas masks donned but bayonets sheathed. In the evening a two-hour march of nearly two thousand protesters wound its way around the campus, with a smaller amount of rock throwing and window smashing than in previous nights, though windows were broken at the Illinois Bell building and the Armory, and a police car windshield was broken. A student-government representative attempted to calm the crowd but was shouted down by Michael Parenti, a visiting professor of political science from Yale University, where he had been a radical leader in the antiwar movement. Parenti called the student rep "a half-assed liberal pushing for representation in a powerless group," then urged the crowd on—"To the Armory!"[9] Another self-described revolutionary, Frank Balanger, rationalized the shift to violence: "People don't understand the issues that are involved. GE and the whole corporation complex is getting obscured with Kunstler, free speech and cops on campus. We've learned that a sit-in is not enough.... The first duty of a revolutionary is to make a revolution and the second is not to get caught." RU member Harriet Spiegel offered her perspective: "We've learned that the only thing that will end oppression is a material attack on the system.... This campus will never be the same." By 10:30 the crowd had dwindled to three hundred diehards, and the guardsmen marched into the crowd, breaking it into smaller groups. Police began rounding up those remaining, herding them onto buses that carried them to a nearby station, where they were given curfew-violation citations then sent home for the night.

By week's end, President Henry had expressed his "shock," Chancellor Peltason his "sadness," and the trustees their "warnings of clear and present danger," but remarkably, at the time, few articulated what seems obvious in hindsight. After years of peaceful protest against what the students considered an unjust, immoral, and illegal war, with an unresponsive government and a university perceived as complicit with the war, the protesters' well of patience was running dry. By this point, the great majority of students at Illinois and other campuses were opposed to the war and wanted it ended. Though committed revolutionaries such as Parenti, Balanger, and Spiegel represented only a tiny minority advocating violence, widespread frustration was spreading through the movement, both at Illinois and nationally, and anger was building toward any and all figures of establishment authority.

CHAPTER 34

April: Quiet between the Storms

The GE protests represented the most violent period in the hundred-year history of the University of Illinois to that point. But by the following week, GE was gone and the campus experienced a relative calm—only to be disrupted the week after when someone tossed a firebomb through a window at the Federal Building in downtown Champaign; fortunately, there were no injuries and only minor damage. A midweek rally on the steps of the Auditorium developed into a heated debate regarding the justification of violence between Parenti and Richard Boghartz, assistant professor of psychology, the latter suggesting that rioting would only increase President Nixon's popularity and bring more police and repression to campus. John Lee Johnson, in the unusual position of referee, intervened and counseled the debaters and the audience that they needed to learn more about the actual workings of the university before they could expect to influence it.

The Radical Union held several meetings to continue their attacks on the Illiac project, while Slotnick and his team continued to defend it. Interminable faculty and student senate discussions were held on the week's violence. A group of law students rescheduled Kunstler's appearance, "with or without university approval." Another firebomb, failing to ignite, was discovered in Lincoln Hall; one that did ignite was thrown through a broken window of the Air Force Recruiting Station in Urbana, spreading fire and virtually destroying the office, causing more than one hundred thousand dollars in damages to the building and adjoining structures. Roger Simon, *DI* columnist, shared his thoughts on the growing anarchy:

Nobody is in charge of the University anymore. Competing groups roam around grabbing parts of the action. The Board of Trustees grabs a chunk, the governor grabs a chunk, the mayors of Champaign and Urbana and the county sheriff take a chunk, and the kids in the street make a bid, too. President Henry and Chancellor Peltason are pretty well ignored by all the other groups. . . .

This University is being run by men who deplore violence rather than embracing justice, who send troops to preserve peace rather than making troops unnecessary, and who will smash the skulls of their students to preserve the property and "rights" of businessmen. It is not rocks that make violence, but rather, men, fat with power, who will not make this University, this nation, and this world responsive to the people who populate it.

Anything but change. Anything but that. . . . never give in. Hold that line.[1]

By week's end the chancellor announced that due to a new state law, the twenty-six students arrested during the week's disorder would lose their scholarships if found guilty of charges filed against them. Though he had argued against the bill as it passed through the legislature, Peltason said simply, "We have to comply with it now that it is law."[2] Representative Clabaugh, still in office, applauded the chancellor's statement, adding, "The only way you're going to cure these punks is to cut off their financial aid."[3]

On March 19, President David Dodds Henry announced his retirement to the board of trustees. Nearing age sixty-five, Henry told the trustees, "I believe that I should change to a less demanding work schedule." The role of university president in this era was extremely challenging; Henry and his peers faced great pressure from all sides—the legislature, the board, students, faculty, parents, newspaper editors, and the general public. Earlier in the decade the president of Indiana University had coined the term "presidential fatigue" when announcing his resignation, as he moved to a less stressful position as head of the National Audubon Society.[4] Henry suggested that the change in personnel at Illinois might bring a new outlook to the campus, hopefully improving the tense student-administration relations. James Eggleston, BSA spokesperson, disagreed, issuing a statement that likely reflected the thoughts of many activists, black and white: "In relationship to the entire system, the resignation of David Dodds Henry does not really make much difference. The system will only choose another racist to take his place in the machinery."[5] Clabaugh denied any influence in Henry's decision and added, "I don't blame any college president for wanting to get out as quick as he can."[6]

In the last week of the month, with trustees finally lifting their ban, William Kunstler was allowed to appear on campus, at Assembly Hall, to a cheering crowd of more than six thousand. The intrepid defender of the Chicago Eight declared his position on violence: "No one would say he desires violent revolution when there are alternatives. We are in an age now where there are alternatives." But he warned, "We have reached a period of time where these alternatives are beginning to vanish."[7] The same week, one student who had chosen such a nonviolent alternative, Steve Schmidt, was freed from federal prison after the U.S. Supreme Court ruled that draft boards had exceeded their powers in punitively drafting persons who had allegedly violated Selective Service regulations.

Relatively speaking, April was a quiet month. The world watched entranced as Apollo astronauts managed to repair a disabled spacecraft and return to earth. Vice President Spiro Agnew warned that America's college students were being swept away "on the wave of the new socialism." Major antiwar disruptions took place at Columbia, Harvard, Penn State, and the University of Kansas. The first annual Earth Day was celebrated with gatherings across the country, and the liberal mayor of New York shut down Fifth Avenue for the day. The government of Cambodia was reported to have asked the United States for aid in dealing with North Vietnamese soldiers based in their country.

At Illinois, undergraduate Jim Larabee, one of the Weathermen-SDS faction on campus, was called to testify at a hearing on the March disturbances. He presciently predicted that worse riots were in store for the university "in a week or two, or a month." In his opinion, the disturbances were "a protest against the network that holds power in the United States and the way that power has been used." He added other reasons for the troubles, including, "a conspiracy between the University and GE, the protection of GE by military power, and 'hippie nationalism'."[8] Later in the week Larabee would be among nine students arrested in a "Festival for Life," an attempted "liberation" of the campus Armory during a ROTC activity. The festive student troupe, carrying a large black flag with "YIPPIE" printed on it, danced and sang and ran in circles around the assembled, uniformed ROTC cadets.[9]

At the end of the month, a "blue ribbon national committee," the Special Committee on Campus Tensions, created by the American Council on Education to identify and analyze the causes of unrest on U.S. campuses published their report, which concluded, "Campus turmoil is not likely to cease unless genuine progress is made toward curing social ills." The committee, composed of "present and former high-level college administrators, students, a university trustee, faculty members, and prominent private citizens," worked for eight months to discover the causes of campus disorder. The report's anticlimactic recommendation was that colleges should increase and improve communication among students, faculty, administrators, and trustees. Not optimistically, the report warned that conditions were likely to get worse before they got better. "Until the nation ceases to force young men to fight in a war they believe unjust, a major source of campus tensions will remain."[10]

CHAPTER 35

May: The Final Month

The final stage of the Illinois student protest movement played out with the two imperatives of the decade interwoven—the treatment of black Americans by the dominant white society, and the anguishing, seemingly never-ending calamity of the war in Southeast Asia. The final drama began on the last day of April.

Edgar Hoults was a young black resident of north Urbana, a 1965 high-school graduate from a small town in southern Illinois across the river from St. Louis, Missouri. Following high school Edgar wed his wife, Alice, after a three-and-half-year courtship during which, according to his father, Ulys, neither dated any others. After marrying, the couple moved several times as Edgar searched for steady work, and when he found a job as a security guard at Follett's Bookstore on the Illinois campus, he and Alice finally began to feel settled. Edgar's father would tell reporters his son "did not drink, smoke, curse or stay out late at night. . . . He went bowling sometimes with some of the men at work but usually stayed home with his family and they all watched television together."[1] In 1970 Edgar was twenty-three years old, Alice twenty-one. They had two small children, and Alice was pregnant with a third.

In the last week of April, after a recent firebombing at the bookstore, Edgar was asked to work all-night shifts at Follett's to help protect the store. As he worked through the night, Alice slept in the upstairs bedroom of their north-end duplex apartment. Early one morning, she awoke suddenly to the sounds of "sirens, racing automobiles and men running." She got up from bed, thinking that it was nearly time for her husband to return from work. As she looked out the front window of her home, hoping to see him arriving, she heard a gunshot at the rear of the house. When she opened the back door, she saw her husband face down in a field of grass, bleeding. "I started shaking and crying," she said. She attempted to go to her husband but was held back by neighbors. She saw Edgar lifted into an ambulance, and that was the last she would see of him until shown his body at a local funeral home. No police came to her to talk about the shooting; no city official visited to explain the killing to her and her children.

The next day's newspapers reported that Hoults had been shot in the back, killed by Champaign police after a high-speed chase that began on campus in the alley behind the bookstore, ran through north Champaign, and ended in the empty field in northeast Urbana behind his family home. The chase had begun early in the morning as Hoults drove away from the store, having finished his shift. Police would later report that they could not determine any reason Hoults might have fled from police except that he was driving with an expired driver's license. The manager of Follett's characterized the young man as a "good and loyal employee" and announced a pledge of one thousand dollars from the store to the family of the deceased, a family that now consisted of the widowed, pregnant Alice and her two small children.

The day the story ran, more than one hundred university students staged an impromptu march from campus to the downtown Champaign police station; they demanded details of the killing but were rebuffed by city manager Warren Browning, who advised, "Don't pass judgment till you know all the facts."[2]

In the second thread of this final act, that same day a White House statement was released, announcing that American advisers would be accompanying South Vietnamese army troops on an offensive excursion into Cambodia, striking at North Vietnamese supply camps. The announcement said that President Richard Nixon would deliver a television broadcast to the nation that evening to explain this major departure from previous policy.

That night, at the Champaign city office, the North End Ministers' Alliance attended an emergency city council session, calling for the resignation of Chief of Police Harvey Shirley for Hoults' killing, a ban on police use of the type of bullet that killed him, and the immediate hiring of twenty blacks into the city's all-white police force. Sporadic gunfire was heard in the distance while the meeting ran, and the shooting would continue throughout the evening in northeast Champaign and on the north side of the campus. Fires broke out sporadically across both cities, and firemen chased false alarms all night. A spokesperson for the ministers summed up the blacks' feelings: "The black community doesn't trust the city council or the police department."[3]

As the ministers were speaking to the council, President Nixon was speaking to the American people in his nationally televised broadcast from the Oval Office. The "advisers" entering Cambodia, Nixon now explained, were actually several thousand U.S. combat troops supported by B-52 "Stratofortress" bombers, air cavalry helicopter gunships, and covering artillery. With baffling logic, Nixon looked into the cameras and stated bluntly, "This is not an invasion of Cambodia.... We take this action not for the purpose of expanding the war into Cambodia but for the purpose of ending the war in Vietnam and winning the just peace we all desire."[4]

Back in Champaign, as the city council meeting ended, the city manager released a statement identifying patrolman Fred Eastman as the policeman who shot and killed Hoults; Eastman was now relieved of duty pending an investigation. In his statement, the *DI* reported Eastman claimed "he slipped and lost his balance as he pulled his revolver from his holster, causing the gun to discharge."[5] Hoults had been brought down by a .38-caliber hollow-point "dumdum" bullet, shot from behind as he left his car and ran from police. Such exploding bullets were not standard issue for the Champaign police force; patrolman Eastman had purchased the shells himself. That night five people were shot and five businesses firebombed in the north end of the twin cities in a second night of violence. Asked if he had reached out to black leaders to attempt to cool down the tense situation, Chief Shirley replied gruffly, "There are no black leaders in this community. The only time a black comes into my office is to demand something, not to talk."[6] He added that if the violence continued, he would simply call in as many men as needed to control the city.

Alice Hoults said adamantly that she "saw no purpose" to the violence that was sweeping the cities. "We don't approve of bombings and shootings," she said. "What I want is justice. Whoever committed this crime should be punished." The manager of Follett's came to her home with two weeks of her husband's pay, seventy-five dollars in donations raised by fellow employees, and a personal check from store owner Dwight Follett for one hundred dollars, in addition to the thousand-dollar pledge from the store. As for her future, Alice told a reporter she could not stay in Urbana and would probably return to her family in the St. Louis area. When asked what she would do there, she began crying and was unable to answer. The older Hoults child was less than two years old, the second was seven months old, and the young widow was only months away from her third.

Bill Groninger, a popular columnist for the Urbana-based Courier, expressed a minority-held opinion on the shooting and its aftermath:

> Although Officer Eastman says the shooting was accidental, the prevailing opinion on white streets seems to be that even if he had done it on purpose he should not be prosecuted.
>
> The race issue aside, if such a thing is possible, the feeling seems to be that if you run from a cop you must have a reason, and that reason is warrant enough for the

cop to shoot you. Well it isn't, not by anyone's book, yet many people, reasonably intelligent in other areas, seem to think it is.

The black community, or at least its vocalists, are mad, and you can't blame them. ... Mr. Hoults was a black man and he was shot by a white cop. ... Further, there is every indication that the Champaign Police force, headed by Chief Shirley, and the city administration, took sides in the matter. Chief Shirley withheld Officer Eastman's name for more than 24 hours ... a courtesy not extended to any black I've ever heard of who has been involved in a shooting in Champaign. Mayor Virgil Wikoff summarily slammed shut the Monarch Tavern, a black night-spot ... [which] strikes me a little like trying to put out a fire by dousing it with gasoline.[7]

That week, in Washington, the Senate Foreign Relations Committee under Senator William Fulbright responded to Nixon's "non-invasion" announcement by unanimously demanding a face-to-face meeting between the president and their committee—the first since 1920, when Woodrow Wilson attempted to push a League of Nations proposal through the congress—and questioned the constitutional powers of a president to send U.S. troops into a neutral country without congressional approval. The *DI* ran a front-page editorial with the lead "Have we come nowhere in nine years?" The paper's editors lamented, "Too many of our brothers have marched too many miles, organized too many actions, spent too many years in jail, written too many editorials to, in our hearts, believe this country could now be embarking on yet another Great American Campaign—this time with a war in Cambodia."[8]

Campus disturbances began within hours of Nixon's broadcast. Student and/or faculty declared strikes at Princeton, Yale, Smith, Stanford, and the Universities of Maryland and Oregon; on countless campuses windows were shattered and firebombs tossed while police responded with tear gas and nightsticks. Thirty-seven college and university presidents, including those of Columbia, Princeton, Cornell, Notre Dame, Dartmouth, and Stanford, but not Illinois, sent a letter to President Nixon calling for an end to the war. The Student Mobilization Committee pushed for mass demonstrations on the nation's campuses, and the National Student Association suggested a nationwide student strike.

Nixon answered his critics bitterly. "These bums ... blowing up the campuses. Listen, the boys on the college campuses today are the luckiest people in the world ... and here they are burning up the books ... storming around," and then he added, perhaps with unintentional insight, "I mean ... get rid of this war, there'll be another one."[9] Former president Lyndon Johnson called on the nation to support their president, saying Nixon deserved the backing of "all people who love freedom."[10] The *Chicago Tribune* despaired, asking if the nation's universities were too far gone to be saved: "American universities have been politicized by revolutionaries to such an extent that it is a serious question whether they can be saved . . . particularly those which have suspended classes in support of student demonstrations and strikes for reasons which have nothing to do with the function of a university."[11]

Three days after Hoults's fatal shooting, on a Sunday, Champaign patrolman Fred Eastman was arrested and charged with voluntary manslaughter. The next day, May 4, Ohio National Guardsmen shot and killed four protesters on the campus of Kent State. A junior, Gene Williams, witnessed the murders, telling reporters he was hiding in a doorway when he saw the troops turn on the crowd and assume a shooting position "in unison, as if responding to a command, and fire into the crowd. Bullets ricocheted off the walls beside us and students fell to the ground to avoid them." Williams told reporters, "A coed fell 15 feet in front of the men into the arms of a male student. A bullet had gone into her neck and lodged there." He saw another shot in the chest. The mostly young, nervous, and poorly trained guardsmen would claim they had heard a sniper's shot, but later review found no evidence to support the claim. President Nixon made a quick judgment: "When dissent turns to violence, it invites tragedy." Vice President Spiro Agnew, soon to resign from office under indictment for bribery, lectured the press about "the grave dangers which accompany the new politics of violence and confrontation that have found so much favor on our college campuses."[12]

CHAPTER 36

Strike: The Final Days

On the Illinois campus, students' attention swiveled from Hoults's death to Nixon's invasion to the deaths at Kent State. On Monday, activists called for an evening rally at the Champaign city office to protest Hoults's killing, then called another for Tuesday for a vote to join the nationwide strike. *DI* editors jumped the gun, announcing support for the strike even before the rally vote took place. Demands discussed among the students ranged far and wide—freeing all political prisoners, ending repression of Black Panthers, impeaching Nixon, abolishing ROTC, ending university complicity with the war, and, of course, immediate withdrawal of all troops from Southeast Asia.

A new group on campus, previously unheard of, the "Revolutionary 26," sent a letter to the *DI* claiming credit for the latest firebombing, this one at Lincoln Square, a new downtown Urbana shopping mall built in 1964. Calling the bombing "an act against capitalistic exploiters," the group characterized the stores as examples of "exclusive white bourgeois Amerika."[1] The bombers railed, "While brothers are being shot down in the streets by Chief Shirley's racist pigs, we will not tolerate the continued peaceful existence of retail establishments that are by and for the bourgeois exploiter class." The militant missive ended on a note of confidence: "This is war, and we will win. History is on our side." Yet another newly formed group, the "Black Liberation Party of Champaign," issued a set of demands to the Champaign Police Department, calling for a federal investigation into Hoults's killing, that half the jury for Eastman's trial be black, and that the department commit to a hiring goal of 25 percent blacks. Chief Shirley ignored their demands.

Black ministers met again with the city council on Wednesday evening, where Roy Williams, representing a local umbrella group, "The Black Coalition," called the Hoults killing "senseless, wanton violence" and condemned "this murder, and similar firings upon blacks, as a genocidal conspiracy being carried out—wittingly or not, by armed enforcers masquerading as our protectors and preservers of law and order."[2] He and his group demanded an end to the conspiracy. One ultraconservative citizen stood and presented a minority view, suggesting "the police department was doing an 'excellent' job," adding "all they needed was more firepower to insure safety on the streets." Loudly heckled by the audience, this speaker "urged that each policeman be issued a .45 caliber submachine gun and each fire engine have a mounted .30 caliber machine gun in order to provide 'instantaneous retaliation' for any attack."[3] Mayor Virgil Wikoff quieted the jeering audience, demanding they allow the man to finish his speech. Vernon Barkstall of the Urban League followed and expressed his grave concern that too many white Americans would agree with the previous speaker. "He speaks for the many, not the few."[4] Wikoff then quickly adjourned the meeting.

Up and down the state, Illinois college students acted quickly in response to Nixon's expansion of the war and to the Kent State deaths. At Chicago Circle, students occupied the administration building and vowed to hold it for the night. At Northern Illinois University, students broke into the administration building and smashed windows at the ROTC building; when evening came, they marched on downtown DeKalb, breaking windows and wreaking havoc. At Northwestern, a rally of five thousand presented demands to the administration and to the community. In response the chancellor cancelled all classes and closed the university for three days, ostensibly to honor the deaths at Kent State, likely hoping the shutdown would provide a cooling-down period. In Carbondale twenty Southern Illinois University students were arrested, two police were injured, and firebombs were thrown at police cars from dormitory windows. The *Champaign News-Gazette* reported, "All parts of the country and all kinds of colleges—from the old and prestigious to the little teachers' colleges—were involved in the outpouring of youthful emotion."

On the Urbana campus, reaction to the invasion began quickly and turned violent almost immediately. The Radical Union held their Tuesday-night meeting in the Auditorium, where the audience overruled a speaker's suggestion of a Thursday strike and voted to begin the strike the next day, Wednesday. They passed resolutions for cancellation of the Illiac IV project, for an impartial investigation into the Hoults killing, and for "liberation classes" to be held on the quad for the duration of the strike—all nearly unanimously approved. As the meeting seemed to near an end, one student rose in frustration and criticized the group. "They're doing things at every other campus in this country. We're the only ones who are sitting around at a meeting."[5] This charge initiated a lengthy debate on the use of violent tactics, following which the meeting attendees and hangers-on, several thousand in all, began an impromptu march around campus to various dormitories, notifying residents of the strike, shouting details, encouragement, and invitations to join both the evening's march and the next day's strike. On their roundabout campus tour the students paused long enough to break windows at Peltason's office in the English Building and at the Administration Building, then wound their way past an ever-favorite target, the Armory, inflicting more damage, then finally weaving through Campustown, battering favorite targets such as Follett's and McBride's. Police, of insufficient numbers to intervene, stayed in their cars and observed from a distance. That night, activists firebombed the Chemistry Annex and the Illinois Bell office near campus. The chancellor, momentarily trapped by students while he toured the campus in a police car, found himself under a barrage of rocks until his driver could manage a quick escape from a crowd that nearly surrounded their car.

The next day, the first day of the strike, Illiac protesters, newly reorganized into a group known simply as "The People" and not wanting their issue forgotten in all the excitement, announced an "Illiaction," a Saturday rally with speakers Jon Froines and Rennie Davis, two defendants in the Chicago Eight trial. In addition, Black Panther Bill Hampton, brother of murdered Panther Fred Hampton, would speak. "The People" had sent invitations to other universities and claimed that students from across the Midwest would be arriving for the rally. By this time the Illiac opponents had made a shift in their strategy. No longer protesting the presence of the machine on campus, "The People" were now focused on stopping the specific military purposes for which the DoD might use it, and they announced a march to follow the rally, one that would prove eventful, from the quad to the new structure under construction to house the supercomputer.

The same day the Saturday Illiaction was announced, eleven faculty in the Political Science Department under the leadership of Lou Gold and Phil Meranto formed another new group, "Faculty for Resistance" (not to be confused with the earlier group, Faculty for University Reform), with the purpose of reorienting all classes henceforth to discussions of political repression and resistance in the United States. The Law School and the Urban Planning Department became the first of many academic units to vote support for the strike. Even the Illiac project team was not immune to the political fever, as eight members of the team working under project leader Slotnick (though not Slotnick himself) published a statement "deploring the brutal, immoral and unconstitutional acts committed by the police, the military and the President of the United States in Champaign, Kent State, and Cambodia." Professor Slotnick admitted that given the prevailing campus mood, he was reevaluating the overall project, saying, "I have grave doubts as to whether this project can continue on this campus while under defense sponsorship."[6]

Within a few days of Nixon's broadcast, more than sixty U.S. colleges and universities had either announced plans to strike or were already on strike. After the deaths at Kent State, the number of strike actions exploded, with more than 450 university, college, and high school campuses across the country shut down by student strikes and an estimated four million students participating.[7] Campus ROTC offices, always an easy target, took a heavy toll—thirty such facilities were bombed and/or went up in flames—while National Guard units were mobilized on twenty-one campuses in sixteen states.[8] Not all student reaction was without at least some gallows humor though, as students at New York University hung a banner out their dormitory window that read "They Can't Kill Us All!"[9]

At Illinois on Wednesday morning, the first day of the strike, hundreds of students manned picket lines at dozens of campus buildings, not stopping students who chose to attend classes but attempting to persuade them otherwise. At noon, four thousand people attended a rally on the quad, listened to fiery speeches, then peacefully dispersed. However, in the afternoon violence flared when a large crowd of twenty-five hundred protesters blocked the driveway to the loading dock of the Illini Union, preventing trucks from making deliveries. Paul Doebel, now the university's chief security officer, did not hesitate to call in local police and state troopers, who made fifty arrests. Michael Parenti and Phil Meranto were among those arrested, the former suffering serious cuts and bruises, some requiring stitches, from rough treatment by state police, who then proceeded to disperse the crowd. The state police would quickly earn a reputation as the most physically aggressive of law enforcement authorities while they were on campus. That evening, a gathering of nearly four thousand on the quad self-divided into a nonviolent group and a "street action faction," but the combined law-enforcement forces, out in strength, kept the crowd confined to the general area of the quad; as the curfew neared again, the crowd quietly dispersed.

At this point an increasingly concerned Governor Ogilvie called up an additional five thousand Illinois National Guardsmen and published a statement in the *DI*: "I call upon every student in our colleges and universities to cooperate with duly constituted authorities and stop the violence which threatens to destroy these schools." Recognizing the likely response to that request, his next bid was to the state's moms and dads: "I also request the parents of every young man and woman on an Illinois university campus to call the students and urge them to comply with the regulations of the institutions and the laws of the State of Illinois." The governor ended his statement with an uneasy warning: "We cannot and will not permit a small group of revolutionaries to destroy our institutions and tear our society apart."[10]

Published alongside Ogilvie's warning, and lining up squarely behind the governor, Chancellor Peltason issued a statement condemning the strike and exhibited little sympathy or patience for the protesting students. The generally liberal administrator stood firmly and self-righteously on the weak straw-man argument of "the right of students to attend classes," at a time when most students were choosing not to attend classes, and prioritized normal "operation of the university" above the moral issues that motivated the students, who considered the situation anything but normal. "I for one will have no part of any effort to deny students the right to attend classes. Students on this campus ... do not have the right to interfere with the operation of this University." The administrator gave a nod to the serious social and moral issues driving the protests—"I mourn the deaths and senseless violence that are so much in evidence today"—but he chose not to support the majority of his students. Throughout the strike he would continue to stand on his belief that keeping the university open and operating as normally as possible was of the greatest import. "Neither this [the deaths and senseless violence] nor other problems that this society faces will be solved by disrupting our educational institutions."[11] The statement, of course, placed him in complete opposition to the striking students, who felt that the far-from-normal events taking place—the Kent State killings, the Hoults shooting, the ongoing war they perceived as never-ending, unjust, and immoral—must take precedence over normal operation of the university. From the students' perspective, Peltason's decision to prioritize "university operations" over "senseless deaths" was not only morally unacceptable, it placed him in the same camp with Richard Nixon, the Ohio National Guard, and the Champaign police. His words and actions throughout the strike would largely infuriate students.

Despite Ogilvie's and Peltason's words, the Illinois strike, which ran from Wednesday, May 6, through Friday, May 8, succeeded at emptying most classrooms and freed thousands of students to express their frustration and anger toward the government and, by proxy, their university. On Thursday, the second day of the strike, a crowd of approximately one thousand gathered in front of the university fire station across from the Union on Green Street, where they urged station personnel to lower their flag to half-mast in honor of the Kent State deaths. The firemen at first refused but finally agreed, on the condition that the students move out of the fire lane driveways. But when the students complied the firemen changed their minds and refused to lower the flag, angering the students, who then moved back into the fire lanes, closer to the station, and attempted to take control of the flag. One hundred state troopers appeared and moved the students back from the station, onto Green Street, where they stayed, blocking traffic.

Doebel then arrived onsite with a compromise, offering to lower the flag across the street, in front of the Illini Union, to half-mast if the students would clear Green Street. By this time the crowd had doubled in size, and with tempers rising on all sides, Doebel wanted to avoid a repeat of the previous day's loading-dock fracas, when his quick call for police had been roundly criticized. Again the students complied with the request, cooperating with police and guardsmen to clear Green Street. The flag at the Illini Union was lowered to half-mast. However, when additional guardsmen and troopers soon arrived, they roughly moved the students away from the front of the Union and back onto the quad. Once the students were moved away from the front of the building, the state troopers immediately raised the flag.

On the quad an afternoon rally with more than two thousand attendees was underway. The rally, sponsored by yet another newly formed group, the Peace Union, whose members wore yellow armbands, were intent on counteracting the image of student violence from the previous days. A spokesperson set the tone for this rally: "We will not break windows, we will not yell and chant, we will light candles and peacefully protest." Not all in the crowd were in sync, though, as junior Julie Jensen warned, "I am not going to be non-violent. If I am arrested I am going to resist."[12]

Later that evening, a huge crowd of ten thousand students and faculty gathered peacefully on the quad, facing the Auditorium steps for a candlelight memorial service to honor the four slain at Kent State and Edgar Hoults. Nine hundred guardsmen stood nearby. A Catholic priest from the Newman Foundation prayed for understanding. A McKinley Foundation minister led the students in a litany to "affirm a new way." A rabbi from the Hillel Foundation urged the students to rededicate themselves to the sacredness of life.

In the crowd yellow armbands mingled with red ones, the latter worn by those rejecting nonviolence, one of whom warned, "You're going to be talking about nonviolence when they take you to Auschwitz." Another offered, "You get the National Guard to wear yellow armbands, then we'll be non-violent." Debbie Senn, a Strike Committee coordinator, urged both to "get together and work to make the strike a success." Ed Pinto, newly elected undergraduate student chairman, announced that 37 percent of all classes had been cancelled by the second day of the strike and that approximately 90 percent of Illinois students were honoring the strike. He expressed optimism that the strike would be virtually 100 percent effective by the third day. The participation rate of the Illinois strike was high but not unique, as the National Student Association declared the strike a nationwide success, with 437 of the nation's fifteen hundred colleges, nearly 30 percent, on strike or closed outright by end of day Thursday.

Following Pinto's speech, Meranto and Parenti, who were bailed out and released from jail only hours earlier, spoke to the crowd. Meranto drew cheers with his charge that "David Dodds Henry, Jack Peltason, and Paul Doebel all work for the biggest pig of all—Nixon."[13] Parenti, face bandaged, drew a laugh as he quipped, "Yesterday I practiced non-violence. The only trouble is, they forgot to tell the other side."[14] He continued more seriously, reminding the crowd that "all the violence ever done by radicals in this country doesn't compare with that done on our first day of fighting in Cambodia."[15] He urged his listeners not to "equate trashing of a few windows with the violence perpetrated by administration bombing in Vietnam." He charged, "The men in control of this society are resorting to control of our bodies with physical force since they can no longer control our minds"; he called the week's police violence "a symbol that the country's power system is fast approaching crisis." The conflict, he argued, "helps liberate our minds." Dramatically, he offered that "it isn't so bad to get arrested, and maybe it isn't so bad to die when our cause is just . . . one day we will be able to tell our children that in the moment of truth, we fought for social justice, and did not give our lives to the tawdry pursuits of gadgets and gimmicks and houses in the suburbs." He closed his speech, fist in the air, shouting, "The future is ours," and his audience rose and cheered loudly.[16] Following Parenti's speech, a small group lowered the American flag flying at half-mast at the Auditorium, set it ablaze, and raised it again, drawing widespread shouts of disapproval from the crowd followed by a voice vote formally condemning the action. Neither Parenti nor Meranto would have long careers as Illinois faculty, as following the tumultuous semester, both would depart the campus for greener pastures elsewhere.

Thursday had been a day of decision for Chancellor Peltason. College presidents across the nation were determining whether or not to close their schools to avoid violence. Preparing for the worst, Peltason had written a draft statement, directing the shutdown of his campus:

> The Urbana campus of the University of Illinois has experienced this week the protest and disruption common to hundreds of colleges and universities across the country. Yesterday and earlier today I pledged our commitment both to the right of non-disruptive protest, and to the right to attend classes. I am convinced at this point, after extensive consultation with students, faculty, employees, security forces, and concerned citizens, that our basic educational objectives cannot be achieved under the conditions that presently exist on our campus. With this large community very few have defied regulations or incited violence. But isolated incidents of destruction and threats of further violence cannot be ignored. We will not capitulate to terror tactics, but we cannot jeopardize the safety of students or staff at this tense moment. Issues outside of the university's sphere of influence have combined to temporarily negate the requirement for teaching and for learning.
>
> Accordingly I am closing the University until ~~further notice~~ Wed. Residence halls will be closed as of _____. All other facilities will be closed _____. I urge all the constituents of the campus community to spend this extended weekend in serious thought and discussion with their families and friends concerning the deaths and senseless violence of the week, so that we may reestablish and strengthen the functions and traditional values of this institution of higher education.[17]

The chancellor chose not to issue this statement, which is now available in the university archives with a handwritten note at top, "Draft by Peltason 5/7/70—not used." As an indicator of the pressure Peltason and his peers faced, the next day brought the announcement that after four days of rioting on the Madison campus, the president of the University of Wisconsin, in another example of the aforementioned "presidential fatigue," had submitted his resignation, claiming that although "he had planned the move for some time, it was unfortunate that it came at this time of crisis."[18]

With Peltason's decision to keep the university open at all cost, the final day of the strike, Friday, began with nervous anticipation on all sides. It would prove to be a day of turbulence. The day started on an upbeat note for the strikers when the College of Engineering, one of the more conservative departments on campus, held a public meeting of students and faculty on the lawn of the Electrical Engineering Building and voted to officially support the strike, as many, if not most, other departments had already done. But trouble developed later when a large crowd of more than two thousand students, attempting to block the University's Central Receiving Depot on the southwest edge of the campus, formed a peaceful picket line to try to prevent delivery trucks from entering. Soon, university police appeared, and with state troopers, cleared the students out of the road, allowing teamster drivers, much to the students' dismay, to cross the now broken picket line. Smaller groups of students then moved farther up the road, attempting to talk drivers into stopping their trucks, but troopers went after them, swinging riot batons, and chased the students across open fields all the way to Memorial Stadium. A few quick-thinking protesters then slipped behind the troopers' lines and back to the parking lot and began letting air out of the police car tires, making the troopers reverse direction to chase after them. Eventually, the inevitable bottles and rocks flew, police made arrests accordingly, and the students were cleared out of the area. At the end of the day, Governor Ogilvie ordered the remainder of his National Guard reserves to report for duty, bringing the total of guardsmen stationed at Illinois colleges to now over nine thousand. In effect, the entire Illinois National Guard was now guarding the state's university system from the state's university students.

On Friday, Illinois Superintendent of Public Instruction Ray Page delivered a stinging speech in Springfield to a gathering of the Illinois Federation of Republican Women, condemning the state's radical students along with the college presidents who "coddled them." He called on the responsible people of the state to "smite the false prophets, the Judas goats," apparently referring to activist campus leaders. Regarding a group of college presidents who had recently met with President Nixon to protest the Cambodian invasion, Page accused the administrators of attempting "to muzzle, yes muzzle, the president and vice president of the United States," and declared the effort repugnant. He challenged university administrators instead to "put a muzzle on the William Kunstlers, the Rap Browns, the Abbie Hoffmans, and the other apostles of anarchy." Closing the universities was simply an easy way out, he suggested, and he accused the presidents of avoiding their responsibilities. Page warned Illinois students: "Beware of false prophets, do not follow like sheep; reject the spineless administrators who crumble with each step." Admitting that he had "spent sleepless nights since the horror which took place on the campus of Kent State University," the angry superintendent did not hesitate to blame the victims. "Four students that should have known better than to have participated in outright revolt against the forces of law and order lie dead."[19] Thus spoke the highest-ranking official responsible for the education of the children of the state of Illinois.

Unfazed by Page's heated rhetoric, at the end of the week the UI Strike Committee declared the week's action a complete success, announcing 97 percent effectiveness by the final day. The committee reported that classrooms on the side of the quad that were home to the humanities, languages, and social sciences were virtually deserted the entire three days. On the engineering campus, buildings had been more populated, but many of the classes were empty or cancelled. In buildings that housed the mining and metallurgy, physics, and commerce departments, Altgeld and David Kinley Halls, the committee claimed that fewer than half the classes were meeting, and those had but a handful of seats filled.

The lame-duck President Henry, on the occasion of the first student strike in the hundred-year history of his university, issued a statement Friday evening and took the extraordinary step, for him, of finally stating a public position on the Vietnam War. This unprecedented action, speaking out even mildly against the nation's foreign policy, was only warranted, Henry said, because of "the present situation on the campuses of the nation and the interaction between public issues and University affairs." The president admitted, though, that "doing so runs counter to past practice." After years of refusing students' requests to do so, Henry finally and publicly stated, "I personally deplore the war in Southeast Asia, and I hope for its early conclusion. I believe the objective of 'victory' is wrong.... I join all of those who would bring the fighting to a close as expeditiously as possible." He expressed "apprehension" over the success of the Cambodian operation to shorten the war. After years of entreaty and demands by his Illinois students, the mild-mannered, diminutive administrator had finally conceded and supported their position: "I respect the depth of feeling and the interests of our students whose generation is fighting this war and who will live their lives with the results of it," recognizing that "casualties of the war, at home as well as overseas, have already marred our future."[20]

Meanwhile, in Washington, President Richard Nixon, speaking to the press, took a curious approach in responding to the latest growing student unrest and claimed that his decision to send U.S. troops into Cambodia was entirely in sync with the goals of the protesting student demonstrators. "I agree with everything they are trying to accomplish. They're trying to say they want peace . . . to stop the killing . . . to get out of Vietnam. . . . Everything I stand for is what they want. . . . I know how deeply they feel." In response to a question about the chaotic state of American society, Nixon, the man who a few years later would stare into the cameras and unconvincingly tell the American people "I am not a crook," just as unconvincingly on this occasion reassured the American people that despite the first successful nationwide student strike in U.S. history, "This country is not headed for revolution."[21]

Peltason also issued a statement late Friday, jointly with nearly one hundred of his vice chancellors, deans, department heads, and directors. Although lining up behind Henry, the chancellor, with dire words, would repeat his steadfast, stubborn dictum that the university must stay open: "The universities of these United States face their greatest crisis in the life of this republic." Like Henry, he too finally gave in to his students' request of many years and took a public stand against the war: "We too believe the Indochina war must be brought to an early end before it tears this great nation apart." With a nod to the killing of Hoults, he added, "We too deplore the tragic deaths at Kent State and in this community. . . . We share concern over injustice and racial prejudice wherever it exists in society." But the chancellor could not stop himself from once again arguing that "no attempt be made to coerce those who wish to attend classes, and that no efforts be made to impede University operations." The reality, which Peltason well knew, was that no students who chose to were being prevented from attending classes, that many of those classes were canceled anyway, and that the majority of students were of their own volition supporting the strike; he chose not to acknowledge this. The chancellor continued, arguing, "We do not believe the existing system has failed. . . . We do not believe the university has failed, but we see its weaknesses and pledge to do our best to correct them." He urged "all members of the academic community to rededicate their commitment to orderly inquiry and rational discourse. . . . [J]oin with us in doing everything possible to keep the campus open so that the educational process can go on." The chancellor ended by quoting the *New York Times* editorial of the day, conveniently supporting his position, which criticized those higher-education institutions that had chosen to support their striking students:

> The best way that the academic community can demonstrate that there are civilized roads to a more responsible society is to stay open and concentrate on the effective harnessing of ideas to action. The irrationality of escapism is no answer. That only leaves the field to the Philistines.[22]

However, any hopes for "orderly inquiry," "rational discourse," and a "more responsible society" would be dashed on this weekend, as more Philistine-like attitudes would prevail. Weather reports for Saturday called for a chance of showers and thunderstorms; in fact, there would be plenty of thunder, and eventually showers too. A special Sunday edition of the *Daily Illini*, published not on newsprint but on standard eight by eleven mimeograph paper and run off at a local co-op print shop, would tell the story of the tumultuous weekend to those few Illini who did not personally witness the events. These were extraordinary times, as the paper's makeshift masthead demonstrated.

CHAPTER 37

Extra at the End

Throughout the three days of the spring strike, with sunny weather and mild temperatures and no classes to attend, groups of students would loosely form, disperse, and re-form throughout the campus and especially on the quad. Saturday's planned activities included a wide variety of workshops and teach-ins on the quad—on the Iliac project and university complicity in the war, on the evils of campus ROTC and the upsides of cooperatives, on communal living, underground newspapers, women's liberation, self-defense, and communist Cuba. Live music was to begin at noon, followed by the Iliac rally. Planned speakers included Lee Weiner of the Chicago Eight, Linda Quint and Nick Ridell of the Chicago 15 (another group of antiwar protesters with a trial underway in Chicago), all to be followed by a protest march to the Illiac IV site.

The predicted showers held off Saturday and a sometimes festive, sometimes riotous spirit was in the air as thousands of students hung out across the campus enjoying the weather. A *Chicago Tribune* reporter captured the atmosphere of those days: "Students struck classes, blocked truck deliveries, held massive rallies, taunted state police and national guardsmen . . . [but] also spent afternoons away from classes, lying in the warm sun listening to rock bands and talking in small groups with national guardsmen who lined streets."[1]

The peaceful "Illiaction" rally drew a crowd of thousands. But the mood didn't last, as following the rally a long, chanting line of students began the march from the quad toward the Illiac construction site, walking in the middle of city streets, leaving blocked traffic in their wake. However, the march never made it to the

THE DAILY ILLINI — EXTRA
Serving Illini Since 1871   SUN., MAY 10, 1970

This special edition of The Daily Illini appears in this form because of our responsibility to bring our readers the news as quickly as possibly during this crisis situation. The Daily Illini would like to thank the Print Co-op.

102 arrested

By the staff of The Daily Illini

DI masthead, strike week, Sunday edition. Photo courtesy of the *Daily Illini*.

planned destination. Once again, a few protesters began throwing rocks at windows along the way, and then, at Wright and Green, the crowd came to a stop and blocked the intersection, some marchers sitting down, in an attempt to hold the intersection, until Champaign's Chief Shirley arrived, personally warning them on his megaphone to clear the streets or face arrest. Soon, eight were in custody and the intersection was cleared, but large crowds of students continued to mill restlessly on the campus streets and the quad throughout the afternoon.

Then, around 6:00 P.M., with no warning, state police, with guardsmen in support, disembarked from buses on Green Street and began an unexpected sweep south, through and around the Illini Union, tersely gathering up groups of students, pushing and shoving them toward the quad. More state troopers appeared on the sides of the quad, surrounding the now confined students. Then, with neither warning nor explanation, the troopers abruptly began arbitrarily grabbing individual students, making arrests, and loading their captives onto three large buses waiting nearby. A *News-Gazette* reporter at the scene barely managed to escape arrest herself, and reported the action this way in the next day's paper:

> No information.
> No explanations.
> The National Guard came from the northwest side of the quadrangle.
> The state police were on the east side of the quad,
> They closed ranks and arrested everyone on the grassy section which has traditionally been the favorite gathering place of University of Illinois students.
> Some had been flying kites,
> Some were enjoying the spring weather with their dates.
> Some were taking pictures—or perusing the scene for the local news media—or observing the activities of the striking students.

Some reportedly had thrown rocks at state police.
All were arrested.

What were the charges?
No one would answer.[2]

State police made more than one hundred seemingly random arrests. (Some would claim white-arm-banded legal-support personnel were especially targeted.)[3] The buses filled and rolled away, the arrested students to spend time in the Great Hall below Memorial Stadium before being moved on to police stations for formal arraignment. The troopers and guardsmen then moved off the quad and left campus. The surprising, unexplained arrest sweep left thousands of shocked and angry students behind on the quad.

Trouble erupted again at 8:00 P.M., when someone pulled a fire alarm in the Union and then minutes later a union employee called police to quell a separate disturbance at the candy counter. Instead of police, state troopers responded and again began roughly moving all students out of the Union and onto the quad. What little patience the troopers had was likely exhausted by a few students responding to the rough tactics by "smashing glass, overturning ashtrays, and setting fire to a sofa."[4] After clearing the building, the troopers departed the area again. At 8:30, about a thousand of the crowd began a march from the quad to Memorial Stadium to demand the release of those students arrested earlier, stoning police cars and smashing windows on the way. Those who remained behind roamed the quad, damaging Altgeld Hall, the Administration Building, and any other targets they could find.

At 10:00 the state police returned to the campus, along with 750 National Guardsmen, both groups pelted with rocks by angry students upon their arrival. The guardsmen surrounded the quad and slowly cleared it while troopers charged up John Street, swinging their riot sticks and clearing the streets. Other police then moved up Sixth and west on John to clear those areas, making arrests along the way. Slowly, the entire campus area was cleared by the overwhelming joint forces of state troopers, guardsmen, and local police. Finally, around 11:00 P.M., the predicted hard rain at last began to fall, forcing the few remaining diehard students to seek cover. By 11:30 the quad was deserted, and with this rainy, confusing Saturday night, the violent phase of the Illinois student protest movement quietly and unexpectedly spluttered to an end.[5]

No one could ever explain why the troopers made their sudden and unanticipated arrest sweep when they did. Most likely they acted on their own initiative. As Roger Simon had described during the March riots, no one seemed in charge of the campus at this point. Over the next weeks a great deal of faculty and administrators' time would be focused on chains of command and who exactly was in charge of whom, what, when, and where on the campus. No clear answers were found. Neither President Henry, finishing out his final days in the office, nor Chancellor Peltason seemed to play a significant role in the Saturday-affair. "Henry retired at 10:30 P.M. and left orders not to be awakened," his spokesman reported. Dean of Students Hugh Satterlee offered his colorful judgment when asked his thoughts on the university's handling of Saturday's disorder. "How do you capture in print the sound of me throwing up?" William K. Williams, now with the title of "Campus Ombudsman," summed up the general feeling: "I sweat for the students arrested . . . this was simply an agonizing affair that has exhausted us all."[6]

On Sunday the *News-Gazette* gave prominent editorial-page position to syndicated columnist David Lawrence, who argued that now was the time the "silent majority must speak." The column, while purporting to seek an answer to "the unprecedented unrest of the younger generation," in fact was a strident call to arms for socially conservative readers to rise up and combat this seemingly out-of-control generation before it was too late. Lawrence quoted Vice President Agnew on the protesting students:

> For the first time in history a great nation is threatened not by those who have nothing, but by those who have almost everything. . . . We have listened to these elitists laugh at honesty and thrift and respect and self-denial. Why then are we surprised to discover we have traitors and thieves and perverts and irrational and illogical people in our midst?
>
> There is no greater problem confronting the American people than this. There must be an intellectual counter-attack made against the cynics, the moral relativists, the creators of the "era of moroseness." In our colleges, in our pulpits, in our forums, we must once again hear the principles of western freedom defined and defended.

Lawrence called for "large segments of the population to exert their influence in each community." Such calls for reaction were not new but would be heard more broadly and loudly from the conservative media in days to come and would not go unheeded. Lawrence's column was just one more locally visible indicator that the reactionary counterattack from the right was in full swing.[7]

Seemingly unaware of any such backlash, on the following Monday fifteen hundred Illinois students marched to the Champaign police station demanding answers about Edgar Hoults's death. Thirty police in full riot gear met them there, supported by two fire engines with hoses facing the demonstrators. Chief Shirley agreed to meet with the students, not at his station, but back on their turf, on the south patio of the Union, where within the hour he, Doebel, and George Frampton would engage in a heated dialogue with about five hundred students. Shirley provided no answers to questions of the Hoults killing. "It is up to the courts to decide

... let the chips fall where they may." When asked if he would outlaw hollow points, Shirley said he would, just as soon as he received "a guarantee nobody was going to shoot at policemen with hollow point bullets." The crowd booed, and somebody yelled the chief was a "fucking dum-dum."[8] Doebel squirmed when asked about the state troopers' Saturday-night tactics, saying, "I didn't ask anybody to come in and bust heads, but just to clear the area." Frampton, more conciliatory, agreed with the students that the mass arrests Saturday night were indiscriminate and unjustified, conceding, "That never should have happened."[9]

Chancellor Peltason, attempting to come to terms with what was now clearly an antiwar majority sentiment on the campus, announced he would authorize alternatives to regular classes in the coming week, suggesting that faculty members lead classroom discussions around the challenges facing society, how the university might help meet those challenges, and how individual students and faculty might play a useful role. The faculty senate quickly voted overwhelmingly to endorse Peltason's suggestion but rejected five separate motions to explicitly support the strike in one manner or another. Three hundred students in the audience booed and hissed. The *DI* called for the chancellor's resignation, labeling him a failure: "The blatantly repressive sweep arrests conducted Saturday on the Quadrangle most graphically demonstrate the inability of Chancellor Peltason and his staff to maintain control of this campus after they had made the decision to allow it to be turned into an armed camp."[10]

Meanwhile, as reaction against the students began building in the state legislature, Anthony Scariano, one of the few representatives sympathetic to the students' goals, warned, "Those people [his fellow legislators] ... have the finest twelfth century minds in the state. If we were living before the days of the Revolutionary War, they would call themselves the Committee on un-British Activities."[11] Champaign mayor Virgil Wikoff shared his thoughts in a speech to the campus Young Republicans, declaring the decision to conduct the Saturday arrest sweep a good move, though he admitted he had no idea who had ordered it. The mayor defended the law-enforcement agencies in total, pointing out that, relative to other parts of the country, "there has been no serious injury, no shots fired, no one has been shot"—completely overlooking the death of Edgar Hoults.[12]

Two days after Wikoff's comments, Mississippi state police killed two black students and injured sixteen others at predominantly black Jackson State College in Jackson. In a firestorm lasting thirty seconds, forty state troopers shot more than 140 shotgun shells into a student dormitory from close range. The police would claim a sniper had been spotted on the building's upper floors. No evidence for the claim was ever found, nor were any charges ever filed against any of the troopers.

Later in the month, the Illinois House of Representatives opened hearings on the wave of student unrest on the state's campuses. Henry, Peltason, and undergraduate student chairman Ed Pinto were invited to appear. In his prepared speech, Pinto straightforwardly listed the reasons for student anger: "The war in Indochina, white racism, the urban crisis, the killing of students in Ohio and Mississippi, police overreaction which 'provoked as much disorder as it prevented,' the absence of 'positive leadership' among faculty and administrators, and 'harsh and arbitrary decisions made by the government'," the *DI* reported. The student-government leader bluntly laid responsibility for the strife not with students but at the feet of authorities: "It is the deaf ear turned to us by both the national administration and the University administration which I feel is the main cause of student dissent." Asked if he supported the violence, Pinto said simply, "I can understand the frustration which leads some of my fellow students to engage in such acts."[13]

Daniel Slotnick would soon be named head of a newly created Center for Advanced Computation at the university, which would come to a joint decision with the Department of Defense, approved by the trustees, that the Illiac IV computer would not be housed on the university campus. According to a spokesperson, the $24 million machine, which Slotnick and team designed and the Burroughs Corporation in Green Valley, Pennsylvania, was constructing, would likely be installed on a military base, where it would be "safer."[14] The university time-sharing arrangement with the Defense Department, two-thirds for military purposes and one-third for academic research, would not be affected by the placement decision. The announcement included no mention of the months-long student fight against the supercomputer or the role the issue had played in the events of Saturday, May 9.

The week following the strike saw most classes back in session, although many instructors, following the chancellor's direction, used the time for discussions about the war, the strike, and myriad social issues. In the last weeks of the month a normality of sorts returned to the campus and final-exam week proceeded, though many exams were cancelled. The majority of the Illinois students who had entered the university in the mid-sixties were now leaving school to face a new challenge, finding their way through life after college. Unfortunately for them, the Department of Labor would announce that month the highest rate of unemployment in ten years.

Normality would not soon return for the widow of Edgar Hoults, now a single mother of two (and soon to be three) small children. Alice Hoults would face her own challenges finding a way forward in life. In October an all-white Champaign County jury would take two hours to determine that patrolman Fred Eastman was innocent of all charges in the killing of her husband, Edgar. Alice Hoults would then file a civil suit against the Champaign police department, and after six years of legal struggle she would receive an out-of-court settlement of $59,000.[15]

CONCLUSION

On Agency

We are now a half century on from the sixties, with the country again deeply divided. To many veterans of the decade, now senior citizens reaching an age of reflection, those earlier times can feel like yesterday and engender the most intense memories. The current political climate bids some to look back on the sixties and attempt to make sense of the time, to look for parallels, for keys of understanding, perhaps to help others do better today what they tried to do then. Following the sixties, I, like many peers, had some shuffling years: taught school in a ghetto, drove a taxi, worked with emotionally disturbed children, ran a community newspaper, finally fell into the high-tech revolution, climbed corporate ladders, married and raised a family. This book is an attempt, now that there is time to do so, to look back from the sunset years and try to make some sense of that rebellious time of youth, perhaps to find lessons in the history.

What significance should we attach to that turmoil in the Illinois heartland, against a background of national and even international generational conflict? Our starting point must be the setting, the state's large flagship university situated amid the corn fields, the great "multiversity," as the journalist Nicholas von Hoffman labeled it, the education factory chartered to produce the graduates to fill the jobs created by the booming postwar economy. Though more intellectual than its surrounding central Illinois communities, the institution was still conservative like them, and rejected the East Coast internationalist George Stoddard, looked with great suspicion on the former communist Edward Yellin, and sent the offbeat Leo Koch packing with no hesitation. This staid institution, seeking notoriety in

Illini at March on Washington, November 1969. Photo courtesy of the *Daily Illini*.

academics and athletics—certainly not in political activism or loosening of social mores—provides a unique lens to view and understand the period and discover its lessons, a lens that can reveal aspects of the time that are similar to but different from more extreme examples at Berkeley, Madison, or Columbia.

Into this setting came a generation raised in the heartland of the world's wealthiest nation at a time of unprecedented economic growth for their families, members of that ill-defined and exceedingly elastic construct, the American middle class. The university enjoyed the bounty of the era too, expanding in budget, campuses, physical plant, faculty and staff, and student enrollment. The confident baby boomers entered that environment reflecting the attributes of the era that formed them—its good fortune, economic plenty, and the moral rectitude of a country that had won a world war, stood up to godless communism, and declared itself the undisputed leader of the free world. They were products of their time, raised in love of country, taught to believe in and respect authority, to know right from wrong.

On reaching their majority, these youths found themselves confronted with moral questions, conflicts between their society's stated ideals and actions, issues that today might seem unambiguous—at the center a deplorable foreign war but overlaid with issues of race and inequality, issues around the society's culture and their privileged position within it. A small but persistent segment of the generation responded by questioning and speaking out—drawing on agency nurtured throughout childhood by doting, hardworking, war-veteran parents and teachers—but they received unsatisfactory answers. To paraphrase Port Huron, a significant minority of this comfortable generation simply could not accept the world as offered. So they challenged authority, but their challenges were rebuffed. They persisted and still were rejected, by government, university, and, often, parents. Frustration grew and some turned to violence, soon squelched by an overpowering establishment. But their movement had impact and in the end led the nation to stop the deplorable war.

This is a first lesson. The students of the sixties protest movement accomplished an extraordinary thing; as mere teens—at most young adults—they led the fight to end a bad war, and eventually they won that fight. Their movement deserves a place in the long tradition of American antiestablishment protests, of abolitionists and suffragettes, labor and civil rights movements, Midwest populism and East Coast progressivism; their movement was of that tradition. They fought against long odds and brought an end to their country's support for a misbegotten war. This should be recognized and recorded in the nation's history; a memorial would not be unreasonable.

These students would leave college life behind, enter the "real world," and face its harsh realities—an end to the postwar boom, economic difficulties in the seventies, decades of reactionary politics and neoliberal economics. Eventually, most would sort their way through, find jobs, raise families, take on mortgages, and fit in as best they could to a world not of their making—though not all would. In the early seventies, the body of twenty-one-year-old James Larabee, the radical Illinois Weatherman, would be found hanging in a mountain cabin thirty miles north of Boulder, Colorado. His suburban Chicago hometown newspaper reported that he had found his way to the mountainous area, "a remote valley ... dotted with tents and small shacks ... to become part of a loose commune of young people ... young and old children of the Movement [who] nourish themselves with organic foods and they use drugs." His death was ruled a suicide by the county coroner. The report called Larabee "a creature of his generation ... because of the whims and shifts of time and history ... a child of revolution, an agent of the changing attitudes which have come to be called the Movement." His final years "were spent on the road or in the heart of the revolutionary movement ... a repudiation of his earlier years and typical of a lot of kids of his generation who broke loose from their roots to harken to different tunes of glory."[1]

A seemingly disproportionate share of Illinois sixties rebels, a majority of those interviewed for this book, would build careers in service professions. Vic Berkey would leave Illinois behind, earn a master's in education at Antioch, a law degree at UCLA, successfully litigate before the Ninth Circuit and the California Supreme Courts, and build a practice representing farm workers in California's central valley. Vern Fein would convert to Christianity in the mid-1970s, work as a community-outreach pastor and special education teacher, found and manage a large food bank providing millions of meals annually to needy central Illinoisans, and publish poetry and writing on the confluence of his Christian beliefs and radical politics. Phil Durrett would leave Illinois after the Dow affair for Amherst College, be featured in a *Life* magazine photo carrying a young daughter in his arms through his graduation ceremony to protest the college's all-male enrollment, then work as a welfare worker and union officer for years and then, exasperated with his country's politics under Ronald Reagan, move to Switzerland and spend most of his adult life as an expat. After Illinois, Patsy Parker would go on to medical school and practice for thirty years in Minneapolis, Minnesota. Lester Wall would become a psychologist and therapist, Patricia Engelhard a lawyer, Bernard Gershenson a college English professor, and Joanne Chester an elected township office holder for thirty-five years. Paula Shafransky knew Jim Larabee, would feel "haunted" by his early death, and remembers him today as "a very gentle soul."[2] About her career as a special education teacher she says, "The sixties made me want to find a job where I could do some good in the world."[3] But for all the good they would do, the sixties generation did not change the world the way they had hoped. The established order they railed against did not fall.

Therein is a second takeaway. The movement failed miserably at political revolution. Such prospects proved no more than youthful fantasy—"numbskull adventurism," as one historian called it.[4] Even worse, unintended consequences prevailed. The mayhem of the sixties was followed by the political reaction of a silent majority that is still with us today, a reaction that gave us the right-wingers Nixon and Reagan, two Bushes, and Trump, while allowing none more liberal than the centrists Carter, Clinton, and Obama. The twentieth-century progressive wave, from Teddy Roosevelt's reforms through FDR's New Deal and LBJ's Great Society, came to a screeching halt with the end of the sixties. Politicians of both parties ushered in a neoliberal era, unwinding progressive achievements, reducing welfare for the poor, diminishing the power of unions, deregulating businesses, privatizing public services, deemphasizing public education, and moving the political center far to the right. And in a brilliant stroke, with consequences that even such a masterful politician could not have foreseen, Richard Nixon began the era's privatization of public services by ending the hated draft and opening the door to today's professional army, to outsourced military adventures, and to quiescent campuses. Without the existential threat of the draft, would there have been the sixties student movement? Impossible to know, though we do know that at Illinois it was not the draft but free speech that initiated the movement, which then evolved to become antiwar, then grew into more. But we also know that since Nixon's move there has never again been a serious campus antiwar reaction, not to Bush's Iraq disaster or to the never-ending Middle Eastern wars in which we seem perpetually enmeshed. So not only did the sixties student movement fail at political revolution, it grossly underestimated the strength of the established order, with unintended consequences prevailing ever since.

The energy of the sixties students did fuel other movements—for women, the environment, minorities, LGBTs—as well as dramatic cultural changes. But if

America's establishment was shaken by the sixties, it was never close to overthrown. The reactionary forces regrouped and intensified their efforts in the decades that followed. Most disillusioned graduates of the sixties would acquiesce, "accept reality," and grow into their middle-aged lives as citizens, workers, and contributors to an established order they had sought to overthrow or at least evade.

However, those who participated in the movement would not forget the experience. Though their victory was certainly not much celebrated, they would remember, on some level, that as students, mere youths, they stood up in opposition to their government, universities, and often their parents, and they had an effect. They knew that they had found within themselves sufficient agency to change history, and the knowledge of that has not gone away.

Therein lies a third lesson. The movement was not a historical dead end, a detour on a road that went nowhere. Memories have afterlife, and the sixties movement lives on in the participants' shared memory. And if it could happen once. . . . Ellen Willis, who lived through it, said of the movement, "It couldn't happen, according to the reigning intellectual currents of the fifties, but it did." So, at other times when it couldn't, might it not happen again? The one-time Illinois Young Socialist president Durrett argues that the sixties movement did not end, that the forces behind it, subordinated for decades to careers and families, have only grown stronger. "Yes," he concedes, "*they* are more in control now than ever . . . but the movement is stronger too," and he points to "the Sanders campaign . . . support for single payer . . . the huge post-inaugural 2016 Women's Marches in every town and village." He argues, "The struggle continues . . . participation in the struggle is the most important thing."[5] He believes the movement lives.

If so, it lives in unforeseen ways. Historian Robert Daniels suggests that "revolution's essence is a turnabout, whether permanent or temporary, in the basic values that hold a society . . . together and legitimize its character."[6] If we accept this, then something much like a revolution did happen in the decade. The society has never again been as it was before. At a minimum, the social values of the movement lived on, with changed attitudes toward drugs, sex, gender, education, and religion. But just as influential, the movement stimulated a profound change in American political discourse. Today, any new issue—really all new issues—from wealth inequality to voting rights to healthcare to war and peace, immediately become topics of debate in a much enlarged, post-sixties public sphere, albeit with a quality of discourse that varies widely, given the explosion of social media, the blogosphere, cable news and talk radio, and the diversity of loud voices, from Fox to MSNBC.

"Sixties values" began a war that has raged in this public sphere ever since, pitting a no-longer-silent, change-averse "moral majority" against proponents pushing for change. If mostly in the former's favor, the battle has swung back and forth, demonstrated in the election of the country's most liberal president, Barack Obama—though a man of the center, his election was certainly stirred by sixties values—followed by the most conservative, Donald Trump—carried to victory by reaction to those values. In response to Obama, the Right was reinvigorated with the activism of the Tea Party and the clatter of the birthers. In response to Trump, nationwide activism swelled on the Left, with many veterans of the sixties emerging once again, engaging with a new generation of protesters, offering the experience of their youthful battles. So the war continues. The decade was a watershed in attitudes and values, representing a discontinuity, a radical break from the past. Students of the generation before lived a completely different college experience. Those who followed may have felt they missed out but gratefully accepted the changes the decade wrought.

Jack Peltason, like many of his generation, maintained that the "student unrest" of the sixties was inexplicable, that no one knew why it happened. Looking back from fifty years on, it's not a mystery. The sixties student-protest movement happened because a significant segment of a generation, when confronted with a moral challenge, exercised agency, acted independently, and demonstrated free will in the face of overwhelming opposition and thus affected history. Their movement was inspired by forces of the era, black Americans rejecting oppression, colonial peoples throwing off empire, and an Asian David bloodying a western Goliath. The students and their movement were very much of their time, and those who lived through the time cannot easily forget. That may be the most enduring lesson of the sixties—that those who lived through the decade, and those who hear of it or read of it, will remember and know that in the arc of history, when conditions arise, when stars align, when the times demand, it can happen again.

Contributors: In Their Own Words

Victor Berkey-Moheno

I was born in Mexico City and grew up in Los Angeles, where I graduated from Hollywood High School as president of my senior class. I attended UC Berkeley, where I graduated with a major in zoology (I wanted to be a dentist) and two minors in history and Spanish. I entered San Diego State University, where I did two years of graduate work in embryology. At that time, I knew more about the effect of Thyroxin on the development of skin in chick embryos than anybody in the world.

My parents were Democrats, although they voted for Eisenhower. Neither one was a college graduate. My older brother was student-body president at Hollywood High School and went on to Stanford, graduating as a chemical engineer. Then he went to Cornell, where he earned a doctorate in astrophysics.

I was not really politically active as an undergraduate at Berkeley, although I was aware of the House on Un-American Activities Committee when they held hearings in San Francisco, and several teachers lost their jobs simply because they were subpoenaed.

My first direct action while at Berkeley was a sit-in at the U.S. Attorney's office in San Francisco. He was Cecil Poole, who incidentally was African American. Our demand was for the federal government to send U.S. Marshals to the South to protect civil rights workers. This was right after three civil rights workers were murdered (Goodman, Schwerner, and Cheney). There were no arrests, and the sit-in remained peaceful. The free-speech movement took place the fall after I left Berkeley.

I recall debating a State Department representative on the radio about the Vietnam War when I was at San Diego State. (The government espoused the domino theory, that if the communists were not defeated in Vietnam, they would invade the United States.) After two years at San Diego State, I entered grad school at the University of Illinois.

Phillip Durrett

I was born in Chicago in 1943, the youngest of four children. My father joined the navy shortly after and served in the Pacific on an aircraft carrier during the war. One of my uncles was killed when his B-17 was shot down over Belgium. Another uncle was a marine, serving in the Pacific, "liberating" islands captured by Japan. Both sets of my grandparents were farmers in Iowa. My mother's parents owned their farm; my father's parents were tenant farmers. My father ended his education after eighth grade and went to work on a farm. He met my mother while helping harvest crops on her parents' farm. After my two sisters were born, my parents moved to Chicago, and my father enrolled in a government training course to learn IT (before digital computers, working with punch cards).

After the war ended, we moved every two to three years and lived in small cities in Illinois, Indiana, and Kentucky. I graduated high school in Quincy, Illinois, in 1961. I had no clear idea of what I wanted to do, so I joined the air force in September shortly after my brother had also joined. Both my sisters had married air force members, so it seemed like a good idea at the time. I served four years as a weather observer in Morocco and in Georgia. I was on a SAC base in Morocco (with nukes) during the Cuban missile crisis and thought we would be at war. One-third of the bombers were placed airborne, one-third on the end of the runway with their engines running, and one-third within ten minute takeoff. Fortunately, JFK ignored General LeMay, who wanted a first strike.

Growing up, I had no firm political opinions. My parents were both Republicans, but I can't remember any political discussions at home. My political education really started in Georgia. I married in 1964, my fiancée moving from Illinois (a student at the U of I) to Atlanta. She got a job at Emory University in a cardiac lab, and we rented an apartment in Atlanta. Emory University had a Christmas party for "white" employees, and a separate party for "Negro" employees (excuse the language, but those were the words used then). My wife was trained by her black co-worker, who earned half of what my wife earned. My wife and I did not attend the "white" party, but we were invited by her black co-workers to their party. She was called into the office and threatened with firing for attending the "wrong" party.

I remember people cheering in Atlanta when JFK was assassinated. Lester Maddox (later the governor of Georgia) owned a restaurant in Atlanta. When the civil rights laws were changed, he closed his restaurant rather than integrate. He placed a coffin in front of his restaurant, put Uncle Sam in it, and sold baby-, mama-, and poppa-sized axe handles.

My enlistment ended in 1965, and we moved to Urbana and I registered at the university. I have no clear memory of when my politics changed from apathetic to progressive to socialist. I soon realized that the history I had been taught growing up was either incomplete or wrong. The Vietnam War was increasing daily, and students (unlike me) were being forced to choose a course of action upon graduation—enlistment, getting drafted, or going to Canada. I knew racism was wrong; unlike in Georgia, it was less visible in Illinois but nevertheless present throughout America. My wife was hounded from her dorm when she dated a black student before we were married. Illinois is named after a tribe of Native Americans, but that was never mentioned in my history courses in high school.

My brother was serving in Vietnam, my brother-in-law was refueling bombers from Thailand, and I joined protests against the war. During one of my rare visits to my parents' home, we were watching CBS coverage of the war and protests; my father said the protestors should be shot, knowing full well I was one of those protestors. I don't think we ever fully recovered, and we never revisited those times. There are so many victims of that war (I don't count myself as one of the victims).

Looking back, I have no regrets for my actions (except for perhaps they were too few). I'm very proud that my daughters are feminists, for which I take very little credit. I'm happy that we can't (or shouldn't) imagine a progressive movement mostly led by men (although we can easily imagine regressive movements like that). I'm equally depressed and hopeful for the future. All my daughters were involved in the protests against Trump, and we'll see what next year's elections will hold. As someone once said, "Now is the time for all good (wo)men to come to the aid of their country!"

Patricia (Patsy) Engelhard

My parents met in Washington, D.C., just after World War II. My father was a German Jew whose family had lived in the United States for generations. My mother was barely a first-generation Orthodox Jew whose parents escaped pre-revolution Russia. My parents were liberal in their DNA and passed on their views of the world and humanity and our responsibility to take care of each other.

I grew up in an idyllic community south of Chicago where my father was a musician and a writer and never earned enough for a family of four. My mother worked from the time she was sixteen, including throughout my childhood. She was the first working mother I knew. She worked for U.S. Congressman Sidney R. Yates for forty years. Life was good and seemed easy until 1963, when my father died and two months later JFK was assassinated. The world as we knew it had changed.

I began at the U of I in the fall of 1965 on merit and needs scholarships and the GI Bill. My sister followed me there a year later. In the spring semester of my sophomore year I dropped out of school and moved to Berkeley, California, just before the Summer of Love. I came back to school for spring semester '68.

I participated in nearly every antiwar protest, rally, and march during the time I was on campus, and I was involved with the early stages of the women's movement at the university. I graduated in the spring semester of 1970—with no grades in my final semester due to the Kent State strike. I was an activist from my freshman year, as was everyone I knew. We did not see any other way to cope with the world we faced.

After graduation I taught in an [Office of Economic Opportunity]-funded school for one year and returned then to Chicago. In the fall of 1972 I began law school with the first wave of women who entered in large numbers. It seemed we all had the idea at the same time—that the law was the tool we needed to change the world. I graduated from DePaul Law School in 1975. I married, had two children and did not work full time for ten years—a decision I have never regretted. My professional career was in nonprofit administration. I worked for a U.S. congressman, was a dean at Northwestern University, and held four different jobs at the American Bar Association. Of course, much happened during all of that, but those are the topic sentences.

I am grateful to have gone through the sixties and grateful for the people who were there too—good friends with a sense of purpose and belief. Do you think young people feel it is possible to change the world now? Do you think they care? We were very lucky. And no matter what history says, we did change the world. It is not the same. What is not better now is because we never fully understood the power of the military-industrial complex that went into full attack mode post-sixties and so now . . . here we are. I wonder if this is what they all meant to happen?

Vern Fein

I was raised by a nonparticipating Jewish father and a closet-Catholic mother, a nearly unheard-of marriage in the 1930s. My father was involved in the tavern business and became fairly wealthy from doing that, though he came from a very poor background. I distinctly remember my family being not only pro-Eisenhower but definitely anti-Stevenson in Illinois, and I also remember the strange sensation of liking what Adlai said, even though I was only twelve. But I was not political, so when I went to Cornell College in Iowa, the only political thing I can remember doing was spitting at people who were holding signs against nuclear weapons because I thought they were communists.

From there, after undergrad, I went to the University of Illinois as an English major and almost completed my PhD. In an Old English class, a couple challenged me about the Vietnam War, and I began to learn about it and realize how wrong it was. Then the free-speech and antiwar and civil rights movements came all together, and I—working alongside Vic Berkey, who was the acknowledged leader, and others from this group Mike interviewed for the book—protested everything that moved until the movement ran its course in the early seventies.

For a period I participated in the burgeoning counterculture that existed around most university campuses in an effort to preserve and promulgate our '60s values and politics. I did not finish my PhD but took a job at the local junior college, from which I was fired due to my antiwar activities, resulting in an ACLU lawsuit that ended in a hung jury. After that I worked in a special education school in town for thirty-four years and retired in 2010. I am fortunate to have a wife of forty-three years, three lovely adult children, and four grandboys. All of my three children are very active in the radical politics of this time in history, the middle son even starting and maintaining an online magazine with an emphasis on progressive political and cultural change; it's called Smile Politely—you can google it. I am finding plenty to do regarding community outreach work to help those in need through various churches I have attended, and I'm even writing some poetry, which I really enjoy, on the side.

Bernard Gershenson

My parents were liberal Democrats in Park Forest, Illinois, a very conservative Chicago suburb (65 percent Goldwater in '64). They often discussed politics, and one of my early memories is of them watching the Army-McCarthy hearings on TV (don't know whether this was live or a newsreel), but I couldn't watch whatever it was I wanted to watch. My first politically active moment happened when some of my eighth-grade friends and I held Kennedy signs while Nixon was speaking from a platform in front of Goldblatt's department store. Some adult ripped the signs out of our hands. I was dumbfounded. I didn't know adults did things like that.

My parents were very pro–civil rights and, similar to what Les points out in his piece, as a Jew in the wake of World War II, I was made sensitive to any mistreatment of minorities. I read newspapers, but I wasn't politically active in high school, where I was a good but not great student. My senior year of high school I was aware of LBJ's recent escalation of the war in Vietnam, which seemed to have no reason—not that I knew very much, but when I registered for the draft in early

August, I knew that there was no reason for me to fight and possibly die in Vietnam. The United States wasn't threatened in any way.

I attended an SDS meeting sometime during freshman year that attracted a handful of people. Keenan Sheedy seemed to be in charge, and I remember one or two others who were there, but that's about all I remember. They were talking variations of Marxist politics and I didn't understand a thing. I didn't go back. But as war escalated, so did my knowledge of what was going on and so did my opposition to it. I became more active in the spring of '67.

After the U of I, I served in Teacher Corps, which included a master's in education, got a master's in creative writing from San Francisco State after that, and then began a teaching career that started at SF State (seven years) and continued at College of San Mateo (twenty-eight years). During that time I published three books of poetry. I was politically active in the nuclear freeze movement in the early 1980s, but not much after that; I protested the Iraq war, made phone calls for Obama, took part in local environmental demonstrations from time to time, was re-energized by Trump and am currently involved in the sanctuary-cities movement and helping detainees fight deportation.

Robert Justin ("Bob") Goldstein

I grew up in Bethesda, Maryland, and was a University of Illinois undergraduate political science major between 1965 and 1968 (also lived in Champaign-Urbana most of the time I was a graduate student at the University of Chicago between 1968 and 1974, from which I received a PhD in 1976). While a UI undergrad, I covered the "New Left," including the DuBois Club and Clabaugh Act controversies, for the *Daily Illini* and for the (now-defunct) *Champaign-Urbana Courier*. I edited the first two editions of *The Advisor*, a published, book-length, student-teacher course evaluation, in 1968 and 1969, and founded and managed The Used Book Store in the YMCA basement on Wright Street between 1971 and 1974 (under other managers, the store lasted until 1999). I taught political science at San Diego State University (1974–76) and at Oakland University (Rochester, Michigan, 1976–2005) and since 2004 have been a research associate at the Center for Russian, Eastern European and Eurasian Studies at the University of Michigan at Ann Arbor, where I have lived since 1985. My academic specialty is the history of civil liberties / political repression / political dissent in modern American and European history and politics, and I have published/edited almost twenty books on those subjects, including books on nineteenth-century European censorship, on the American flag desecration controversy, and on the American post–World War II "red scare." My most well-known book, *Political Repression in Modern America*, was published in a 2001 second edition by the University of Illinois Press, and I am currently updating and revising the book for the press.

Like everyone else who lived through the '60s, especially on an activist college campus, my life (and my life's work) was profoundly shaped by my experiences at the University of Illinois, and I remain friends with quite a few of my friends from those times. When the '60s rock group "The Doors" sang in one of their songs "No one here gets out alive," they proved to be literally correct with regard to some, like their lead singer Jim Morrison, but even for all others, no one "escaped" without ideas, hopes, dreams, and, often, scars.

Joseph Hardin

When I got to the U of I, the thought of political activity was not on my mind. I was interested in setting the curve in my intro chemistry class and seeing what in the world panty raids could possibly be about. By my sophomore year I was checking out the groups on campus talking about the war and civil rights. I had been called to take my physical by my draft board the previous summer and had decided I should look into this Vietnam War business.

A friend and I went to meetings about fair housing—that is, discrimination in selling and renting based on race—and I went to an SDS meeting and understood half of what was said. I spent the coming summer washing test tubes and reading and talking with people about the war and the movement for equality in the South. And listening to Dylan. By the beginning of my junior year I was convinced something had to be done about some of this and became active in the antiwar movement. I helped start what was then called an "underground" newspaper that spoke about the world from the perspective of young, disenchanted, often angry, occasionally stoned viewers of the disturbing, evolving scene in our country and halfway across the world.

I spent the next couple of years trying to convince enough people that the war should be ended and the capitalist system kinda sucked. We could do better. After drifting for a while I came back to Urbana and went to grad school for an exceptionally long period, taught at the University of Georgia for a year, and then was asked to help out with a new National Science Foundation–funded computer center being established at the U of I. I spent the next few years introducing people to this idea of computer networks and managing the development of software to help people work with the center's supercomputers over what came to be called the internet. One of the first Web browsers came out of this work, as did other tools for communicating on the emerging Web.

I helped found a group, the International World Wide Web Conference Committee, that still holds annual conferences on internet technologies and how they impact the world. Then I moved to the University of Michigan, helped with a lab engaged in Web and tech research, and focused on educational tech for a while, starting up the Sakai Foundation, which helps coordinate the development of an open-source software system used by 350 or so colleges and universities around the world to help faculty and students deliver, manage, and enhance courses. Open systems of all types, open software, open access, open courseware, open educational resources, and open research efforts occupied my time until I retired in 2010.

Since then I have done some consulting on internet patent suits, on the side of those trying to fight claims made under the ridiculous patent regime in the United States, and sailed a boat on Georgian Bay in Ontario, Canada, where I live in an old farmhouse with my wife of seventeen years now. Last summer I introduced a grandson to sailing on the Great Lakes. Recently, I got a 1970 BSA 650 Thunderbolt motorcycle. And a very good helmet.

Keven Roth

I grew up in Park Forest, an ideal planned community of the 1950s on the fringes of south suburban Chicago. My parents were both college educated. My father worked on the Manhattan Project (I was born in Los Alamos), and after the war he went back to medical school and pioneered the use of radioactive isotopes in medicine. My mother was a frustrated writer and actress, turned involuntarily into a housewife. It was a very intellectual household. Graduate students and visiting foreign professors were frequent visitors in our home, and my father enjoyed taking them on trips to see America. I usually went on those trips. We also traveled abroad on trips associated with medical conferences my father attended. There was a lot of art and music in our house. I was not fond of classical music. There was never a doubt about all three kids going to college.

We were serious Democrats. My grandmother said she prayed for us every night, because we didn't go to church and we were Democrats. We had a mock election in my third-grade class, and I was one of only two who voted for Adlai Stevenson.

I started college at U of I in 1966. My roommate was my best friend from high school. Our first semester was rather boring until we discovered that the more interesting students hung out in the Union cafeteria. After that, we were part of every antiwar event on campus, including a protest at the local draft board in Champaign and the Mobilization to End the War in Vietnam in New York in spring of 1967, both marches in Washington, as well as the attempts to remove "women's hours" that would have allowed us to stay out after 10:00 P.M.

I would like to say that a feminist awakening led me to protest our restrictive hours, but the actual case was less clear-cut and more reflective of the times. Like many women, I did find that locking women up at 10:00 P.M., while the men could do what they wanted around the clock, was unfair. While women muttered about this among themselves, at a meeting of SFS in the back lounge of the union, the usual leaders of meetings, the guys, started talking about successful efforts at other colleges to abolish women's hours and maybe we should do something. I asked what we could do. I became the leader of the effort.

I got my degree in geography and went on to eventually work for the U.S. Geological Survey as a cartographer.

Steve Schmidt

My parents were both from small Mississippi River towns in Iowa where the Depression weighed on their childhoods. Neither was politically active, and politics was not much discussed at the kitchen table, probably because my father was a conservative Republican while my mother was a Roosevelt Democrat. My older brother and I were born in Denver, my younger brother in Pennsylvania. We grew up in small-town Iowa, but I went to high school in Lincoln, Nebraska. The advantage to me of our move to Lincoln was that the large school had a debate team. Debating the extension of Social Security benefits to include medical care (Medicare) was my first exposure to research and formal discourse on a political topic—heady stuff for a fifteen-year-old.

Ours was not an intellectual household, but my two brothers and I were told from an early age that college was expected to be a part of our education. With that much guidance, I began at the U of I in 1966 as a James Scholar in pre-med. The pre-med curriculum was time-consuming, so it took me a few months to discover the Union cafeteria and the disputatious students who gathered there. Beginning in spring 1967, I took part in almost all of the free-speech, antidraft, and antiwar protests on campus over the next several years, as well as the protests in Chicago during the 1968 Democrat Party convention. My direct involvement in these protests was interrupted for about nine months by a federal incarceration for my antidraft activities. Unfortunately, the war in Vietnam had only expanded during my absence, so there was more than enough to do when I was free from jail again in the late spring 1970. Demonstrations, marches, sit-ins, and speeches continued right on through the protest against the so-called "Christmas bombings" in December 1972.

As the war wound down in 1972, I went to law school in Washington, D.C. I guess many activists saw the law as a possible way to continue the struggle for justice. With the Watergate scandal heating up and the congressional hearings underway, it was a very "interesting time" to be in Washington, especially with professors like Charles Ruff teaching us criminal law. But after a year of that, I realized that lawyering was not for me. So I returned to Urbana and helped to foster "counterculture" institutions like Earthworks Garage.

After a few years of that, I returned to the U of I to get undergraduate and graduate degrees in economics and political science. From there, I went back to D.C. to work in the federal government. I worked for Senator Paul Simon for a brief time, then worked for the Department of Labor for twenty-two years. Meanwhile, I married, raised two children, coached basketball and soccer teams, and tried to support social justice groups: ACLU, Planned Parenthood, Southern Poverty Law Center, Just Neighbors, and others.

Lester Wall

I grew up on the south side of Chicago and went to South Shore High School, which was three-fourths Jewish. Three South Shore basketball starters went on to Amherst, Harvard, and the University of Chicago. My mother loved Adlai Stevenson, my father not so much, but he was a Democrat. It was a mostly Democratic neighborhood.

I was an economics major in the business school. The Holocaust in Germany was the biggest determinate of my political beliefs. I was a strong supporter of the civil rights movement, the free-speech movement, freedom and equality issues in general. The lies of the Johnson administration and in particular the immorality of the soldiers were instrumental in focusing me on Vietnam. America seemed the clear oppressor, in great part because civilian populations were often considered Viet Cong and treated as enemy soldiers.

I met the author when he was a small-town boy largely unfamiliar with the ways of the world. With prodigious effort on my part and with painfully slow results I was able to open his eyes on life, love, politics, fate, and sex. With little appreciation I might add. In return he introduced me to life-altering substances and fast motorcycles, putting me in life threatening situations more than once. I should have listened to my mother's warnings, but the Slim Jim snacks sent from his home proved irresistible to me.

Acknowledgments

This was a story that deserved to be told, and I am fortunate to be the one to tell it. Such a task requires a great deal of support. This where I thank folks, not just for helping with the book, but for keeping me sane. A famous author said he wrote for self-preservation. Me too. I don't much like retirement, and desperately needed something that offered purpose, intellectual stimulation, and interaction with people. This project did that, thus helped keep me sane.

Thanks to Bernard Gershenson for reading and editing every page of the manuscript, repeatedly, and improving it every time. He spent his adult life teaching people to write and, in the end, even managed to teach me some. Thanks to James Engelhardt of the UI Press for considering the concept worthwhile. To the University of Illinois archivists, especially Anna Trammell and Ellen Swain, for treating me as a serious researcher. To Lester Wall for being a best friend in the sixties and teaching me more than I'll admit. To Joseph Hardin, from whom I learned most of what I know about politics yet still managed to lose every political bet I ever made with him. To Patricia Engelhard for loving the idea of this project from the beginning. To Mara Stolurow and Paula Shafransky for both humoring me and taking me seriously. To my high school history teacher, Brother Wayne Dupuis, and my first college history prof, Paul W. Schroeder, both of whom taught me the joy of history, and Professors Mary Pickering and George Vasquez who showed me it's still fun at this age. And to the patience of my wife Katherine, who is still not entirely sure what I was doing all those days I claimed to be working at the library.

Without the participants in the Illinois student movement there would have been no movement to write about, nor any memories to draw on for the writing of it. Thanks to the leaders, Phil Durrett, Vern Fein, and Victor Berkey Moheno; to all the contributors, Joanne Chester, David Eisenman, Nancy Engelhard, Belden Fields, Larry Geni, John Hackman, Dan'l McCollum, Robert Outis, David Ransel, Keven Roth, Paul Schroeder, Roger Simon, Marty Shupak, Steve Schmidt, Rick Soderstrom, and Vincent Wu; and to all the others involved, mentioned and not. The movement happened at Illinois because of their collective efforts.

My thanks to Professor William Maher and Angela Waarala of the University Archives for their help recovering fifty-year-old, yellowed images and to Phojoe.com for masterfully restoring them to usable condition, to Debbie Ross of the Abraham Lincoln Presidential Library in Springfield, Illinois for locating all the film reels I asked for, to Mary Datoc of the Santa Clara County Library System who procured them for me, and to the Saratoga Library for providing a place to work.

My special gratitude goes to Professors Mary Ann Wynkoop and Robert Goldstein for their valuable and insightful critiques.

All problems, inaccuracies, and omissions are of course entirely my fault. Thank you all for my sanity.

Notes

Preface

1. Fein interview, September 9, 2016.
2. Berkey interview, April 11, 2017.
3. Wall interview, April 16, 2017.

Introduction

1. Roger Simon, "Up Against It," *Daily Illini*, March 10, 1970, 8.
2. "New Beginning Freshmen, Fall 1968, 'Unofficial' Demographic Profile," *UIUC Student Enrollment, University Division of Information Management*. Self-reported race/ethnicity data collected for the first time in 1968; author subtracted "Native American" (likely error noted in report) and "Unknown" from total. http://dmi.illinois.edu/stuenr/frosh/frosh68.html. "UIUC On-Campus Student Enrollment by Curriculum, Sex, and Residency," *University of Illinois Division of Management Information*. http://dmi.illinois.edu/stuenr/ethsexres/ethsex67.htm.
3. Thirty-nine percent represents 1967 Cook County undergraduates. "UIUC Student Enrollment, updated 1/31/2018," *University of Illinois Division of Management Information*. http://dmi.illinois.edu/stuenr/#county.
4. The 1962 founding manifesto of Students for a Democratic Society, written primarily by Tom Hayden, in Port Huron, Michigan, at the group's first national convention.
5. Gellhorn, *States and Subversion*, 56.
6. Ibid., 66.
7. Ibid., 138.
8. Engelhard, Geni interview, September 18, 2017.

9. Hardin interview, April 5, 2017.
10. Ibid.

Chapter 1. The New Yorker: George D. Stoddard

1. "U.I. Trustees Still Have Responsibility," *Champaign-Urbana Courier*, July 27, 1953, 6.
2. "Monday's News Fodder; Korean Peace, U.I. War," *Champaign-Urbana Courier*, July 27, 1953, 3.
3. "George Stoddard Dies at 84; Educator Led 4 Universities," *New York Times*, December 29, 1981.
4. "Ban AYD Bill Awaits OK by Green," *Daily Illini*, July 2, 1947, 1.
5. "What Is 'The Ivy Affair'?" *Chicago Daily News*, July 25, 1953.
6. David Lieberman, Chicago Illinois, to Wayne Johnston, Wayne A. Johnston Papers, 1945–1967, University of Illinois Archives, Urbana.
7. "Stoddard Ouster Might Aid Livingston as Candidate," *Champaign-Urbana Courier*, July 26, 1953, 1.
8. George Tagge, "State's GOP Urged to Oust Party Phonies," *Chicago Tribune*, August 12, 1950, 1.
9. "Livingston Calls Stoddard 'Pain in the Neck' and 'Snob,'" *Champaign-Urbana Courier*, August 5, 1953, 16.
10. "Faculty Group Plans Protest of Ousters," *Champaign-Urbana Courier*, July 26, 1953, 1.
11. "Board's Action Unjust, LAS Heads Say," *Champaign-Urbana Courier*, July 29, 1953, 3.
12. "U. of I. Faculty Told to 'Stick to Education,'" *Champaign-Urbana Courier*, July 30, 1953, 3.
13. Ibid.
14. "Stoddard Rips Livingston for Ouster Vote," *Chicago Tribune*, July 30, 1953, 1.
15. "Stoddard Statement Draws Ire," *Champaign-Urbana Courier*, August 4, 1953, 28.
16. "Livingston Calls Stoddard 'Pain in the Neck' and 'Snob,'" *Champaign-Urbana Courier*, August 5, 1953, 3.
17. "George Stoddard Dies at 84; Educator Led 4 Universities," *New York Times*, December 29, 1981, https://goo.gl/4F6JG1.
18. "Stratton Says Stoddard Tried to Set Policies," *Champaign-Urbana Courier*, July 28, 1953, 3.
19. "Crime and Punishment," *Daily Illini*, July 28, 1953, 6.
20. "'Stoddard Case' Continues to Draw Varied Comment," *Champaign News-Gazette*, July 31, 1953, 18.
21. "I 'Felt Badly' on Stoddard Secret Meet—Red Grange," *Champaign News-Gazette*, July 28, 1953, 3.
22. "Stoddard Defends His Regime at U. of I.," *Chicago Sun-Times*, August 3, 1953.
23. "Politicians Finally Liquidated Stoddard," *Chicago Sun-Times*, July 29, 1953.

Chapter 2. The New Guy: David Dodds Henry

1. Larry Beaupre, "Henry Refused Presidency When Offered," *Daily Illini*, July 1, 1965, 12.
2. Ibid., 12.
3. Goldstein interview, December 29, 2017.

4. Robert McG. Thomas Jr., "David D. Henry, 89, President of Illinois U. in Time of Tumult," *New York Times*, September 7, 1995.

Chapter 3. The Communist TA: Edward Yellin

1. "UI Student's Trial Today," *Daily Illini*, March 9, 1960, 3.
2. "Loyalty Oaths Ordered for City Teachers," *Chicago Tribune*, June 19, 1955.
3. "Yellin Faces U.S. Trial on Contempt," *Champaign News-Gazette*, March 8, 1960, 6.
4. "Yellin Found Guilty of Contempt," *Champaign-Urbana Courier*, March 12, 1960, 3.
5. Lange, "Who Can Define?" 86.
6. "Wall Reinstates Yellin," *Daily Illini*, March 26, 1960, 1.
7. Editorial, "What's the Yellin About?" *Daily Illini*, March 22, 1960, 6.
8. Editorial, "All Over but the Shouting," *Daily Illini*, March 26, 1960, 4.
9. Ibid., 96.

Chapter 4. The Sexual Rebel: Leo Koch

1. "Advice on Sex," *Daily Illini*, March 18, 1960, 7.
2. Ken Braun, "University Fires Koch," *Daily Illini*, April 8, 1960, 1.
3. Ibid.
4. "Prof. Koch Relieved of UI Duties for Sex Views," *Champaign News-Gazette*, April 8, 1960, 3.
5. Lynn Ludlow, "Suspended for Sex Views, U.I. Biologist Will Appeal," *Champaign-Urbana Courier*, April 8, 1960, 1.
6. "President Henry Hanged in Effigy," *Champaign-Urbana Courier*, April 8, 1960, 1.
7. Allyn, *Make Love Not War*, 43.
8. Bilgrami and Cole, *Who's Afraid of Academic Freedom?* 73.
9. "Dad's Leaders Back Henry in Koch Decision," *Champaign News-Gazette*, April 10, 1960, 3.
10. "Students Protest Koch's Firing," *Champaign News-Gazette*, April 10, 1960, 3.
11. Lynn Ludlow, "He's Really against Free Love, Prof. Koch Reports," *Champaign-Urbana Courier*, April 10, 1960, 14.
12. "Group Defends Koch's Right to Opinions," *Champaign News-Gazette*, April 9, 1960, 10.
13. Tom Kacich, "C-U Was One Happening Place 50 Years Ago," *Champaign News-Gazette*, December 30, 1989.
14. "U. of I. Board Blocks Revival of Sex Controversy in Firing," *Chicago Tribune*, March 21, 1963.
15. "Koch Firing Justified," *Chicago Sun-Times*, April 12, 1960.
16. "Sex: Profound Revolution," *Daily Illini*, March 22, 1960, 1.
17. Allyn, *Make Love Not War*, 44.

Chapter 5. The Civil Rights Movement and the University

1. Roger Ebert, "Urge Vigil Participation," *Daily Illini*, September 20, 1963, 1.
2. "Divine's Followers Give Aid to Strikers: With Evangelist's Sanction They 'Sit Down' in Restaurant," *New York Times*, September 23, 1939.

3. Carol Stevens, "Begin Champaign Sit-In," *Daily Illini*, October 2, 1963, 1.
4. "Henry Outlines UI Civil Rights Policies," *Daily Illini*, October 3, 1963, 1.
5. Barb Whiteside, "Thurmond to Receive Apology," *Daily Illini*, November 14, 1963, 1.
6. "To Protest McMullin Arrest," *Daily Illini*, November 22, 1963, 1.
7. Ibid.

Chapter 6. Civil Rights, Free Speech, and War

1. Dixie Cowan, "Students Protest Berkeley Policy," *Daily Illini*, December 5, 1964, 3.
2. "Keyes Guilty of Refusing Draft," *Daily Illini*, January 6, 1965, 2.
3. "Negroes Ask for Protection," *Daily Illini*, February 12, 1965, 1.
4. Editorial, "28 Students," *Daily Illini*, March 5, 1965, 8.
5. Vicki Packer, "Students Here Join in Selma Protests," *Daily Illini*, March 13, 1965, 1.
6. *Daily Illini*, March 27, 1965, 1.
7. "Students Protest War Policy; Establish Viet Nam Committee," *Daily Illini*, April 6, 1965, 2.
8. Vicki Parker and Margaret Converse, *Daily Illini*, March 18, 1965, 3.
9. Dan Balz, "Hold Student Vigil," *Daily Illini*, October 2, 1965, 1.
10. Dan Balz, "Students Aid Soldiers," *Daily Illini*, October 22, 1965, 1.
11. Howard Rothman, "SDS Criticizes Blood Drive," *Daily Illini*, November 11, 1965, 3.
12. Wu interview, January 12, 2018.
13. "Seek Clabaugh Act Repeal," *Daily Illini*, April 22, 1966, 9.
14. Sue Engel, "To Open Coffee House for Radicals," *Daily Illini*, May 27, 1966, 1.
15. John Schmadeke, "300 Protest U.S. Bombing in North Vietnam," *Daily Illini*, July 7, 1966, 1.
16. Fein interview, September 19, 2016.

Chapter 7. A Spark: W.E.B. DuBois Club

1. Bob Goldstein, "Campus Groups Merge," *Daily Illini*, September 27, 1966, 3.
2. "SDS Holds First Meeting of the Year," *Daily Illini*, September 23, 1966, 2.
3. Goldstein, "Clabaugh Promises to Fight Organization of Local Chapter," *Daily Illini*, September 27, 1966, 1.
4. Ibid., 4.

Chapter 8. The University Reacts

1. Bob Goldstein, "Weigh Dubois Action," *Daily Illini*, September 28, 1966, 1.
2. Ibid., 4.

Chapter 9. The University Delays

1. Statement from Dean of Students, September 28, 1966, Public Information Office, Student Protests Subject File, 1954–74, University of Illinois Archives, Urbana.
2. Robert Goldstein, "Millet Defers Decision on DuBois Club Request," *Daily Illini*, September 29, 1966, 1.

3. Schmidt interview, January 15, 2018.
4. Brian Braun, "YAF Tables Clabaugh Stand," *Daily Illini*, November 2, 1966, 2.
5. "A Cause for Concern," *Daily Illini*, November 3, 1966, 8.
6. Robert Goldstein, "SDS to Sponsor Vietnam 'Speakout,'" *Daily Illini*, November 5, 1966, 1.
7. Phil Durrett, email to author, December 9, 2017.
8. Goldstein interview, December 29, 2017.
9. Ibid.
10. Robert Goldstein, "SDS Speakers Attack U.S. Policies," *Daily Illini*, November 8, 1966, 1.
11. Robert Goldstein, "Millet to Decide DuBois Petition," *Daily Illini*, November 19, 1966, 1.
12. Robert Goldstein, "Millet Defers DuBois Decision," *Daily Illini*, December 2, 1966, 1.
13. Ibid., 5.
14. Ibid.
15. Brooke Cultra, "Meredith: Make a Decision," *Daily Illini*, December 2, 1966, 1.

Chapter 10. Passing the Buck

1. Robert Goldstein, "Henry Hands DuBois Problems to Trustees," *Daily Illini*, December 13, 1966, 1.
2. Brian Braun, "Faculty Senate Makes Public Millet Letter," *Daily Illini*, December 13, 1966, 1.
3. Robert Goldstein, "Henry Barred Reds at Wayne State," *Daily Illini*, December 13, 1966, 1.
4. Ibid.
5. "Millet: Student Rights vs. Privileges," *Daily Illini*, December 16, 1966, 1.
6. Editorial, "What's the Deal," *Daily Illini*, December 21, 1966, 8.

Chapter 11. The Board Surprises

1. Robert Goldstein, "Board Hears DuBois Issue," *Daily Illini*, January 14, 1967, 1.
2. John Schmadeke, "DuBois Club Wins Battle," *Daily Illini*, February 10, 1967, 1.
3. Ibid.
4. Editorial, "Berkeley Comes to Illinois," *Chicago Tribune*, February 11, 1967.
5. Robert Goldstein, "React to DuBois Decision," *Daily Illini*, February 11, 1967, 1.
6. Ibid, 2.

Chapter 12. The Legislature Speaks

1. Robert Goldstein, "Illinois Senate Seeks Ban of Local DuBois Chapter," *Daily Illini*, February 16, 1967, 1.
2. Ibid., 2.
3. Robert Goldstein, "Urge DuBois Recognition," *Daily Illini*, December 2, 1967, 1.

4. Letters, David D. Henry Personal Papers, 1922–84, University of Illinois Archives, Urbana.
5. Ibid.
6. Brian Braun, "Clabaugh Act in Legislature," *Daily Illini*, February 17, 1967, 1.
7. Robert Goldstein, "Illini Hold Viet War Protest," *Daily Illini*, February 17, 1967, 4.
8. Robert Goldstein, "Set up Anti-war Group," *Daily Illini*, February 7, 1967, 5.
9. Robert Goldstein, "Delay DuBois Recognition," *Daily Illini*, February 18, 1967, 1.
10. Ibid.
11. Brian Braun, "Scariano Hits Clabaugh," *Daily Illini*, February 21, 1967, 2.
12. Editorial, "Toward a Crisis," *Daily Illini*, February 21, 1967, 12.
13. "DuBois Affiliation Stalemates Talks by Millet, Bennett," *Daily Illini*, February 24, 1967, 1.
14. "Refuse to List SDS Students," *Daily Illini*, February 21, 1967, 10.
15. "Wisconsin Students Continue Protest," *Daily Illini*, February 24, 1967, 15.
16. Bob Snyder, "Protest Use of Illini Union," *Daily Illini*, February 25, 1967, 3.
17. Kenneth J. Heineman, "Defense-Related Grants as a Proportion of Overall Federal Obligations to the Largest Private and Public University Military Contractors, 1966," in *Campus Wars*, 15.
18. Arthur W. Galston, "Science and Social Responsibility: A Case History," *Annals of the New York Academy of Sciences* 196, no. 4: 223–35. Available at http://beck2.med.harvard.edu/week13/Galston.pdf.

Chapter 13. A Movement Is Born

1. Brian Braun, "Circle Students Hold Sit-In," *Daily Illini*, February 28, 1967, 1.
2. Robert Goldstein, "Protesters Ask UI to Repeal Clabaugh," *Daily Illini*, March 1, 1967.
3. Bruce Zumstein, "Groups Stage Quad Protest," *Daily Illini*, March 2, 1967.
4. Fein interview, September 19, 2016.
5. Vern Fein, e-mail to author, December 12, 2017.

Chapter 14. Henry Responds

1. Robert Goldstein, "No Official Position: Henry," *Daily Illini*, March 4, 1967, 1.
2. "No Chance to Get Repeal: Clabaugh," *Champaign News-Gazette*, March 8, 1967, 3.
3. Editorial, "Trying His Patience," *Champaign-Urbana Courier*, March 12, 1967, 38.
4. J. R. Pierce, "DuBois Club a Front?," *Champaign-Urbana Courier*, March 12, 1967, 38.
5. Lucile Drake, "Clabaugh Act Is Backed," *Champaign-Urbana Courier*, March 22, 1967, 44.
6. Lewis H. Peter, "Dr. Henry Upholds Law," *Champaign-Urbana Courier*, March 22, 1967, 44.
7. Dan Balz, "Trustees Must Act: Millet," *Daily Illini*, March 11, 1967, 1.

Chapter 15. The Board Reverses

1. Tony Burba, "Shadow of 'People of Illinois' Hovers over Deliberations on DuBois Club," *Champaign News-Gazette*, March 16, 1967, 21.

2. "U.I. Trustees Turn Down DuBois Plea," *Champaign-Urbana Courier*, March 15, 1967, 9.

3. Robert Goldstein, "Board Reverses Stand on DuBois Recognition," *Daily Illini*, March 15, 1967, 1.

4. Dorothy Wetzel, "U.I. Trustees Turn Thumbs Down on DuBois Club on Campus," *Champaign-Urbana Courier*, March 15, 1967, 3.

5. Ibid., 2.

6. Robert Goldstein, "React to Board's Action," *Daily Illini*, March 16, 1967, 1.

7. "Rep. Clabaugh to Explain Purpose," *Champaign News-Gazette*, March 19, 1967, 3.

8. Brian Braun, "Millet Declares Student Test No Violation of the Clabaugh Act," *Daily Illini*, March 16, 1967, 3.

9. Dan Balz, "Henry Interprets DuBois Decision," *Daily Illini*, March 18, 1967, 1.

Chapter 16. Students for Free Speech

1. Robert Goldstein, "Plan Free Speech Moves," *Daily Illini*, March 18, 1967, 7.

2. Robert Goldstein, "SFS Plans for Diskin," *Daily Illini*, March 21, 1967, 3.

3. Ransel interview, February 18, 2018.

4. Editorial, "Take a Long Look," *Daily Illini*, March 21, 1967, 10.

5. Mary Hughes, "Senate Recognizes DuBois," *Daily Illini*, March 23, 1967, 1.

6. Ibid.

7. Robert Goldstein, "Communist Spokesman Talks to 2,000 Students," *Daily Illini*, March 24, 1967, 1.

8. Carolyn Spear, "Diskin Views Self as Decent Human Being," *Champaign News-Gazette*, March 24, 1967, 21.

9. Paula Peters, "Diskin Advocates Greater Student Voice in U. of I. Decision Making," *Champaign-Urbana Courier*, March 24, 1967, 3.

10. Goldstein, "Communist Spokesman," 3.

11. Bruce Zumstein, "Call SFS Commies," *Daily Illini*, March 24, 1967, 3.

12. Outis interview, January 3, 2018.

Chapter 17. Henry Reverses

1. "DDH Opposes Clabaugh Act," *Daily Illini*, April 7, 1967, 1.

2. David Dodds Henry statement, "Confidential: To the Board of Trustees Report from the President," April 10, 1967, 3, David D. Henry Personal Papers, 1922–84, University of Illinois Archives, Urbana.

3. Robert Goldstein, "Henry: Clabaugh Act Unworkable," *Daily Illini*, April 8, 1967, 1.

4. Don Ruhter, "Free Inquiry Not Violated," *Daily Illini*, April 12, 1967, 1.

5. Dan Balz, "Trustees, Students, to Meet," *Daily Illini*, April 20, 1967, 1.

6. Mary Hughes, "SFS Undecisive [sic] on Course of Action," *Daily Illini*, April 20, 1967, 3.

7. Mary Hughes, "Kill Clabaugh Repeal Act," *Daily Illini*, April 27, 1967, 1.

8. Roger Simon, "Leaders Ponder SFS Future," *Daily Illini*, April 29, 1967, 8.

9. Ibid.

10. Dan Balz, "Trustees Hear Millet on Unrest," *Daily Illini*, June 29, 1967, 1.

11. Casey Banas, "U. of I.'s Henry Explains Student Unrest," *Chicago Tribune*, June 10, 1967, 86.

Chapter 18. Spring/Summer '67: Women Rising

1. "UIUC On-Campus Student Enrollment by Curriculum, Sex, and Residency," University of Illinois Division of Management Information, http://dmi.illinois.edu/stuenr/ethsexres/ethsex67.htm.

2. Two large *Daily Illini* ads with names affixed provide insight. The first, from October 31, 1967, page 20, lists 212 male names and 136 female names declaring their complicity in the 1967 Dow sit-in, 61 percent male to 39 percent female. The second, from April 2, 1968, page 20, lists the names of seventy-two males who stated their refusal to be drafted. Below those were names of additional individuals, twenty-two males and ninety-five females, declaring their support for those above, the total names nearly 50/50.

3. E-mails to author, January 24, 2018.

4. Shafransky interview, June 6, 2017.

5. Chester interview, December 18, 2017.

6. Ibid.

7. Patricia Engelhard, email to author, December 17, 2017.

8. Nancy Engelhard, email to author, December 17, 2017.

9. Shafransky interview.

10. Mary Hughes, "Patsy Wins," *Daily Illini*, April 28, 1967, 1.

11. Margaret Converse, "SCOPE Raps Housing Laws," *Daily Illini*, November 4, 1965, 4.

12. John Schmadeke, "SDS, SCOPE Give Views," *Daily Illini*, February 26, 1966, 6.

13. Don Ruhter, "Sooo Wonderful to Win," *Daily Illini*, April 28, 1967, 3.

14. Roger Simon, "SFS Talks Meetings, Dances, Patsy," *Daily Illini*, April 28, 1967, 1.

15. Roger Simon, "UI Activists Unsure about Goals," *Daily Illini*, September 19, 1967, 6.

16. Keven Roth, email to author, April 6, 1917.

17. Roger Simon, "Unruly Crowd Disrupts Midnight Protest Rally," *Daily Illini*, May 13, 1967, 1.

18. Roth interview, April 7, 2017.

19. Keven Roth, e-mail to author, December 4, 2017.

20. Jack A. Smith, "SDS Sets Out on Radical Path," *National Guardian* 19, no. 41, http://www.sds-1960s.org/Guardian1967-07-15.pdf.

21. Berkey interview.

22. De Groot, *Student Protest*, 193.

23. Smith, "SDS Sets Out on Radical Path."

24. Barber, *Hard Rain Fell*, 117.

25. Fein interview.

26. Joseph Hardin, e-mail to author, "67 SDS Meeting," April 11, 2017.

27. Wu interview.

Chapter 19. Fall '67: A Hectic Beginning

1. Seth Rosenfeld, "How the Man Who Challenged 'the Machine' Got Caught in the Gears and Wheels of J. Edgar Hoover's Bureau," *San Francisco Chronicle*, October 10, 2004.
2. Don Ruhter, "Chancellor Discusses Plans," *Daily Illini*, September 12, 1967, 1.
3. Roger Simon, "SFS Ends Formal Structure," *Daily Illini*, September 23, 1967, 1.
4. Ibid.
5. David C. Jones, "Peltason Supports Academic Freedom," *Daily Illini*, September 26, 1967, 1.
6. Roger Simon, "Draft Resisters Won't Go," *Daily Illini*, September 26, 1967, 1.
7. Schmidt interview, January 15, 2018.
8. "Henry Sees More Progress," January 15, 2018, September 26, 1967, 2.
9. Editorial, "Henry's Year Ahead," January 15, 2018, September 27, 1967, 10.

Chapter 20. A New Focus: The War

1. "Gripe-In Discusses Viet War," *Daily Illini*, September 27, 1967, 1.
2. Roger Simon, "Call for Massive Protest," *Daily Illini*, September 27, 1969, 1.
3. Roger Simon, "UI Students Protest War, U.S. Marines," *Daily Illini*, September 29, 1967, 1.
4. Ibid., 10.
5. Ibid., 1.
6. Keven Roth, e-mail to author, April 6, 2017.
7. Roger Simon, "Green Beret Raps Draft," *Daily Illini*, September 3, 1967, 1.
8. Ibid.
9. Carl Schwartz, "Leader Cites New SDS Job," *Daily Illini*, September 4, 1967, 3.
10. Roger Simon, "SDS: Senate Move Bad," *Daily Illini*, September 6, 1967, 7.
11. Ibid.

Chapter 21. Draft Resisters Act

1. Roger Simon, "Dow Demonstrations Discussed," *Daily Illini*, October 10, 1967, 9.
2. Marcia Kramer, "DRU Explains Draft Protest," *Daily Illini*, October 13, 1967, 2.
3. Schmidt interview.
4. Roger Simon, "Schmidt, Weeks Explain," *Daily Illini*, October 13, 1967, 3.
5. David Ransel interview, January 18, 2018.
6. Simon, "Schmidt, Weeks Explain."
7. "Card Burners Talk against 'Slave Army,'" *Champaign-Urbana Courier*, September 17, 1967, 3.
8. Soderstrom interview, December 13, 2018.
9. "Card Burners."
10. Robert Goldstein and Larry Finley, "Ten Arrested in Draft Protest," *Champaign-Urbana Courier*, October 17, 1967, 7.
11. Dan'l McCollum notes provided with interview, September 22, 2016.

12. John Finley, "That's Better," *Champaign-Urbana Courier*, September 19, 1967, 8.

13. Schmidt interview.

14. Ed Borman, "Draft Protesters Indignant at Bail Requirement," *Champaign News-Gazette*, October 17, 1967, 3.

15. "Intervention," *Daily Illini*, October 19, 1967, 8.

16. "Draft Resistance Union Demonstration on October 16," Student Protests Subject File, 1954–74, University of Illinois Archives, Urbana.

17. Ibid.

Chapter 22. Then There Was Dow

1. "Wisconsin Students Riot, Plan to Strike," *Daily Illini*, October 19, 1967, 1.

2. Maraniss, *They Marched into Sunlight*, 118.

3. Linda Picone, "SDS to Demonstrate against Dow," *Daily Illini*, October 20, 1967, 6.

4. Linda Picone, "Plan Protest against Dow," *Daily Illini*, October 24, 1967, 1.

5. Roger Simon, "Illini Demonstrate in D.C.," *Daily Illini*, October 24, 1967, 1.

6. "Rusk Blasts Demonstrators," *Daily Illini*, October 25, 1967, 5.

7. McCollum notes, 2016.

8. "Call for Restraint," *Daily Illini*, October 25, 1967, 10.

9. Bernard Gershenson and Joseph Hardin emails, July 12, 2017.

10. Roger Simon, "Protesters End Dow Visit," *Daily Illini*, October 26, 1967, 1.

11. Letter from Richard S. Bogartz to Peltason, November 8, 1967, Dow Demonstrations Folder, University of Illinois Archives, Urbana.

12. Simon, "Protesters End Dow Visit."

13. Robert Goldstein, "U.I. to Discipline Demonstrators," *Champaign-Urbana Courier*, October 26, 1967, 11.

14. Jack W. Peltason statement, "Dow Demonstrations," November 9, 1967, Dow Demonstrations Folder, University of Illinois Archives, Urbana.

15. Letter from F. A. Kumerow to Peltason, November 1, 1967, included in "Peltason Report to Board of Trustees," December 1967, Dow Demonstrations Folder, University of Illinois Archives, Urbana, quoted in McGuire, "Preserving the Image of Authority."

16. Ibid.

17. Editorial, "A Reasonable Reaction," *Daily Illini*, October 27, 1967, 12.

18. Roger Simon, "Dow Protesters Submit Statements," *Daily Illini*, November 7, 1967, 1.

19. Ibid.

20. Letter from Herbert D. Sloan to Herbert Gutowsky, November 1, 1967, Herbert S. Gutowsky Papers, 1963–69, University of Illinois Archives, Urbana.

21. Letter from Daniel Curley to Robert Rogers, November 25, 1967, Daniel Curley Papers, University of Illinois Archives, Urbana, quoted in McGuire, "Preserving the Image of Authority."

22. "Peltason Faces Activists," *Champaign News-Gazette*, November 8, 1967.

23. Roger Simon, "Student Power Call at Gripe-In," *Daily Illini*, November 3, 1967, 1.

24. Elise Cassel, "Davidson: SDS Must Resist," *Daily Illini*, November 3, 1967, 5.
25. Simon, "Student Power Call."
26. "Dissent," *Daily Illini*, November 1, 1967, 8.

Chapter 23. The Aftermath

1. Phillip Durrett, e-mail to author, September 13, 2017.
2. Durrett interview, August 7, 2017.
3. Roger Simon, "300 Protest Expulsions," *Daily Illini*, November 29, 1967, 1.
4. Ibid.
5. Letter to Dean Stanton Millet, November 28, 1967, Dean of Students Subject File, 1966–2011, University of Illinois Archives, Urbana.
6. Keven Roth, e-mail to author, April 6, 2017.
7. Letters, David D. Henry Personal Papers, 1922–84, University of Illinois Archives, Urbana.
8. "Protesters 'Fast for Peace' in Camp-Out on Quad Today," *Daily Illini*, December 1, 1967, 4.
9. Roger Simon, "Five Turn in Draft Cards," *Daily Illini*, December 5, 1967, 1.
10. Bruce Zumstein, "Trustees See Card Burning," *Daily Illini*, December 21, 1967, 1.

Chapter 24. 1968: The Wildest Year

1. Schmidt interview.
2. Joseph Hardin, e-mail to author, December 16, 17.
3. Angela Jordan, "The time has come, the Walrus said . . . ," University of Illinois Archives, https://archives.library.illinois.edu/blog/time-has-come-the-walrus-said.
4. Editorial, *Walrus* 1, no. 1 (February 1, 1968): 1, University of Illinois Archives, Urbana.
5. Linda Picone, "Socialist Asks Withdrawal," *Daily Illini*, February 8, 1968, 1.
6. Linda Picone, "Woman Details Viet Visit," *Daily Illini*, February 10, 1968, 1.
7. Marcia Kramer, "'The Pill' Safe, Effective," *Daily Illini*, February 14, 1968, 7.
8. Dennis Sodomka, "No Wild Trip but Quite a Show," *Daily Illini*, February 15, 1968, 1.
9. "Women's Union," *Daily Illini*, March 8, 1968, 23.
10. *Daily Illini*, April 26, 1968, 18.
11. Elise Cassel, "Females Form Union," *Daily Illini*, September 25, 1968, 6.
12. David Ransel, e-mail to author, January 25, 2018.
13. Bernard Gershenson, e-mail to author, January 24, 2018.
14. Linda Picone, "New Left to Quiet Down," *Daily Illini*, February 17, 1968, 4.

Chapter 25. Race Returns to Center Stage

1. John Grady, "Revolutionary Blasts Whites," *Daily Illini*, February 17, 1968, 1.
2. "John Lee Johnson," *Champaign-Urbana Local Wiki*, https://localwiki.org/cu/John_Lee_Johnson.

3. Carl Schwartz, "Girls Touch Off Panty Raid," *Daily Illini*, March 29, 1968, 4.
4. Carolann Rodriguez, "Negroes Predict Violence," *Daily Illini*, April 5, 1968, 1.
5. Ibid.
6. "Chronology of Campus Protests, University of Illinois at Urbana, 1948–1972," University of Illinois Archives, Urbana.
7. Darrell Kindred, "Henry Promises UI Action on Racial Discrimination," *Champaign News-Gazette*, May 7, 1968, 3, 50.
8. Sally Wagner, "Fail to Pass Open Housing," *Daily Illini*, April 17, 1968, 3.
9. "Memphis Workers End Strike," *Daily Illini*, April 17, 1968, 9.
10. Cottrell, *Sex, Drugs, and Rock and Roll*, 162.
11. "CRJ Talks Recruitment," *Daily Illini*, April 18, 1968, 3.
12. Ellen Asprooth, "Ask for More UI Negros," *Daily Illini*, April 19, 1968, 1.
13. Ellen Asprooth, "CRJ Attacks New UI Plan," *Daily Illini*, April 20, 1968, 1; Carolann Rodriguez, "BSA Reveals Plan," *Daily Illini*, May 1, 1968, 5.
14. Lieberman, *Prairie Power*, 122.
15. Sally Wagner, "Young Analyzes Youth," *Daily Illini*, April 27, 1968, 1.
16. "Police Disrupt Week-Long Sit-In," *Daily Illini*, May 1, 1968, 7.
17. Carolann Rodriguez, "UI to Enroll 500 Blacks," *Daily Illini*, May 3, 1968, 7.

Chapter 26. Spring Sputters to an End

1. Marcia Mayeroff, "Kornibe: Power for Students," *Daily Illini*, February 13, 1969, 2.
2. Linda Picone, "New Left Loses Appeal," *Daily Illini*, May 10, 1968, 5.
3. "Students Seize Universities," *Daily Illini*, May 5, 1968, 2.
4. Carolann Rodriguez, "Addison Elected BSA President," *Daily Illini*, May 5, 1968, 3.
5. Marcia Kramer, "YRs Condemn Student Protesters," *Daily Illini*, May 15, 1968, 3.
6. Marcia Kramer, "Peltason: Near Exciting Period," *Daily Illini*, May 18, 1968, 3.
7. S. M. E. "Does Student Power = Democracy's Strength?" *Phi Delta Kappan* 50, no. 1 (1968): 1, http://www.jstor.org/stable/20372206.
8. Schroeder interview, December 19, 2017.

Chapter 27. Summer '68: The Turning Begins

1. Mark Rudd, "The Death of SDS," *Mark Rudd Blog*, http://www.markrudd.com/?sds-and-weather/the-death-of-sds.html.
2. Joseph Hardin, e-mail to the author, June 11, 2017.
3. Bernard Gershenson, e-mail to the author, June 10, 2017.
4. Patricia Engelhard, e-mail to the author, August 14, 2017.
5. Paula Shafransky, e-mail to the author, June 14, 2017.
6. Thomas Powers, "Anti-War Protesters Battle Police," *Chicago Tribune*, April 28, 1968.
7. Bernard Gershenson, e-mail to the author, December 3, 2017.
8. Patricia Engelhard, e-mail to the author, December 6, 2017.
9. Lester Wall interview, April 6, 2017.
10. Bernard Gershenson, e-mail to the author, November 29, 2017.

11. Sale, *SDS*, 418.
12. Grathwohl and Reagan, *Bringing Down America*, 103.
13. Heineman, *Campus Wars*, 188.
14. Patricia Engelhard, e-mail to the author, August 18, 2017.
15. Joseph Hardin, e-mail to the author, July 18, 2017.
16. Ransel interview, January 18, 2018.
17. David Lawrence, "Aura of Fear Threat to Orderly Demo Convention," *Chicago Sun-Times*, August 27, 1968.
18. Soderstrom interview, December 13, 2018.

Chapter 28. Fall '68: Project 500

1. Clardy, *Management of Dissent*, 35.
2. David Eisenman interview, September 21, 2016.
3. Ibid.
4. "An Old Problem," *Daily Illini*, September 11, 1968, 1, 12.
5. Carl Schwartz, "Union Incident 'Damn Foolish'—Rep. Clabaugh," *Daily Illini*, September 13, 1968, 1.
6. Marcia Kramer, "BSA: Dismiss Charges," *Daily Illini*, September 13, 1968, 3, 6.
7. David Eisenman, "Project 'Too Great' a Success," *Daily Illini*, September 11, 1968, 13.
8. "Chancellor's Statement," *Daily Illini*, September 25, 1968, 2.
9. Carolann Rodriguez, "Clabaugh Criticizes Sit-In," *Daily Illini*, October 24, 1968, 5.
10. For further details on the black student movement at the university, see the excellent history by Joy Williams, *Black Power on Campus: The University of Illinois, 1965–75* (Urbana: University of Illinois Press, 2003).

Chapter 29. Spring '69: Heating Up, but Not Boiling Over

1. L. Picone Hansen, "Berkey Dismisses Rumors of Abduction by Panthers," *Daily Illini*, January 14, 1969, 3.
2. Carolann Rodriguez and Wendy Rafilson, "Students Confront Marines," *Daily Illini*, February 7, 1969, 1.
3. Meg Gunkel, "UI Current Events Forum Questions Whether New Left Justifiable in Use of Violence," *Daily Illini*, February 7, 1969, 7.
4. John Hundley, "Hogan Quits Football for Politics," *Daily Illini*, February 12, 1969, 1, 2.
5. Ibid.
6. L. Picone Hansen, "Whites Hold March, Vote against Union Sit-In," *Daily Illini*, February 12, 1969, 1, 2.
7. Ibid., 2.
8. L. Picone Hansen, "Whites Hold March, 200 Appear at Dr. Henry's Door," *Daily Illini*, February 12, 1969, 1, 3.
9. Roger Simon, "Students Want Change in University Structure," *Daily Illini*, March 12, 1968, 5.

10. Elise Cassel, "Reform Group Issues Manifesto," *Daily Illini*, March 13, 1968, 5.

11. "Disorders Continue in Madison," *Daily Illini*, February 14, 1969, 3.

12. Joel Summer, "Blacks Delay Any Action: Senate Council Meets Today to Hear Student Demands," *Daily Illini*, February 15, 1969, 1, 2.

13. Joel Summer, "Blacks Delay Any Action: 'Must Meet All Demands,'" *Daily Illini*, February 15, 1969, 1, 2.

14. "Ten Days to Shake the Empire," *Daily Illini*, February 2, 1968.

Chapter 30. Black and White Together

1. "Advance Rioter Bill," *Daily Illini*, February 20, 1969, 1.

2. Alan Mutter, "Congress Backs Proposed Strike," *Daily Illini*, March 18, 1969, 1.

3. Evelyn Bowen, "Peltason Evaluates Project 500," *Daily Illini*, March 21, 1969, 6.

4. Marge Ferroli, "Dorms Lock Doors," *Daily Illini*, May 28, 1969, 3.

5. "The Year Ends," *Daily Illini*, June 3, 1969, 6.

6. John Hundley, "4,590 Graduate from UI," *Daily Illini*, June 16, 1969, 1.

7. Schmidt interview, January 15, 2018.

8. "Steve Schmidt Begins Serving Four Year Term in Penitentiary," *Daily Illini*, July 9, 1969, 1.

Chapter 31. A Sign of the End: Weathermen Come to Town

1. "Jones Foresees Armed Struggle," *Daily Illini*, September 18, 1969, 4.

2. Joseph Hardin, e-mail to the author, July 7, 2017.

3. Vernon Fein, e-mail to the author, July 8, 1969.

4. Marcia Kramer, "Local SDS Quits National," *Daily Illini*, September 26, 1969, 5.

5. "Okay Moratorium," *Daily Illini*, October 2, 1969, 3.

6. "Nixon Tells of Undisclosed Timetable for Troop Withdrawal from Vietnam," *Daily Illini*, November 4, 1969, 1.

7. Editorial, "Nixon's Plan," *Daily Illini*, November 5, 1969, 10.

8. Erskine, " Polls."

9. Vern Fein, e-mail to the author, September 21, 2017.

10. UPI, "1969 Year in Review: War Protests," http://www.upi.com/Archives/Audio/Events-of-1969/War-Protests.

11. Marcia Kramer and John Hundley, "300 Blacks March for Slain Panthers," *Daily Illini*, December 9, 1969, 1.

12. David Ransel, e-mail to author, January 18, 2018.

13. Ransel interview, January 18, 2018.

Chapter 32. Spring '70: The Final Semester

1. Carl Schwartz, "Department of Defense to Employ UI Computer for Nuclear Weaponry," *Daily Illini*, January 6, 1970, 1.

2. Ibid., 3.

3. Evelyn Bowen, "FUR Votes to Oppose Illiac IV; Stop Operation by Any Means," *Daily Illini*, January 9, 1970, 3.

4. "RU Demands Abolition of Illiac, ROTC," *Daily Illini*, January 14, 1970, 1.

5. G. Robert Hillman, "Arraign Alleged Arsonist," *Daily Illini*, January 16, 1970, 1.

6. Rick Fitch, "Radical Groups Report Increase in Membership," *Daily Illini*, January 23, 1970, 10.

7. Kathy Reinbolt, "Spock Justifies Revolution," *Daily Illini*, February 25, 1970, 3.

8. Heineman, *Put Your Bodies*, 3.

Chapter 33. March: Patience Spent, the Storms Begin

1. "Police, Protesters Clash in Fighting over GE Recruiting," *Daily Illini*, March 3, 1970, 1.

2. Victor S. Navasky, "Right On! With Lawyer William Kunstler," *New York Times*, April 19, 1970.

3. Marcia Kramer, "Trustees Veto Kunstler's Presence," *Daily Illini*, March 3, 1970, 3.

4. "Police, Youths Clash; Cities Impose Curfew," *Daily Illini*, March 4, 1970, 1.

5. Earl Merkel, "300 of Guard Used in Campus Disturbances," *Daily Illini*, March 4, 1970, 1.

6. David Ransel, e-mail to the author, January 19, 2018.

7. David Ransel, e-mail to the author, January 18, 2018.

8. "Chancellor Peltason 'Appalled at Events,'" *Daily Illini*, March 4, 1970, 7.

9. "Nine Students Suspended in Third Night of Disorders," *Daily Illini*, March 5, 1970, 1.

Chapter 34. April: Quiet between the Storms

1. Roger Simon, "Up Against It," *Daily Illini*, March 10, 1970, 8.

2. "26 Charged in UI Disorders May Lose Scholarships," *Daily Illini*, March 12, 1970, 3.

3. "Going to Cure UI Punks," *Daily Illini*, March 18, 1970, 3.

4. Wynkoop, *Dissent in the Heartland*, 63.

5. Barbara Roth, "Student Leaders View Retirement," *Daily Illini*, March 19, 1970, 5.

6. Ira Teinowitz, "Politicians Comment on DDH," *Daily Illini*, March 19, 1970, 5.

7. Marcia Kramer, "6,519 Hear Kunstler Speak," *Daily Illini*, March 24, 1970, 1.

8. Kathy Reinbolt and Debbie Daro, "Larabee Warns of More Rioting," *Daily Illini*, April 21, 1970, 3.

9. Earl Merkel, "9 Arrested Following 'Liberation' of Armory during ROTC Drill," *Daily Illini*, April 4 22, 1970, 1.

10. Paul Ingrassia, "Continued Campus Tension Seen," *Daily Illini*, April 29, 1970, 3.

Chapter 35. May: The Final Month

1. Alan D. Mutter, "21-Year-Old Widow Can't Find Words Kids Can Understand," *Champaign-Urbana Courier*, May 3, 1970, 3.

2. "Quiet March Protests Killing," *Daily Illini*, April 30, 1970, 1.
3. "Death Sparks Violence in Cities," *Daily Illini*, May 1, 1970, 1.
4. "Nixon Says No Invasion," *Daily Illini*, May 1, 1970, 1.
5. G. Robert Hillman, "Policeman Relieved of Duty after Edgar Hoults Shooting," *Daily Illini*, May 1, 1970, 1.
6. "More Violence in Cities; Five Shot," *Daily Illini*, May 2, 1970, 1.
7. Bill Groninger, "Right Decision Won't Win Votes," *Champaign-Urbana Courier*, May 3, 1970, 3.
8. Editorial, "Stop New War," *Daily Illini*, May 2, 1970, 1.
9. "Cambodian Invasion Sparks Violence on U.S. Campuses," *Daily Illini*, May 2, 1970, 3.
10. "LBJ Asks Support for Nixon from All Who Love Freedom," *Daily Illini*, May 2, 1970, 3.
11. Editorial, "Are the Universities Worth Saving?" *Chicago Tribune*, May 8, 1970, 20.
12. "Four Kent Protesters Dead," *Daily Illini*, May 4, 1970, 1.

Chapter 36. Strike: The Final Days

1. "Radicals Take Credit for Fire," *Daily Illini*, May 5, 1970, 4.
2. Tom Slocum, "Citizens Demand Police Dept. Changes," *Champaign News-Gazette*, May 6, 1970, 3.
3. Ibid.
4. Jim Kroemer, "Anger over Shooting Unleashed on Council," *Champaign-Urbana Courier*, May 6, 1970, 3.
5. Ellen Asprooth, "Vandalism Follows UI Strike Call," *Champaign News-Gazette*, May 6, 1970, 3.
6. "8 on Staff Favor Strike," *Daily Illini*, May 8, 1970, 8.
7. "Nixon: A Presidency Revealed," television program, History Channel, dir. Joe Angio (February 15, 2007).
8. Gitlin, *Sixties*, 410.
9. "1970 Timeline," New York University, http://www.nyu.edu/library/bobst/collections/exhibits/arch/1970/1970-2.html.
10. "Governor Ogilvie Lashes Out at 'Revolutionary Group,'" *Daily Illini*, May 7, 1970, 10.
11. Ibid.
12. Barbara Demski, "2,500 at Peace Union Rally for Non-violent Protest Here," *Daily Illini*, May 8, 1970, 1.
13. David Hood, "Anti-violence Students Protest as Flag Burned on Quadrangle," *Champaign-Urbana Courier*, May 8, 1970, 3.
14. "Evening Rally Quiet," *Champaign-Urbana Courier*, May 8, 1970, 3.
15. Ellen Asprooth, "Thousands Jam Quad; Strikers Remain Peaceful," *Champaign News-Gazette*, 5.8.70, 3.
16. Ellen Asprooth, "Parenti Comes Close to Bringing Crowd Together," *Champaign News-Gazette*, May 8, 1970, 19.
17. Draft statement, May 8, 1970, Office of the Chancellor, subject file 1967–80, University of Illinois Archives, Urbana.

18. "President of UW Resigns," *Champaign News-Gazette*, May 8, 1970, 20.
19. "Page Blisters Dissident Students; College Heads," *Champaign News-Gazette*, May 9, 1970, 1.
20. "Dr. Henry Explains," *Champaign News-Gazette*, May 9, 1970, 1.
21. Walter R. Mears (AP), "President, Students Agree," *Champaign News-Gazette*, May 9, 1970, 1.
22. Chancellor's statement, May 8, 1970, Office of the Chancellor, subject file 1967–80, University of Illinois Archives, Urbana.

Chapter 37. Extra at the End

1. Sheila Wolfe, Joseph McLaughlin, "Our Reporters on Campus See Many Moods," *Chicago Tribune*, May 10, 1970.
2. Bonnie Blankenship, "No Information, Explanation—All Were Arrested," *Champaign News-Gazette*, May 10, 1970, 3.
3. "102 Arrested," *Daily Illini*, May 10, 1970, 2.
4. Terry Michael, "105 Arrested on Campus," *Champaign News-Gazette*, May 10, 1970, 1.
5. "102 Arrested," *Daily Illini*, May 10, 1970, 2.
6. "Officials Distressed," *Daily Illini*, May 10, 1970, 1.
7. David Lawrence, "Silent Majority Must Speak," *Champaign News-Gazette*, May 10, 1970, 4.
8. Ibid.
9. Barbara Dembski and Ron Chafetz, "Protesters March to Police Station," *Daily Illini*, May 12, 1970, 18.
10. Editorial, "The Chancellor Has Failed," *Daily Illini*, May 12, 1970, 8.
11. Paul Ingrassia, Chuck Steirman, "Campus Unrest Brings Backlash," *Daily Illini*, May 13, 1970, 1.
12. Robert C. Cooper, "Wikoff Calls Decision to Clear Quad Saturday 'A Good One,'" *Daily Illini*, May 14, 1970, 5.
13. Marge Ferroli, "House Session on Unrest Hears University Presidents, Students," *Daily Illini*, May 26, 1970, 1.
14. Carl Schwartz, "UI Seeks to Move Illiac Off Campus," *Daily Illini*, June 22, 1970, 1.
15. Kerry L. Pimblott, "The Struggle for Racial Equity in the Champaign County Criminal Justice System." *The Public I: A Paper of the People*, February 8, 2008.

Conclusion

1. "21 Years in the Life of Jim Larabee, a Child of Revolution," *Chicago Daily Herald*, Suburban Edition, July 21, 1972.
2. Paula Shafransky, e-mail to the author, February 6, 2018.
3. Shafransky interview, June 6, 2017.
4. Rick Perlstein, "Who Owns the Sixties?" *Lingua Franca* 6, no. 4 (May 1996), http://linguafranca.mirror.theinfo.org/9605/sixties.html.
5. Durrett interview, August 7, 2017, and e-mail to author, August 29, 2017.
6. Daniels, *Year of the Heroic Guerrilla*, 9.

Bibliography

Interviews

Joanne Chester, December 18, 2017
Phillip Durrett, August 7, 2017
David Eisenman, September 21, 2016
Nancy Engelhard, September 18, 2017
Patricia Engelhard, September 18, 2017, and September 19, 2016
Vern Fein, September 19, 2016
Belden Fields, September 21, 2016
Larry Geni, September 18, 2017
Bernard Gershenson, March 29, 2016
Robert Goldstein, December 29, 2017
John Morrow Hackman, July 19, 2016
Joseph Hardin, January 26, 2017
Dan'l McCollum, September 22, 2016, with nine pages of notes
Victor Berkey Moheno, April 11, 2017
Robert Outis, January 3, 2018
David Ransel, January 18, 2018
Keven Roth, April 7, 2017
Steve Schmidt, January 15, 2018
Paul Schroeder, December 19, 2017
Paula Shafransky, June 6, 2017
Marty Shupak, October 16, 2017
Roger Simon, March 5, 2017

Rick Soderstrom, December 13, 2018
Mara Stolurow, May 24, 2016
Lester Wall, April 6, 2017
Vincent Wu, January 12, 2018

Primary Sources

University of Illinois Archives, Urbana
    Daniel Curley Papers
    David D. Henry Personal Papers, 1922–84
    Dean of Students Subject File, 1966–2011
    Dow Demonstrations Folder
    Herbert S. Gutowsky Papers, 1963–69
    Office of the Chancellor, Subject File 1967–80
    Student Protests Subject File, 1954–74
    The Walrus, 1968–
    Wayne A. Johnston Papers, 1945–67
Champaign News-Gazette
Champaign-Urbana Courier
Chicago Daily News
Chicago Sun-Times
Chicago Tribune Archives, http://archives.chicagotribune.com
Daily Illini, Illinois Digital Collection, https://goo.gl/kCMHBs

Secondary Sources

Ali, Tariq, and Susan Watkins. *1968: Marching in the Streets*. New York: Free Press, 1998.
Allyn, David. *Make Love, Not War: The Sexual Revolution*. London: Routledge, 2016.
Anderson, Terry H. *The Sixties*. London: Routledge, 2011.
Barber, David. *A Hard Rain Fell: SDS and Why It Failed*. Oxford: University Press of Mississippi, 2010.
Bilgrami, Akeel, and Jonathan R. Cole, eds. *Who's Afraid of Academic Freedom?* New York: Columbia University Press, 2015.
Bloom, Alexander. *Takin' It to the Streets: A Sixties Reader*. Oxford: Oxford University Press, 2015.
Breines, Wilson. "Whose New Left?" *Journal of American History* 75, no. 2 (September 1988): 528–45.
Burrough, Bryan. *Days of Rage: America's Radical Underground, the FBI, and the Forgotten Age of Revolutionary Violence*. London: Penguin, 2015.
Clardy, Brian K. *The Management of Dissent: Responses to the Post Kent State Protests at Seven Public Universities in Illinois*. Lanham, Md.: University Press of America, 2002.
Cottrell, Robert C. *Sex, Drugs, and Rock and Roll: The Rise of America's 1960s Counterculture*. Lanham, Md.: Rowman and Littlefield, 2015.
Daniels, Robert V. *Year of the Heroic Guerrilla*. Cambridge, Mass.: Harvard University Press, 1989.

De Groot, Gerard J. *The 60s Unplugged: A Kaleidoscopic History of a Disorderly Decade*. Cambridge, Mass.: Harvard University Press, 2010.
———. *Student Protest: The Sixties and After*. London: Routledge, 2014.
Ebert, Roger, ed. *An Illini Century*. Urbana: University of Illinois Press, 1967.
Erskine, Hazel. "The Polls: Is War a Mistake?" *Public Opinion Quarterly* 34, no. 1 (1970): 134–50.
Fields, Belden. *Academic Freedom and the Board of Trustees at the University of Illinois: A Historical Perspective*. Urbana, Ill.: Campus Faculty Association, 2014. https://cfaillinois.org/2014/10/09/academic-freedom-and-the-board-of-trustees-at-the-university-of-illinois-a-historical-perspective.
Gellhorn, Walter, ed. *The States and Subversion*. Ithaca, N.Y.: Cornell University Press, 1952.
Gitlin, Todd. *The Sixties: Years of Hope, Days of Rage*. New York: Bantam, 1987.
———. *Swept Away in the Sixties*. American Prospect, September 12, 2016. http://prospect.org/article/swept-away-sixties.
———. *The Whole World Is Watching: Mass Media in the Making and Unmaking of the New Left*. Berkeley: University of California Press, 1980.
Grathwohl, Larry, and Frank Reagan. *Bringing Down America: An FBI Informant in with the Weathermen*. New York: Arlington House, 1977.
Heale, M. J. "The Sixties as History: A Review of the Political Historiography." *Reviews in American History* 33, no. 1 (March 2005): 133–52.
Heineman, Kenneth J. *Campus Wars: The Peace Movement at American State Universities in the Vietnam Era*. New York: New York University Press, 1994.
———. *Put Your Bodies upon the Wheels: Student Revolt in the 1960s*. Chicago: Dee, 2001.
Isserman, Maurice. "The Not-So-Dark and Bloody Ground: New Works on the 1960s." *American Historical Review* 94, no. 4 (October 1989): 990–1010.
Kennedy, Patrick D. "Reactions against the Vietnam War and Military-Related Targets on Campus: The University of Illinois as a Case Study, 1965–1972." *Illinois Historical Journal* 84, no. 2 (Summer 1991): 101–18.
Lange, Eric. "Who Can Define the Meaning of Un-American? The Story of Ed Yellin and the Era of Anti-Communism." Master's thesis, University of Michigan, 2010.
Lee, Phillip. "The Curious Life of *In Loco Parentis* in American Universities." *Higher Education in Review* 2011:65–90. http://scholar.harvard.edu/files/philip_lee/files/vol8lee.pdf.
Lieberman, Robbie. *Prairie Power: Voices of 1960s Midwestern Student Protest*. Columbia: University of Missouri Press, 2004.
Mailer, Norman. *The Armies of the Night: History as a Novel, the Novel as History*. New York: New American Library, 1968.
Maraniss, David. *They Marched into Sunlight: War and Peace, Vietnam and America, October 1967*. New York: Simon and Schuster, 2004.
McGuire, David. "Preserving the Image of Authority: The University of Illinois and Anti-War Protest, 1965–1970." Thesis, 1991. University of Illinois Archives, Senior History Honors Theses, record series 15/13/811, box 3.
Pardun, Robert. *Prairie Radical: A Journey through the Sixties*. Los Gatos, Calif.: Shire, 2001.
Peltason, Jack W. *Reactionary Thoughts of a Revolutionary*. Urbana: University of Illinois Press, 1995.

Perlstein, Rick. *Before the Storm: Barry Goldwater and the Unmaking of the American Government*. New York: Nation, 2009.
———. *Nixonland: The Rise of a President and the Fracturing of America*. New York: Scribner, 2009.
———. "Who Owns the Sixties? The Opening of a Scholarly Generation Gap." *Lingua Franca* 6, no. 4 (May/June 1996): 30–37.
Pimblott, Kerry, L. "The Struggle for Racial Equity in the Champaign County Criminal Justice System." *The Public I: A Paper of the People* 8, no. 2 (February 8, 2008).
Rancan, Antonella. "The Academic McCarthyism at the University of Illinois: An Integration." Preliminary draft. http://public.econ.duke.edu/~staff/wrkshop_papers/2008-2009%20Papers/Rancan.pdf.
Resources from Students for a Democratic Society (SDS) and Related Groups and Activities. http://www.sds-1960s.org/index.htm.
Rorabaugh, W. J. *Berkeley at War: The 1960s*. Oxford: Oxford University Press, 1990.
Rossinow, Doug. *The Politics of Authenticity: Liberalism, Christianity, and the New Left in America*. New York: Columbia University Press, 1998.
Sale, Kirkpatrick. *SDS: The Rise and Development of the Students for a Democratic Society*. New York: Random House, 1973.
Stoddard, George D. *"Krebiozen": The Great Cancer Mystery*. Boston: Beacon, 1955.
Suri, Jeremi. ed. *The Global Revolutions of 1968*. New York: Norton, 2007.
Von Hoffman, Nicholas. *Multiversity: A Personal Report on What Happens to Today's Students at American Universities*. Austin, Tex.: Holt Rinehart Winston, 1966.
White, Theodore H. *The Making of the President: 1968*. New York: Atheneum, 1969.
Williamson, Joy. *Black Power on Campus: The University of Illinois, 1965–75*. Urbana: University of Illinois Press, 2003.
Wynkoop, Mary Ann. *Dissent in the Heartland: The Sixties at Indiana University*. Bloomington: Indiana University Press, 2002.
Zakrzewski, Dana. "Students for a Democratic Society." http://www.campusactivism.org/server-new/uploads/undergrad2a-sds.htm.

Index

Addison, David, 151, 179
Adelman, Gary, 118, 123, 147
Ad Hoc Faculty Committee on Vietnam, 34
Administration Building, UI, 62, 146, 151, 209, 220
Air Force Recruiting Station bombing, 199
Allen, Joe, 72, 86
Altgeld Hall, 196, 220
American Association of University Professors (AAUP), 24, 68, 70, 187
American Legion, 6, 57, 70
Americans for Democratic Action, 41
Aptheker, Bettina, 39
Aptheker, Herbert, 62
Armory, 35, 193, 196–97, 201, 209
Auditorium, 33–34, 194, 199, 208, 212–13

Balanger, Frank, 197–98
Bennett, Ralph, 39–49, 54–59, 68–69. *See also* W.E.B. DuBois Club
Berkey (Moheno), Victor: background, 46; CRJ, 150–51; Democratic Party, 90; Dow sit-in, aftermath, 114–16, 124, 126, 130–31; draft resistance 107–8; grovel-in 176–77; Henry, 64; Lynd, 119; moral clarity, xvii; Panthers, 174; Parker, 88; post-UI, 227; SDS, 72, 75, 142, 182; SFS, 64, 79–82. *See also* SACA
Black Panthers, 189, 209; on UI campus, 173–74, 176
Black Students Association (BSA): Hampton murder, aftermath, 189; Henry retirement, 200; institutional racism, 173, 176, 179; King assassination and aftermath, 145, 147–49, 151; Project 500, 147, 149, 165–68
Board of Trustees, UI: Clabaugh Act, 36; draft action, 135; Dubois Club, 39, 50, 53–55, 56, 68–70; Henry, 24, 64, 76–78; Illiac IV, 223; Kuntsler, 195, 200; Peltason, 137, 168–69; Stoddard, 11–16
Bogartz, Richard, 124
Bowen, Harold, 11–12
Briscoe, John, 63
Broyles, Paul, 6, 13, 18, 181

Champaign City Council, 146, 203–4, 208
Champaign draft board, 115, 134, 145
Champaign News Gazette, 119, 208, 219, 221
Champaign-Urbana Courier, 66, 125, 163, 204
Champaign Urbana University Committee, 75
Chandler, Paul, 179, 182–83

Index

Channing Murray: Dow planning, 123; DRU, 107, 115, 134; Halstead, Rothstein, 139; Schmidt, 106; SFS, 79; women's role, 86
Chester, Joanne, 84, 123, 132
Chicago Circle campus, UI, 36, 62, 208
Chicago Democratic Convention (1968), 136–37, 140, 155–57, 161–65, 183
Chicago police, 7, 136–37, 156–57, 163–65, 186
Chicago Sun-Times, 16, 124, 163
Chicago Tribune, 5–6, 54, 118, 167, 205
Citizens for Racial Justice (CRJ), 146–48, 168
Civil rights movement, 30–39, 90, 116
Clabaugh, Charles: academic freedom, 70; anti-communism, 7, 12–13; "damn foolishness,"167; DuBois Club, 39; 44, 48; "free inquiry" and "horse stealing," 77; Henry resignation, 200; "horsehair shirt," "pinkos," and "moving the State House to Moscow," 65; "kooks," 58, 169; "only way to cure these punks," 200; Project 500, 169; trustee actions, 55. *See also* Clabaugh Act
Clabaugh Act: Henry, 51; movement against, 36, 39, 44–46, 50–57, 61–80; passage, 7, 17; repeal attempt, 47, 57–58; struck down, 165; wording, 12. *See* Clabaugh, Charles; SACA
Committee on Student Affairs (CSA), 47–48, 57–58
Committee to End the War in Vietnam (CEWV), 58, 62, 83, 141–42
Communist Party: Aptheker, Herbert, 62, 74–75; Broyles, 181; Diskin, 36, 74–75; DuBois, 39, 48; Henry, 77; SDS, 160; Yellin 19–20; Youth for Democracy, 13 18, 50
Congress for Racial Equality (CORE), 32, 39
Couture, Ray, 131, 134
Cronkite, Walter, 161, 188
Curley, Daniel, 127

Dad's Association, 23
Daily Illini: blank front page, 187–88; call for Peltason resignation, 222; Clabaugh Act opposition, 45; disciplined undergrads, 132; draft card burning, 119; DuBois Club, 58–59; Eisenman Project 500 analysis, 167; farewell to 1967/68 school year, 183; grovel-in, 177; Henry, change of position, 78; Hoults shooting, 204; Illiac IV, 192; Koch letter, 22; "New Left losing steam," 150–51; "Nobody is in charge," 2, 199–200; Parker, 87–88; "Peltason appalled," 197; Peltason on Project 500 arrests, 168; Project 500 arrests, 167; radicals vs. liberals, 128; restraint urged, applauded, 123, 125–26; SACA, 73; Simon-Schmidt interview, 116; as source, xvii; special Sunday edition, 217, 219; Stoddard dismissal 15; student privileges, 52; student strike support, 207
Days of Rage, 185, 187
Democratic Party National Convention, 7, 137, 140, 155–57, 161–65
Dillavoux, Ora, 14, 16
Diskin, Louis, 36, 73–75
Dixiecrats, 31, 90
Doebel, Paul, 210–12, 221–22
Dohrn, Bernardine, 160, 185–87
Dow Chemical Corporation: campus recruitment, UI, 7, 114–16, 137, 142; sit-in, aftermath, UI, 122–35; UW, Madison, 59–60, 121–22
Draft Resisters Union (DRU), 108–10, 113, 115–20, 135
Durrett, Phillip: background, 46; coffee house opening, 36; Dow sit-in, aftermath, 124–25, 131; DuBois 41, 43; economic analysis, 111; movement, 229; SFS resignation, 79–80; SFS transition 107. *See also* SACA

Eastman, Fred, 204–7, 223
Ebert, Roger, xvii, 33
Eisenman, David, 152, 166–68
Electrical Engineering Building, 194, 214
Engelhard, Nancy, 85
Engelhard, Patricia, 85–86, 157–58, 161–62

Faculty for University Reform (FUR), 192, 209
Faculty Senate Committee on Academic Freedom, 48, 50, 56
Federal Bureau of Investigation (FBI), 33, 40, 117–18, 158–59, 189
Fein, Vern: anti-war activities, 37, 150, 174, 188; background, 63; CEWV, 142; CRJ, 151; Dow sit-in and aftermath, 124, 126, 130; empty chair, 63; gripe-in, 111; on revolu-

tion, 186; SACA, 71–72; SAR, 182; SDS, 91–92, 107; *Walrus*, 138; "we were right," xvii. *See also* SFS
Fields, Belden, 196–97
First amendment, 19–20, 43–44, 165, 184
Follett's Bookstore, 195, 202–4, 209
free speech: ad hoc committee in defense of, 43; "against the principles of the government," 56; area, 33, 45; Chicago Circle campus, 36, 62; *DI* ambivalence, 73; Gutowsky, 115, 122; Henry, 71; libertarians, 112; McMullin, 31; Outis, 76; Peltason, 166; rights of Dow, 114–15, 122, 142, 144; SACA, 61–62; SFS, 72–73; shift to antiwar, 73, 90–92, 105–7, 114, 119; Stoddard, 12; Univ. of California at Berkeley, 32–33; Yellin, 20. *See also* SACA; SFS

Galston, John, 60
General Electric, 194–97
Gershenson, Bernard, 138, 141, 156–58
Goldstein, Robert, 18, 46, 177
Gottheil, Fred, 34, 46–47
Grange, Harold "Red," 14, 16
Graves, Goddard, 109, 116
Gregory Hall, 3, 34, 185
Groninger, Bill, 204–5
grovel-in, 177–78
Gutowsky, Herbert, 115–16, 122, 124–25, 127, 142; on academic freedom, 187

Halstead, Fred, 139–40
Hanagan, Mike, 111–12, 115, 131
Hammond, Rodney, 145, 149
Hampton, Fred, 173, 189
Hardin, Joseph, 91–92, 138, 156, 162, 186
Hasagawa, Robert, 36
Henry, David Dodds: background, 16–18; Clabaugh Act, 51, 77; CRJ, 146; *DI* criticism, 110; Diskin, 36, 74–75; DuBois Club, 40–41, 50, 55, 69, 77–78; effigy, 25; governance, UI, 44; Koch, 22–25; Kuntsler, 195; opposition to Vietnam War 215; retirement, 200; role of the university, 184; SACA, 62–67, 71; student unrest, 81–82; university and civil rights, 31; Wayne State, 51, 153–54; "Year Ahead" speech (1967), 109–10; Yellin, 21–24
Hogan, Mickey, 174–76

Hoover, J. Edgar, 40–41, 48, 159
Hoults, Alice, 204, 223
Hoults, Edgar, 202–3, 205, 212, 221–22
House Un-American Activities Committee (HUAC), 19–21, 51–52
Hutchens, Robert M., 6

Illiac, 4, 191–92, 208–9, 218, 223
Illini Union: Diskin speech, 74; demonstrations, 37, 58, 60–62, 112, 144; Dow, 123–24; draft card burning, 118–19, 134–35; flag lowered, 211–12; gripe-in, 81, 107, 111; Project 500 protest, 166–67; state police, 196, 210, 219; Stoddard resignation, 14
Illinois legislature, 5–6, 12–17, 56–59, 80, 222–23
Illinois National Guard, 162–63, 196–97, 210, 214, 218–20
Illinois State Police, 196, 210–14, 218–20
Inter-Fraternity Council, 47, 65, 106
Ivy, Andrew, 13

Jackson State College, 222
Johnson, John Lee, 143–45, 166, 199
Johnson, Lyndon B., 7, 32–33, 37, 136–37, 144
Johnston, Wayne, 14, 69
Jones, Jeff, 185

Katzenbach, Nicholas, 40–41, 48
Kennedy, John F., 31
Kennedy, Robert, 137, 144, 153, 161
Kent State University, 206–12, 215–16
Kerner, Otto, 57, 153
Keyes, Gene, 33
King, Martin Luther, 29, 33; assassination and aftermath, 137, 145–48
Klonsky, Mike, 160
Koch, Leo, 22–25
Kornibe, Jim, 150, 152
Krebiozen, 13–15
Krippendorff, Ekkehart, 174
Krohne, Elizabeth, 24
Kunstler, William, 195, 199–200

Landis, Fred, 80, 88, 122, 131
Larabee, James, 201, 227–28
Leary, Timothy, 140
Lincoln Hall, 3, 199
Livingston, Park, 15

Lucas, Ron, 134, 142, 189
Lynd, Staughton, 114, 119

March on Washington, 29, 109, 123
McBride's Pharmacy, 195–96, 209
McCarren, Pat, 40
McCarren Act, 40, 74
McCarthy, Eugene, 137, 144
McCarthy, Joseph, 5, 12
McCarthy, Laurie, 189–90
McCollum, Dan'l, 118, 123, 144
McMullin, Richard, 31
Men's Independent Association, 44–45
Meranto, Philip, 146, 192, 209–10, 212–13
Midnight Meeting, 88–89
Mikva, Abner, 131–33
Millet, Stanton: Bennett, 59; CRJ, 146; draft card burnings, 119–20; DuBois Club, 43, 48–53, 58–59, 69; end-of-year thoughts, 80; Project 500 students, 166; student protest leaders 64–66; trustees, 81
Mitchler, Robert, 70, 133
Mobilization against the War, 45–46
Morey, Lloyd, 17
Morgan, Thomas, 81, 119, 126–27, 176

National Association for the Advancement of Colored People (NAACP), 30–31, 34, 38, 146, 168
National Coordinating Committee to End the War in Vietnam, 46
Nixon, Richard: agrees with protesters, 215–16; Cambodian invasion 203–6; Chester, 84; nominated (1968), 137; secret peace plan, 188–89

O'Brien, Paul, 113
Ogilvie, Richard, 183–84, 210, 214
Oglesby, Carl, 128–29, 159
Outis, Robert, 64, 67, 74–76

Page, Ray, 135, 214
Pan Hellenic Council, 47, 65, 106
Parenti, Michael, 197–99, 210–13
Parker, Patsy, 86–88, 131–32, 144–45, 152, 177
Peace Union, 212
Peltason, Jack W.: black student demands, 178–79; Dow sit-in, aftermath 125, 132; early days as chancellor, 106–8; named chancellor, 44; Project 500, 147–49, 152, 166, 168–69; Red Herring appearance, 127; riots, 197; student strike, 210–11, 213–14, 222; Vietnam War statement, 187, 216; vigil support 30
Phillips, Herbert, 51
Picone, Linda, 150–51
Pinto, Ed, 212, 223
Plager, Sheldon, 69
Pogue, Herbert, 68
Progressive Labor Party (PLP), 160, 185, 193
Project 500, 149, 152, 165–69, 182–83

Radar, Gary, 113
Radical Union (RU), 187, 192, 194, 199, 208
Ransel, David: establishment power, 163; Fields, 196–97; McCarthy, 190; Reed, 141; Schmidt, 117; SDS, 73
Red Cross, 35–36
Red Herring, 106–7, 113, 127–28, 137, 140
Reed, Gail, 140–41
Reserve Officers Training Corps (ROTC), 60, 139, 192–93, 201, 208
"Revolutionary 26," 207
Revolutionary Youth Movement (RYM), 160, 185, 187, 193
Rossman, Michael, 176–77
Roth, Keven, 89, 112, 123, 132
Rothman, Howard, 64, 130
Rothstein, Vivien, 85, 139–40
Rudd, Mark, 156, 160, 185–87

Saltiel, John, 125, 130
Savio, Mario, 106
Scariano, Anthony, 57–58, 80, 222
Schmidt, Steven: arrest, 184; Dow sit-in, 131; draft resistance, 109, 115–19, 134–35, 139, 190; Henry, 44; Kennedy, Robert, 137; Red Herring, 106–7; release from prison, 201. *See also* DRU
Schroeder, Paul, 153
Semmel, Herb, 46, 130–32
Sewell, William, 122
Shafransky, Paula, 84, 86, 228
Sheedy, Keenan, 45, 55, 58, 62, 158
Shirley, Harvey, 203–5, 207, 219, 221
Shupak, Marty, 177
Simon, Roger, xvii, 116–17, 199–200
Slotnick, Daniel, 192, 199, 209, 223

slush fund, 44
Soderstrom, Rick: Berkey, 46; draft card burning, 117–18; DRU, 107; shift from free speech to anti-war, 112, 114; SNCC, 34, 39
Special Committee on Campus Tensions, 201
Spiegel, Harriet, 197–98
Spock, Benjamin, 193
Stoddard, George D., 11–18, 50
Stratton, Kenneth O., 30
Student Committee on Political Enlightenment (SCOPE), 86–87
Student Mobilization Committee, 180, 205
Student Non-violent Coordinating Committee (SNCC), 31–34, 39, 61–62
Students Against Racism (SAR), 182
Students Against the Clabaugh Act (SACA), 61–73, 75, 78, 83
Students for a Democratic Society (SDS): anti-war activities at UI, 35–36, 45, 58; "Days of Rage," 186–87; Dow sit-in, 114–15, 121–22, 142; DuBois Club, 55; factions, UI, 65, 69, 70, 72,79; free speech/SACA, 46, 62, 64–65; Gregory Hall, 185–86; male domination, 83, 90–91; meetings at UI, 73, 84, 107, 138, 158; Millet appearance, 51; National Convention (1968), 90, 160–61; National Convention (1969), 185; National Council meeting (1968), 159; new generation, 182; Oglesby, 128; Panthers, 173–74; Port Huron statement, 5; Rothstein, 85; "Ten Days of Protest," 147; "Ten Days to Shake the Empire," 180; Urban, 113–14; Weathermen, 156, 160, 192–93. *See also* Progressive Labor Party; Revolutionary Youth Movement
Students for Free Speech (SFS), 72–76, 78–81, 83, 90, 107
Subversive Activities Control Board (SACB), 40–41, 43, 48, 69

Thurmond, Strom, 31

University of California at Berkeley, comparisons to: *Chicago Tribune,* 54; Clabaugh, 65; *DI*, 45, 52, 73; Fein, 71; Mitchler, 70; SFS, 44, 72; YAF, 45
University of Michigan, 34, 59
University of Wisconsin, Madison, 59–60, 121–23, 178, 214
Urban, Vernon, 113–14

Voss, Larry Allan, 192–93
voter registration drives, 29, 31–32, 35

Wall, Lester, 132, 138, 159
Wallace, George, 32, 47
Walrus, 84, 138–39, 148
Warren, Mike, 108, 111
Wayne State University, 17–18, 51, 149, 153
Weathermen, 185–87, 192–93
W.E.B. DuBois Club, 38–41, 43–44, 53–71, 74, 77–78
Weeks, Dennis, 115–17
Werry, Jocelyn, 60, 189–90, 193
Werry, John, 46–47, 127, 132
Wikoff, Virgil, 205, 208, 222
Williams, William K., 41, 73, 120, 125, 221
women in the movement, 31, 46, 83–92, 119, 139–41
Women's Independent Association, 45, 47
Women's Union, 140–41
Wu, Vincent, 35–36, 46–47, 92, 118

Yellin, Edward, 19–21
Young Americans for Freedom (YAF), 45
Young Democrats, 31, 33, 62, 86
Young Republicans, 151, 222
Young Socialists, 36, 41, 61
Youth for Democracy, 13, 17, 50

MICHAEL METZ took part in the student movement at the University of Illinois at Urbana-Champaign from 1965 to 1970. He is retired from a career in high-tech marketing and resides in Saratoga, California, with his wife, daughter, and two dogs.

The University of Illinois Press
is a founding member of the
Association of University Presses.

Composed in 10.25/13 Marat Pro
with Trade Gothic LT Std display
by Lisa Connery
at the University of Illinois Press
Cover designed by Dustin Hubbart
Cover image: Rick Soderstrom and Steve Schmidt
burning draft cards. (*Champaign-Urbana Courier*)

University of Illinois Press
1325 South Oak Street
Champaign, IL 61820-6903
www.press.uillinois.edu